Wayne E. Oates is Professor of Psychology of Religion at the Southern Baptist Theological Seminary in Louisville, Kentucky. He is a graduate of Wake Forest College and Southern Baptist Theological Seminary where he earned the Th.D. and has studied at Union Theological Seminary in New York City. He has written many books about pastoral counseling and is a recognized authority in the field.

Andrew D. Lester is the Assistant Director of the School of Pastoral Care at North Carolina Baptist Hospital in Winston-Salem where he is also Coordinator of the Model Community Project. A graduate of Mississippi College and Southern Seminary, he has had extensive pastoral counseling experience, and served on the faculty at Southern Baptist Seminary, where he received the Th.D. degree.

PASTORAL CARE
IN CRUCIAL
HUMAN SITUATIONS

PASTORAL CARE
IN CRUCIAL
HUMAN SITUATIONS
Wayne E. Oates and Andrew D. Lester

JUDSON PRESS, VALLEY FORGE

to
Scott Wayne Lester
William Wayne Oates
D. Swan Haworth

ACKNOWLEDGMENTS

The editors would like to extend their gratitude to the authors who contributed to this volume. We are personally related to each of them and know them to be excellent students and effective ministers. We appreciate their friendship and their colleagueship. The reader will understand our feelings, after reading these chapters, for both the personal concern and the clinical scholarship of these individual men are evident in their writing.

We are also indebted to our friends in the medical profession who have allowed these ministers to work on the healing team in their respective clinical settings. They have graciously written introductions to most of these chapters describing from their perspective the importance of pastoral care in critical human situations.

We are grateful for the friendship we have with each other which has helped sustain us through our own personal crises.

Andrew D. Lester
Wayne E. Oates

CONTENTS

Andrew D. Lester is Assistant Director of the School of Pastoral
Care at North Carolina Baptist Hospital in Winston-Salem. Wayne
E. Oates is Professor of Psychology of Religion at the Southern
Baptist Theological Seminary in Louisville, Kentucky.

1

THE USE OF
RESEARCH IN PASTORAL CARE

Andrew D. Lester and Wayne E. Oates

The predicaments with which this book deals represent excruciating crises in human lives. They involve extraordinary pain
and stress on the part of the whole person in the context of his
family. Pastors are involved routinely with people under stress.
Some human events and life-situations, however, are seemingly
more threatening to the pastor and to the family than others.
The unalterable life-situation of the mentally retarded and the
disabled, the existence of terminal diseases and emotional ill-
nesses are several examples. All of these situations are treated in
the following chapters.

Many pastors move courageously into these situations with all
the training they have. They minister to the best of their abilities.
Other pastors shrink back from involvements with these types of
crises because they feel inadequate to minister effectively in these
human dilemmas. Every pastor seeks ways to help him fulfill his
function in such difficult situations.

While many pastors have turned to the fruits of research in
pastoral psychology for assistance, few have realized that they
can also share in the research task. By so doing, they will not
only add to the body of material available to all, but they will
find that the observation and accumulation of data in the day-
to-day ministry will provide a wealth of subject material which
will aid them in understanding the life-situations of their parish-

11

ioners. This chapter will suggest the values and characteristics of such pastoral research as a guide to the discussion of specific situations in the following chapters.

"SHIRTSLEEVE RESEARCH"

An untapped source of research in the field of pastoral psychology is the daily observations and interactions of the parish minister. Although many ministers have training that would enable them to conduct such research, only rarely does a working pastor or a service chaplain turn out basic research. More often it is the teachers, both clinical supervisors and professors, who write extensively in the field of pastoral care.

Research conducted from the perspective of the parish minister can add a unique dimension to the literature in the psychology of religion and pastoral theology disciplines. Many areas of pastoral work can be more adequately studied if pastors are willing and receive encouragement to do the research. Pastoral visitation would be an example. What actually takes place when a pastor visits in a home? How could the pastor make home visits more effective? Think of the research on grief that could be provided by the pastors in Memphis, Tennessee, after Martin Luther King's death, or by the pastors in Aberfan, Wales, after the slag slide which tragically snuffed out the lives of many children in the community.

The word "research" often carries overtones of "impersonality," "treating people as guinea pigs," and "deceiving people," or is assumed to involve elaborate statistical machinery and quantitative measuring procedures. These associations might partially explain the hesitancy of pastors to involve themselves in pastoral research. However, as can be seen from the following description, pastoral research is one way in which each unique individual can be taken seriously as a total being. Authentic pastoral research will help to develop relationships which are deeply personal, intimately open and honest, in which each party sees the other as a person, not a thing.

Models for pastoral research can be found among the medical profession and the various psychotherapeutic disciplines. Sigmund Freud's psychoanalytic theories were formulated in the midst of a busy medical practice as he attempted to understand the psychosomatic problems of his patients. After World War II, a

Japanese physician, Michihiko Hachiya, published a book entitled *Hiroshima Diary* in which he chronicled his medical work with victims of this atomic disaster.[1] Something similar is done in the ninth chapter of this book. *Men Under Stress*, a pioneer work in the field of psychiatry by Roy Grinker and John Spiegel, resulted from a careful account of emotional problems confronted by combat troops in World War II.[2] The research materials were gathered under combat conditions.

Ministry and research could just as readily be combined by the parish minister. Anton Boisen produced some very creative ideas while working as a chaplain with mental patients. *The Exploration of the Inner World* told of his work with mentally ill persons and what he learned from them.[3] Such an approach to pastoral research has an illustrious history. Large portions of the New Testament were written within the context of energy-consuming pastoral ministries. James evidently had a large pastoral responsibility while he did his "research" on the relationship between faith and works among early Hebrew Christians. The beloved physician Luke probably carried on a busy medical practice and a vital Christian witness as he compiled the story of the life of Christ and the early church, which he reported in Luke-Acts. Paul the apostle was a busy missionary-preacher during the time that he wrote the letters to Corinth in an attempt to understand and respond to the religious struggles of these new Christians.

DISTINCTIVES OF PASTORAL RESEARCH

Pastoral research is different from "pure" research because the research itself is not the only, or even the primary, objective. A pastor is interested in both research and service. Ministering to persons is the primary objective. Nevertheless, ministry and research are not incompatible with each other, but mutually supportive. Pastors can study pastoral psychology during their day-to-day care of individuals and groups. Teachers have always combined teaching and research. Many other clinicians, psycho-

[1] Michihiko Hachiya, *Hiroshima Diary*, Warner Wells, trans. and ed. (Chapel Hill, N. C.: University of North Carolina Press, 1955).

[2] Roy R. Grinker and John P. Spiegel, *Men Under Stress* (Philadelphia: Blakiston Company, 1945).

[3] Anton T. Boisen, *The Exploration of the Inner World* (New York: Harper & Row, Publishers, Inc., 1936).

therapists, and doctors have combined therapy and healing with research.

Pastoral research honestly accepts the subjectivity involved in research. Some persons in academic circles become quite involved in trying to eliminate the subjective factor in research. But absolute objectivity, as we see it, is not possible in the realm of the study of man. Objectivity is relative. Pastoral research freely admits that clinical research involves subjective interaction with the "human documents" being studied. The researcher seeks to recognize, regulate, and understand the subjective dimension rather than to deny its presence.

Another distinctive of pastoral research is its relationship to phenomenological psychology and existential philosophy. Both these disciplines are interested in the life-situation of an individual as it is perceived, experienced, and responded to by that individual. Existentialism asserts that each person must seek self-actualization within the reality of his own life-situation. B. F. Nel epitomizes the phenomenological approach when he says that persons

> should be viewed in terms of specific situations in the world. The [person] should be seen as an existential being in the process of realizing himself within a particular situation. An analysis should be made of the particular way in which [this person] encounters the world he lives in.[4]

Every human endows the objects and events of the world with meaning. Understanding this meaning and responding to it is one dimension of pastoral research. This function has been summarized by Roy Woodruff after his pastoral research with alcoholics as follows:

> Effective pastoral research not only collects data, it also performs a ministry of concerned listening to and participating in the life of the individual. The pastoral researcher should endeavor to form a faithful friendship with the respondent, taking seriously his developmental pilgrimage, and giving him encouragement in his present circumstances.[5]

The research and writing within the following pages has included such involvement and ministry.

[4] Barend F. Nel, *A Phenomenological Approach to the Problems of Youth,* Vol. VIII, No. 27, of the *Educational Studies by the Work Community for Advancement of Pedagogy as a Science* (Pretoria, South Africa: University of Pretoria Press, 1960), p. 6.

[5] C. Roy Woodruff, *Alcoholism and Christian Experience* (Philadelphia: The Westminster Press, 1968), pp. 128-129.

Conducting this type of research means that the researcher must become a participant in his research. In Harry Stack Sullivan's terms he becomes a "participant observer."[6] The pastoral researcher purposely becomes related to the situation he is studying. The presence of a "participant researcher" changes the nature of that which is being studied, but this change in itself is a phenomenon worth examining. Pastoral research includes the study of such changes.

Pastoral research is characterized by its involvement with people. The subjects of pastoral research are not statistics, or animals, or theories, but are what Anton Boisen has called the "human documents." Individuals in the sample are treated as persons to be related to rather than as objects to manipulate.

Pastoral research takes persons seriously as unique individuals. It follows Gordon Allport in recognizing the "patterned individuality" of every human being.[7] Furthermore, because each person is unique, pastoral researchers learn something a little different from each person. Although general conclusions and understandings can be extracted from pastoral research, the unique responses to life that make up individual life-styles are the most basic ingredient. Since the individuals are taken so seriously they begin to feel like participants themselves. They become the teachers as they introduce the pastor to their life-situation.

Pastoral care and counseling take place in the context of interpersonal relationships; therefore, pastoral psychology, as well as pastoral research, must take seriously not only the parishioner and the pastor but the dynamics which take place in the relationship between them. One of the editors (Lester) has conducted phenomenologically-oriented pastoral research with adolescents.[8] He sought to establish a personal relationship with the adolescents before they were asked to be part of the sample group because he proceeded on the assumption that "adolescents

---

[6] Harry Stack Sullivan, *The Psychiatric Interview* (New York: W. W. Norton & Company, Inc., 1954), pp. 19-25.

[7] Gordon W. Allport, *Pattern and Growth in Personality* (New York: Holt, Rinehart and Winston, 1961), pp. 3-21.

[8] Andrew D. Lester, "Implications of the Needs and Experiences of Selected Adolescents for the Church's Ministry" (unpublished Doctoral thesis, The Southern Baptist Theological Seminary, Louisville, Kentucky, 1967).

could, and would, reveal more about their deepest thoughts and feelings to someone with whom they were personally acquainted and had learned to trust."[9] The results of his study demonstrated that such an approach to research is worthwhile.

In the first place the adolescents themselves appreciated the phenomenological method of research. Their positive response was revealed in their answers to the question, "Would you go through this project again for us?" Their "yes" answers included the following observations:

> In this project I learned about the good home and family and life that I have. Some don't have such good a life as I do. And I never realized it until then. I learned a lot by doing the essays.
>
> Because I learned a lot about myself. . . .
>
> Because it helped me understand myself a little better and how others saw me.
>
> Because it really made me stop and take a second look at myself and my life I had planned for in the future.
>
> Because I've learned a lot about myself. . . .
>
> It made me take a good look at myself and my problems.[10]

The research obviously helped the participants in addition to providing information to the researcher.

The personal relationship which the author had established with the adolescents influenced their willingness to volunteer for the project. Twenty-six of the thirty adolescents in the sample stated that they would have been very hesitant to begin the project with a researcher that they did not know. Some of their reasons indicate the importance of trust and fidelity in pastoral research.

> Because I wouldn't have let anyone share the feelings and the things I wrote, unless I was as sure of them as I am of [the researcher].
>
> I probably wouldn't have trusted him because I wouldn't know if he were a friend or that he would tell what I wrote.
>
> Because I don't think I could really have trusted someone I didn't know with the information on the essays.
>
> Because if I didn't know the person I wouldn't have trusted them [sic] and therefore I wouldn't want them [sic] to know anything about me.
>
> Because if I didn't know this person it would be hard to place all my faith in him.

[9] *Ibid.*, p. 252.
[10] *Ibid.*, pp. 248-249.

Because I proable [sic] would of thought the person just wanted to know about me and my mistakes.

I would not know this person and I feel I couldn't be honest with him or her.[11]

These responses also indicate how difficult it would be for "objective" researchers to gather information in any depth from this group of adolescents. Research in pastoral psychology, when it deals with human life-situations, is incomplete without the types of data gained through the phenomenological approach.

Lastly, Lester's research would indicate that the personal participation of the researcher helped the adolescents to feel that they had been respected as individuals rather than treated as objects. The following responses demonstrate their feelings:

> He made us feel like we were somebody he really cared about and did not treat us as little heathens.

> He would put us at ease and the things we had to do were not like a school test where you are all scared.

> [the researcher] is an older person who is really interested in us. He became a part of us instead of expecting us to become a part of him. He felt he could understand us better if he came into our world instead of expecting us to come into his world. It was easier for him to come down to us than it was for us to come up to him.[12]

The last response is an excellent description of the potential meaning of pastoral research to the parishoner.

CHARACTERISTICS OF RESEARCH IN THIS BOOK

In the first place pastoral research stands or falls on factual observations, brief but accurate record keeping, and an appreciation of the process of development. B. F. Skinner calls this the "cumulative record."[13] Robert W. White calls it "the study of lives in progress."[14] The genius of pastoral research lies in the pastor's "overview" of the continuing flow of the parishioners' individual lives in the context of his own relationship, of the parishioners' family situation, and the strength of the Christian community. Pastoral research cannot abide in an atmosphere of static and

[11] *Ibid.*, pp. 236-237.
[12] *Ibid.*, p. 253.
[13] B. F. Skinner, *Cumulative Record* (New York: Appleton-Century-Crofts, Inc., 1961).
[14] Robert W. White, *Lives in Progress* (New York: Henry Holt & Company, Inc., 1952), p. 4.

stagnant perceptions of human life under God. Rather a dynamic, experiential faith is implied in the practice of pastoral research. The reader will find all of these ingredients in the pages that follow.

A second characteristic of the research in this book is its emphasis on family relationships. Although the subjects of the research are individuals under traumatic circumstances, obviously their response to the stress both influences and is influenced by the family context in which they exist. A pastor who attempts to minister to individuals without seriously considering the family milieu will not be as effective as the one who does. Likewise, pastoral research which does not examine and observe the intra-family relationships will be necessarily incomplete. Human beings are historical entities. Life-styles are developed in the lifelong encounters which people have with their environment. Recognition and appreciation of this fact is a prerequisite to meaningful pastoral care, and, therefore, an important concern of pastoral research.

Lastly, we call attention to the overarching and undergirding theme of the book — *hope*. The pastor represents hope to persons who face the unalterable, the unknown, or the frightening. In some way, each of the following chapters calls attention to the place of hope in human crises. In an age when despair, discouragement, and disillusionment are the predominant emotional dynamics, it becomes increasingly necessary for the Christian faith to unmask, refurbish, and communicate its belief in hope. Currently there is, within theological circles, a flurry of interest in the "theology of hope." This book reveals the existential importance of this renewed concern by demonstrating its relationship to human crises. Pastors represent the Christian hope in their care of persons. We trust that the following pages will provide guidelines for bringing this dynamic in a realistic fashion into human crisis situations.

Mahan Siler, Jr., pastor of the Ravensworth Baptist Church, Annandale, Virginia, earned the degree of Doctor of Sacred Theology from Southern Baptist Theological Seminary. He has had several years of pastoral experience in addition to his academic work.

2
PASTORAL CARE OF FAMILIES AT THE EVENT OF CHILDBIRTH

Mahan Siler, Jr.

The experience of childbirth has profound meaning for all of the members of the family. Because this event is of such crucial importance, a research project was designed to ask: "How does giving birth to a child affect the covenants involving family, church, and God? How can the ministry of pastoral care contribute to the significance of this event?"

This research project, the results of which form the basis for this chapter, was a clinical study of the ministry of a church to twenty families during the event of childbirth.[1] This event was interpreted as a dynamic, developmental process with three discernible phases: pregnancy, hospitalization, and reestablishment as new parents. However, before discussing these three phases in detail, three underlying considerations must be presented which are pertinent to the pastoral care of families throughout all phases of the childbirth event.

[1] The primary research method employed was the focused interview. Intensive interviews were conducted with twenty couples in Crescent Hill Baptist Church in Louisville, Kentucky, who had recently passed through the crisis of childbirth. The clinical research was of an exploratory nature from which explicit hypotheses have been derived. These hypotheses are used here as guidelines for a suggested ministry of pastoral care at the event of childbirth. The findings of other related research are incorporated when they expand, reinforce, or contradict the conclusions of the research project.

The Religious Significance of Childbirth

The event of childbirth can be, but is not necessarily, a bearer of religious significance. The religious potential of personal crises is affirmed by an array of scholars, such as Anton Boisen, Elton Trueblood, Wayne Oates, Paul Tillich, Lewis Sherrill, Karl Barth, Helmut Thielicke, Carl Michalson, and C. W. Brister.[2] This observation is tested by the empirical data of this study.

Twenty-three of the forty parents reported that the experience of childbirth had explicit religious meaning. Some parents regarded the birth of their child as a miraculous gift from God to which their response was gratitude. One parent's comments are representative: "I believe it deepened our faith. Why, you can't go through that without feeling it is a miracle. I felt God was giving me more than I was giving him." Other parents felt a new sense of responsibility expressed in religious terms. As one father said, "It makes us concerned to bring up Mary Sue as God would have us do. . . ." Two parents stated that the experience had contributed to their understanding of God. For one mother the fatherhood of God became more personal: "You are told over and over again how our relationship to God is as a child. This means much more to me now that I have a child of my own. If he [the child] means this much to me, how much more he means to God. The whole idea has taken on greater depth to me." For another parent the significance of Jesus was illuminated: "The incarnation becomes more meaningful . . . in the simple analogy of getting a new child because Christ came as a child. He came helpless into the world: the condescending of God." Seven mothers reported the feeling of ful-

---

[2] Anton Boisen, *Religion in Crisis and Custom* (New York: Harper & Row, Publishers, Inc., 1945), p. 47; Elton Trueblood, *The Common Ventures of Life* (New York: Harper & Row, Publishers, Inc., 1949), p. 61; Wayne E. Oates, *The Christian Pastor* (rev. & enl. ed.; Philadelphia: The Westminster Press, 1964), p. 6; Paul Tillich, *Systematic Theology* (Chicago: The University of Chicago Press, 1951), Vol. I, p. 13; Lewis Sherrill, *The Struggle of the Soul* (New York: The Macmillan Company, 1951), pp. 11-22; Karl Barth, *Church Dogmatics*, G. W. Bromiley and T. F. Torrance, eds. (Edinburgh: T. & T. Clark, 1960), Vol. III, No. 2, pp. 135, 138; Helmut Thielicke, *Out of the Depths*, G. W. Bromiley, trans. (Grand Rapids, Mich.: William B. Eerdmans Company, 1954), pp. 21-50; Carl Michalson, *Faith for Personal Crises* (New York: Charles Scribner's Sons, 1958), pp. 6-13; C. W. Brister, *Pastoral Care in the Church* (New York: Harper & Row, Publishers, Inc., 1964), p. 202.

fillment in being participants with God in his creative work. These mothers spoke of "sharing in creation" and being allowed "to bring children into this world." In addition, for some parents the experience was an occasion for self-examination and a reaffirmation of faith. In the words of one father: "Scott [child] has become a kind of rebirth of faith in me in our relationship to God and in the church and in the world in general."

On the other hand, seventeen out of the forty parents passed through the crises of childbirth with relative indifference to its overt religious dimensions. Yet the dimension of ultimate concern was present within the crisis. The experience brought to the surface such potentially religious questions as: Who am I? Where am I going? Is life worth living? What do I believe? Can I be responsible in the care of another's life?

"I began to look at myself," one father said, "and I didn't want my child to see what I saw. It began a personality change. . . ." Many parents spoke of a "new interest and purpose for living." Goals were reassessed and convictions about life's meaning were deepened because, as one mother said, "if it were just myself, then I would let these things drift." The discovery of an unplanned and unwanted pregnancy forced one mother to question even the worth of living:

> That was my lowest. I felt forsaken as anybody could possibly be. That's the lowest I have ever been. They told me to go home and I didn't want to. I told Sam [husband] to go to work, that I didn't need him. I didn't want to face the children or anything. I just wanted to get a cab and go to a motel somewhere. I was completely shot.

Thus, in the words of one parent, "This whole experience has been one of looking at our lives." Some parents see the event of childbirth as a bearer of explicit religious significance. The pastor's role in such instances is to help parents clarify and express these religious meanings through interpersonal conversation and appropriate acts of worship. For those who detect little religious meaning the alert pastor can be sensitive to the ultimate questions raised in the parents' minds. These ultimate concerns, clothed in the particularity of each parent's unique history, can open the possibility of self-understanding that issues into new or strengthened covenants with God and other persons close to the individual.

The Significance of the Husband

Emotional support from the husband is the primary factor in the well-being of the wife-mother. O. S. English and C. J. Foster in their book, *Fathers Are Parents Too*, lay down a specific challenge: "The functions of motherhood have been both implicit and explicit for centuries. It is time that a father's functions were made clearer and given a more tangible meaning." [3] This challenge becomes all the more urgent if during the event of childbirth the husband-father's support is the primary factor in the well-being of his wife.

The wives who participated in this research project were clearly most sensitive to their husband's response to them and to the coming child. The interviews with seventeen wives were interspersed with remembrances of emotional support. Representative comments follow:

> He was quite excited when he first heard the news.
>
> Every fear I would have, he would say, "That could happen but most likely it won't."
>
> I knew he was with me. It has drawn us so much closer.
>
> I think the most meaningful thing was the look on Jim's face right after delivery. That meant a whole lot to me. He was bursting buttons!
>
> He was excited about the baby. He wanted to know when the baby kicked and what the doctor said.
>
> I guess his optimism, his bright outlook, meant more than anything else.
>
> He became such a part of it.
>
> As we went to the hospital he was very reassuring.
>
> At the hospital he was aware of how I would feel when he would leave.
>
> Well, I think the emotional high point would have been the look on Ron's face when Mike was born.

Conversely, the wives were equally sensitive to evidences of incomplete support from their husbands. The following excerpts from interviews illustrate such disappointment:

> Then, too, I was trying to nurse the baby every few hours. He didn't realize how fast it was wearing me down. I don't think he understood.
>
> Sometimes he teased too much in front of other people. I was afraid that people would think that he didn't want the baby.
>
> He doesn't really seem to be concerned. He is not worried and I want

[3] O. S. English and C. J. Foster, *Fathers Are Parents Too* (New York: G. P. Putnam's Sons, 1951), p. 16.

to be pampered a little, I guess. After the interview with you we talked about some of these things and we talked about how some mothers tend to be emotional during this period. He doesn't think that I am this way at all when I actually think I am.

The pastor, in contrast to the obstetrician, usually has direct access to the husband during the event of the childbirth. If the husband wields such a crucial role during this family crisis, the pastor should include in his pastoral care a concern to assist and encourage the husband in this unique ministry to his wife.

Importance of Interpersonal Communication

As parenthood approaches, the couple face a choice: Either they discover a new kind of intimacy and strengthened covenant, or they drift toward coexistence wherein each partner pursues a separate life. Interpersonal communication seems to be an important factor in actualizing the cohesive possibilities. Nine couples in this study rated highest the positive effect of the crisis upon their marital relationship in bringing about an increased "closeness." The same parents reported and demonstrated effective interpersonal communication.

Mrs. Young became pregnant in the third month of their marriage. She and her husband resented this intrusion into the ordered, intimate early stage of their marriage. Yet they illustrated the importance of effective interpersonal communication in expressing excessive frustration as well as mutual support. Mrs. Young remarked: "We are a lot more honest with each other . . . we didn't ignore the things. We talked about it and about what we would do about the money and all." Later Mr. Young commented: "We saw much of each other's weaknesses. Last night, for instance, I saw in her the worst I think I could ever see in her, and yet this draws a love from me too. . . . I saw her as she is."

In contrast, two couples reported that the birth of their child had a negative effect upon their marital relationship. In both instances the lack of effective communication was a major factor. As one wife commented: "Our togetherness had been shot in the head. We have trouble going to bed together. And we used to sit down and talk and read from the Bible before going to bed. We have trouble doing that anymore." Another wife, after acknowledging the increased "distance" she felt in her marriage, responded: "I think I meant mainly that we don't have enough time together anymore. . . . We don't get to sit down and talk like we used to. Part of it is the baby, but not all."

Thus there seems to be a distinct correlation between marital interpersonal communication and the effect of cohesiveness. If such communication does contribute to a deepened marital covenant during the experience of childbirth, then the pastor must give high priority to the stimulation and facilitation of meaningful interpersonal communication between husband and wife.

These overarching considerations suggest that the pastor must include in his care the following: assisting families in realizing the religious potential for Christian growth which exists in the crisis of childbirth; awakening and encouraging the husband in his distinctive ministry to his family; and giving impetus, content, and guidance to effective communication within the family.

PREGNANCY PHASE

The period of pregnancy is a type of temporary plateau reached by the couple on their way toward the pinnacle of parenthood. From this plateau the couple is disposed to look in three directions: *to look behind* and evaluate the preparation made thus far for the greater tasks of parenthood; *to look within* and reflect upon the soundness of their relationships and values; and *to look ahead* and anticipate the impending parental responsibilities. Generally, pastoral care has been unaware and therefore unresponsive to these teachable moments latent within the period of pregnancy.

Developmental Tasks

There are three developmental tasks of parents during this stage to which the ministry of pastoral care can respond.

Achieving Emotional Acceptance of the Child

One of the savory fictions of our culture is that every baby is a "bundle of joy," eagerly awaited and received by loving parents.[4] However, in fact, not fiction, pregnancy generally is met by diverse attitudes and multiple emotions. Thus a major goal

[4] James H. S. Bossard, *The Sociology of Child Development* (New York: Harper & Row, Publishers, Inc., 1948), p. 87.

during the expectancy period is for the couple to be ready to accept fully the child when he is born. Since the pastor can assist in the cultivation of accepting attitudes, some factors which influence these accepting-rejecting attitudes need to be delineated.

First, good marital adjustment encourages the parental acceptance of childbirth. If the partners have passed safely through the early adjustments of marriage and are sufficiently mature to be able to focus wholeheartedly on someone outside themselves, then they are likely to welcome the childbirth. However, when the prospect of parenthood intrudes upon an immature marital relationship, then resentment and rejection may be felt. One husband expressed this resentment of such intrusion upon the early period of his marriage: "When we realized the baby was coming, I thought of the responsibility. . . . All I could see was her [wife] quitting work, the loss of study, no time to be a young couple. . . . I was as depressed as I could be."

A second factor in the emotional readiness for the child is the expectant mother's attitude toward womanhood. If she is basically content with her role as a woman, then childbearing becomes a way of confirming and expressing her womanhood. However, if she harbors a lifelong resentment toward being a female, she is apt to resent the pregnancy and childbirth. In this sense, the coming of a child crystallizes the mother's attitude toward her biological destiny. One wife regarded her life prior to pregnancy as preparation and prelude to the opportunity of motherhood: "Some people want to be a teacher, and that's fine, but I have always wanted to be a housewife and mother. And I don't think one goes without the other. So now I have accomplished really what I want. And now it's just a matter of striving to be a good mother."

Motivation for parenthood is a third influential factor upon parental attitudes. If a child is wanted, the further question of "why" should be considered. A child may be wanted for inadequate reasons. Parents may want their children in order to meet *their* needs for attention, status, eventual security, or a sense of permanence. Planned pregnancies are not necessarily predictive of acceptance.[5] Also the event of childbirth may frustrate and

[5] Sophie S. Sloman, "Emotional Problems in 'Planned For' Children," *American Journal of Orthopsychiatry*, Vol. XVIII (July, 1948), pp. 523-528.

deter vocational and personal aspirations. This too can be a factor in developing accepting-rejecting attitudes toward the child.

These are some factors to which the pastor should be sensitive as he assists in the formation of attitudes during pregnancy.

Reorienting Basic Relationships

A second need of parents throughout the experience of childbirth is the reorientation of basic relationships. The period of pregnancy marks the beginning of new kinship patterns hammered out amid the heat of this crisis.

Most prominent is the need to recast successful marital roles, especially for first-time parents. The change from being a husband to a *husband-father* and from being a wife to a *wife-mother* does not begin at childbirth; on the contrary, it begins with the discovery of pregnancy.

During pregnancy the emerging maternal role is characterized by a *centripetal force*. The wife is pulled inward in her childbearing.[6] Deutsch refers to this movement as "intensified introversion."[7] The pregnant woman gradually restricts her outside involvements. Her passive receptive needs are heightened as she builds an emotional reserve from which she will draw as a new mother.[8] She looks to the husband and family to supply the additional love and emotional support she craves.

The husband's role during pregnancy is fashioned by a *centrifugal* force. The pull is not inward, as with the wife, but outward toward the dual roles of provider and supporter. His capacity to give material and emotional sustenance must match the wife's heightened receptive needs.

The drama of pregnancy includes not only expectant parents but also expectant grandparents. Their heightened interest fosters either the cohesive or disruptive tendencies in the relationship.

For eleven parents the crisis of childbirth was the occasion for

---

[6] Evelyn M. Duvall, *Family Development* (2nd ed.; New York: J. B. Lippincott Co., 1962), p. 158.

[7] Helene Deutsch, *The Psychology of Women* (New York: Grune & Stratton, Inc., 1945), Vol. II, p. 138.

[8] Aline B. Auerbach, "Meeting Needs of New Mothers," *Child and Family*, Vol. VI (Winter, 1967), p. 12; Therese Benedek, "The Psychosomatic Implications of the Primary Unit: Mother — Child," *American Journal of Orthopsychiatry*, Vol. XIX (October, 1949), pp. 644-645.

renewed and deepened in-law covenants. In the words of one parent: "I feel more of a connection now [with my parents]. We didn't write or call much. Now Jim [child] is a sort of bridge between us."

In other instances the bearing of the first offspring encourages an intense ambivalence of independency and dependency needs. On one hand, the first-time parents strove for independence from parental interference. Yet, in each instance they demonstrated need for physical, psychological, and sometimes financial assistance from parents or a parent substitute.

Thus, the relationships involving parents and relatives are significantly affected by the crisis of childbirth. The pastor has the unique opportunity to assist in the understanding and perhaps resolution of conflictual feelings and to foster the cohesive potential of these role and relational adjustments.

Maintaining Emotional Equilibrium

A third task prominent during the stage of pregnancy is the effort to maintain emotional equilibrium. An emotionally stable pregnancy is desirable, not only for the mother's sake, but perhaps also for the general health and well-being of the infant.

The emotional disturbance of fear was experienced to some degree by each of the women. The loss or malformation of the child was the most frequently mentioned and persistent fear. The fear of delivery was more prominent among women expecting their first offspring. They reported "misgivings," "being fearful a little," and feeling "the natural anxiety a mother would have." The precise fear of death was voiced by three mothers. The pastor can aid in the understanding, expression, and release of some of the anxiety felt during pregnancy, thereby encouraging the desirable emotional equilibrium.

PASTORAL CARE

There are a number of ways a pastor can help the expectant couple to handle these developmental tasks successfully.

Pastoral Visit

The pastor should arrange a visit with both the husband and wife, preferably in their home. Ideally, the visit should be made between the second and fourth month of the pregnancy, after the community becomes aware of the event, yet before the attitudes and feelings toward the coming child have crystallized.

In light of the needs already mentioned, the pastor might carry in his mind the following questions, guiding him to pertinent areas of exploration.

Accepting-rejecting attitudes: How do the expectant parents and siblings feel about their coming child? What seems to be their motivation for parenthood? Is their concept of parenthood realistic or romanticized? How can accepting attitudes be encouraged, rejecting attitudes faced and overcome?

Reorienting relationships: How do the expectant parents feel about the emerging roles? Do they seem to have good interpersonal communication? What effect is the coming child having upon their relationships with the in-laws? How are the other children reacting to the pregnancy?

Emotional equilibrium: Does either parent indicate prolonged depression or anxiety? What are the foci of their fears? How persistent and obsessive do they seem to be? Is there indication of guilt feelings related to the anxiety?

Religious dimension: How explicit are the religious meanings of the event to the family? Is prayer a resource of strength and way of expressing fear and hope? What religious questions has the event stimulated? What potentially religious questions have emerged? (*e.g.*, Who am I? Where am I going? What do I believe?)

Pastoral Care Through Literature

Early in the stage of pregnancy the pastor should acquaint the family with available literature. The literature serves the double function of conveying knowledge and stimulating conversation. Especially recommended are: *A New Child in the Family*, edited by Helen Link; *Pierre the Pelican Bulletins;* and *Messages to Cradle Roll Parents*, Series One: "Your Baby-to-Be." The Mennonite Commission for Christian Education has prepared a small pamphlet entitled *So You're Going to Be Parents* by Rhoda Garber Cressman. In the disciplined context of the Mennonite fellowship, this aid has been put into the hands of their pastors. It can be used by pastors of all faith groups, though. It is inexpensive so that it may be given to the couple. The writer has included in his pastoral care the gift of *A New Child in the*

Family. In each instance the family has been helped by such use of literature.

Pastoral Care to the Husband

The pastor can help the husband to clarify and assume his essential part in the drama of childbirth. Perhaps a luncheon could be scheduled with the expectant father during the pregnancy period. Most important is how the husband feels about the pregnancy. The husband's expressions of tenderness, his sharing in the "nest building" preparations, his understanding of his wife's erratic mood swings, his expressed confidence in her emerging role – all can be discussed as a part of the pastoral care of the husband during the stage of pregnancy.

Pastoral Care Through Instruction

Classes for expectant parents can be very helpful. A group of churches may offer jointly a series of classes. A suggestive procedure for such classes is as follows:

First Meeting – introduction of participants to each other and orientation to the purposes and procedures of the classes

Second Meeting – a discussion of the biblical and theological significance of parenthood

Third Meeting – discussion of the couples' feelings about the pregnancy and about the coming child

Fourth meeting – discussion about the physical and emotional dimensions of the specific experience of childbirth (An obstetrics supervisor or registered nurse could be a valuable resource person; and a visit to the maternity ward of a nearby hospital could also be planned in connection with this class discussion.)

Fifth Meeting – discussion on the anticipated adjustments following the childbirth

HOSPITALIZATION PHASE

The actual birth of the child is the focal point toward which the experiences of pregnancy aim and from which the adjustments of early parenthood arise. The pastor is not concerned with the birth of the baby *per se*. Neither is he primarily concerned with the profound physical changes which must occur in the new mother. These tasks are within the responsibility of the hospital medical staff. Rather, the pastor's ministry is essentially concerned with the *birth of a new relationship* between mother and child and the ramifications of this budding relationship to other basic covenants.

For the mother this initial period of hospitalization allows a moratorium upon the multiple tasks of parenthood. For instance, the full responsibility of baby care, the care of siblings, the reorganization of household routines, and the resumption of community responsibilities are postponed during the period of hospitalization. In addition to physical recovery, time is given for reflection and formation of this new familial relationship.

Pastoral Care to the New Mother

A tradition of pastoral visitation with new parents during the period of hospitalization is generally established. This expectation was articulated by one mother: "I was beginning to think he [the pastor] had forgotten me. I was glad he came because I had been looking for him." The pastor can enter gladly into this historical practice, seeking to fill this traditional form with maximum significance. He symbolizes and communicates the concern of God and the care of a particular congregation to the family at the zenith of the event of childbirth.

Suggestions for the pastor's visit to new mothers are as follows:

1. The pastor should follow the feelings of the new mother rather than project upon her his own feelings concerning childbirth.[9] These feelings, whether they be gratitude and awe, or dismay and inadequacy, can be received and sometimes interpreted by the pastor. If the mother is bewildered by some of her emotional reactions, the pastor may be able to help her both to understand them and to prevent them from becoming serious obstacles in the initial phase of motherhood.

A pastoral visit to one mother illustrates the pastor's effectiveness in receiving and sharing the new mother's spirit of celebration. "The main thing was that I knew he [the pastor] was a man very busy and yet he could find the time. There were many other deeper needs and yet he was not rushed or hurried. . . . He did show real happiness, and I appreciate him rejoicing with us."

The British Baptists have published an "order" of prayer and

[9] Richard K. Young and Albert L. Meiburg, *Spiritual Therapy* (New York: Harper & Row, Publishers, Inc., 1960), p. 129.

worship that can be used on the visit to the hospital or even later in the home or church. Copies of Ernest Payne's and Stephen F. Winward's *Orders and Prayers for Church Worship* (Rev. ed.; London: The Carey Kingsgate Press Ltd., 1965) can be provided for father, mother, and minister. Using the service of "Thanksgiving for Childbirth" from pages 276-278 can be itself a way of communicating steadfastness and security as well as worship and celebration. See also pages 289-290, "Thanksgiving for Childbirth," in John E. Skoglund's *A Manual of Worship* (Valley Forge: Judson Press, 1968).

2. The pastoral visit to new parents may open the way to discussion concerning the relation of the newborn life to God and their own relation to God and the church. During this early phase of parenthood, there may be a keen sense of potentiality and responsibility which could be an entrée into the personal and religious significance of childbirth.

One couple expressed such religious meaning in the following way: First, the husband recalled the visit: "I was there. We were beginning to have dinner. He blessed the meal and said a prayer." "Yes," added the wife, "it was about uniting us for a better future, as one. . . . I especially appreciated it. I felt I needed the care of someone close to God who really cared to bless us as a family."

3. The pastor should also listen for other concerns. The pastoral visit may be the occasion to raise and discuss a marital problem or some personal concern for another member of the family or church. If there are other children at home, the conversation should include the subject of their welfare and reaction to the infant. The pastor, as teacher, could help the mother understand and prepare for the sibling rivalry which will likely occur to some degree upon her return home.

4. If the pastor finds that the mother and/or father have genuine feelings of gratitude and responsibility, it is appropriate that these feelings be expressed in a brief rite at the hospital. The rite should be adapted to the feelings expressed in pastoral conversation. Such a rite might be as follows:

Mrs. _____ and/or Mr. _____, God has entrusted to your care this child. You have shared with me your feelings of gratitude and new sense of responsibility. Together we have discussed what we hope he (she) will become. Don't you think it would be appropriate for us to express some of these feelings in prayer before God?

Prayer: God, our heavenly Father, Creator of life, we praise thee for blessing this marriage with the gift of new life. To thee we express our deep thanksgiving; with thee we desire for this child the achievement of Christian maturity; and in thee we seek the wisdom to teach, the empathy to understand, and the hope which endures. Grant to this family the capacity to love him (her) without worshiping or possessing him (her), reminding us that each of us rightfully belongs to thee. Amen.

The pastor may want to write out his prayer in advance and leave it with the parents. The following Scriptures are appropriate to discuss or read during the brief service of worship: Judges 13; Psalm 127:1, 3; Psalm 103:17, 18; or Luke 2:15-20.

5. The need for a pastoral ministry during the period of hospitalization is intensified when the developing mother-child relationship is obstructed for some particular reason. In instances of miscarriage, stillbirth, or the birth of a malformed child, the pastor is called upon to assist the couple through the grief process.[10] If the mother gives birth to a premature child, the pastor can help the couple verbalize and bear the burden of uncertainty. If the new mother or father reacts to childbirth with excessive emotional disturbance, the pastor should introduce them to psychiatric care.

Pastoral Care to the New Father

During the period of hospitalization the major focus of attention is upon the mother and the infant. However, the husband may be more accessible to fruitful pastoral conversation. He is not so confined by a hospital routine or restricted by the physical adjustments of the postpartum period.

The father himself needs ministry. He too has feelings and fears that need to be received and interpreted. The father needs support and perhaps guidance in the two distinct functions peculiar to his role during hospitalization. The gift of *emotional support* to his wife is most urgently needed during this period. Then, in addition, he is the primary *liaison* between the confined new mother and the larger family and community.

[10] Wayne E. Oates, *Anxiety in Christian Experience* (Philadelphia: The Westminster Press, 1955), pp. 67-73.

REESTABLISHMENT PHASE

At no time during the event of childbirth is change more painfully felt than upon the return home of new parents from the hospital. The reality of a new experience, personified in a newborn child, then becomes an unalterable fact. This abrupt change was expressed poignantly by one mother: "It [baby] was still sort of a toy [in the hospital]. When I brought him home, then it happened! The baby started crying! We had to change the diaper for the first time! It was really different!"

The child is an intruder, welcome though he may be, for which the parents are now primarily responsible. He challenges the personal identities, schedules, and relationships of those within his familial sphere. Indeed, the new experience demands realigned priorities and relationships. The pastor, then, is concerned during this three-month period of reestablishment that the new child become assimilated successfully into the covenants involving the family, church, and God. These covenant relationships can become renewed with the proper incorporation of the child into the family.

DEVELOPMENTAL TASKS

The pastor should be sensitive to the following developmental tasks.

Shifting of Roles

First, the major shift in the husband and wife roles is felt during these first months. During pregnancy and hospitalization the mother is the primary object of attention and the baby is regarded as her achievement. However, during the period of reestablishment, the child clearly assumes the center of the stage. The mother becomes a servant of the child, no longer able to place first her own wishes and plans. Most mothers bring to this new role a combined sense of responsibility and inadequacy. First-time parents particularly wonder about their capacity to be effective parents. One mother reported:

There was for me a feeling of inadequacy. I wanted one and yet dreaded the first three months after birth. During pregnancy I would think of this. . . . If I just didn't have to go through the first three months – well, in this case, it was the first six months. I would wonder if I was doing the right thing.

The pastor is expected to emphasize the importance of parental responsibility. Yet he also should remind parents that they are not *solely* responsible for the life of their child. The parents share this responsibility with God, with the larger family and community, and with the child himself. Undue pressure may be relieved when the parents come to regard themselves as stewards, not possessors, of their child. Also, as the church provides effective resources and encouragement in parental care, the heavy burden of parenthood is lessened because it is shared.

Family Confinement

A second radical change precipitated by the advent of the child is the confinement of familial activity. The freedom of mobility is exchanged for an exacting restriction oriented around the child's needs. This confinement was regarded by those who were interviewed as the major adjustment of the postpartum period. "I would pick up the paper and decide it would be good to go to a movie downtown," one father commented. "And then realize: 'What are we going to do with the baby?'"

Similarly, the parental activity must be rescheduled around the needs of the infant. This schedule is not only different but is more extensive. The coming of the first child increases the household duties by 45 to 85 percent.[11] Parenthood means to new mothers the loss of sleep, chronic tiredness, added duties, long hours of work, and a decline in housekeeping standards. Thus, fatigue looms as a frequent by-product of the demanding child-centered schedule.

Husband-Wife Relationship

A third change forced by the event is in the relationship between husband and wife. One result is strain, as illustrated by the comments of a mother:

She [baby] was sick with the colic for three months. It was cry, cry, cry! We were distraught. Our relationship was strained. "Why don't you do it [take care of the baby], I have been working all day?" This is the type of things we would say to each other.

Yet another frequent result is increased mutual respect and appreciation. While much of the affectional output had to be

[11] R. A. Harper, *Marriage* (New York: Appleton-Century-Crofts, 1949), p. 249.

redirected to the child, for many couples the child himself became a uniting focus and symbol of their love which they felt for each other.

Sibling Relationships

Siblings too are greatly affected by the entrance of another child into the family sphere. For most of the parents with other children, the rivalry of siblings was a problem during the period of reestablishment. The age and number of siblings, the preparation given the siblings, and the response of parents to sibling rivalry seem to affect the intensity of the problem.

Thus, within the family covenant the newborn child is a bearer of considerable change. The familial role, mobility, schedules, and husband-wife and sibling relationships are radically affected. The change is inevitable. The pastor and the church are concerned that the change be constructive. The pastor seeks to assist the family in directing the change toward re-formed and strengthened covenants with each other and God.

THE CHURCH'S MINISTRY TO THE FAMILY

The family's relationship to the church is also changed by the advent of the child. On one hand, the exacting care of the child can become the occasion for exhibiting indifference to the concerns of the church and community. In such instances, the parents' prior covenant with the community of faith becomes defective. On the other hand, the event of childbirth provides impetus for a renewed covenant with the church. Responsibility for the care of a child can give the parents a new stake in the concerns of the church and community. The desire to expose the child to constructive influences may encourage parental interest in the church and other institutions of the community. The pastoral ministry should be sensitive to this perilous postpartum period, assisting the couple in their reentry into the church community as new parents.

If the advent of a child comes in the season of Advent itself, the ministries of the Christian year provide extra resources for the endowment of the birth of a child with Christian significance. The churches of the great liturgies are rich with experience at this time. The *Martin Luther Christmas Book,* translated by Roland Bainton and arranged with woodcut prints of the nativity of Christ, can be a lasting gift by the pastor and/or the church to the child at this season of the year. Luther indicates that the plight of Joseph was little different from the way this present study found fathers today: "Joseph had to do his best, and it may be that he asked some maid to fetch some water, but we do not read that anyone came to help."[12]

Of course, the classic sourcebook to which to turn for the ministry according to the Christian year is *The Book of Common Prayer*, a continuing legacy to all Christians from the Episcopal Church.

What about the relationship of the newborn child to the church? This question brought to the surface considerable confusion and frustration among the interviewees. These parents felt their child was in some sense a part of the church. Yet the status of their child in the church and before God often seemed to have no clear theological moorings.

Pastoral care can take either or both of two forms during the period of reestablishment.

Pastoral visit by telephone: The pastor can visit briefly with new parents by way of telephone during the early months. This method was used as a way to follow-up some of the major interviews. It seemed to be an appropriate way to reach the new mother during the most exacting and confining phase of the reestablishment period. In addition, some mothers appeared to be more comfortable in discussing personal feelings by telephone than by a more direct personal encounter. The telephone call can serve the purpose of conveying the church's concern, extending appropriate encouragement and interpretation, and listening for serious difficulties in the postpartum period.

Pastoral visit in the home: A second plan for ministry is a pastoral visit with the family in their home approximately three months after the birth of their child. The general purpose of this pastoral visit would be to assist the couple in reflecting upon the full meaning of the whole experience for their family. This suggestion actually came from the interviewees. In the words of one mother: "We feel that this sort of questioning about our relationship to the church and to our families is good and something that can be done [by the ministry of a pastor]." Speaking for her

[12] *Martin Luther Christmas Book*, Roland H. Bainton, trans. (Philadelphia: Fortress Press, 1958), p. 38.

husband, another mother added, "Robert said that it was very good for us to express some of the way we feel. We had not really done this. It gave it all a better perspective."

In addition to pastoral care, the new family may share in the corporate worship of the church in significant fashion. In paedo-baptist communions the ministry of the church during the event of childbirth naturally focuses upon the rite of baptism. At such times the thanksgiving and dedication of the parents and congregation are given expression in worship, and the child is received as a member of the church. Some Christians have rejected the rite of infant baptism and its theological implications. Yet, even for them the church's ministry should include some rite, consonant with the congregation's beliefs and accompanied by a teaching and pastoral care ministry. This rite should be a celebrative act of worship wherein the parents' and congregation's gratitude and responsibility is voiced and the relationship of the child to the community of faith established. Then this rite of worship, coming at the termination of this significant event with the family, gathers up and gives expression to the re-formed covenants involving family, church, and God.

In a church not practicing infant baptism, a rationale for this terminal and climactic act of worship which could be given to the family for purposes of discussion might be as follows:

A SERVICE OF DEDICATION

The church has always taken seriously the major events in a person's life. At marriage, there is the wedding ceremony; at conversion, there is the rite of baptism; at death, there is the funeral service.

What does the church offer at the birth of a child? In the Old Testament circumcision was the "spiritual birthmark" which symbolized the entry of the newborn child into the community of faith. Throughout the history of the church, most Christians used infant baptism to elucidate the religious significance of the childbirth experience. However, some Christians have rejected infant baptism as the proper rite to be observed at the outset of the infant's life. Yet the need for an appropriate rite still exists. We need the occasion to affirm publicly that childbirth is sacred, that children are divine gifts, and that the responsibility of parenthood is essentially a religious responsibility. This affirmation should find expression in an act of worship that gathers up the religious significance of the event of childbirth.

For this reason our church proposes a Service of Dedication

during this momentous occasion in the life of your family. This service is a rite designed to be theologically consonant with our church heritage. Its purpose is to enable you, your family, and your church to unite in the expression of gratitude and dedication to God.

Please read carefully this explanation regarding the meaning of the Service of Dedication. The pastor will meet with you prior to this service in order to discuss with you the questions and comments that you may have about this service.

This service seeks to express a threefold dedication: the dedication of you, the parents—your child—and the congregation.

Parental Dedication

You are different persons now. You are either parents for the first time or for a new time. As a result of the advent of your child, every facet of your lives has been affected. Your schedule, your mobility, your resources, your relationships have been challenged and changed—all because of the entry of a helpless infant in your world. This means that your former commitments are inadequate. You are simply no longer the same person that made those previous commitments. The covenants of trust and love you made with God at baptism and with each other at your wedding now need to be updated. These basic covenants require reshaping to include the meaning and responsibility that accompanied the coming of your child.

Thus, one purpose of the Service of Dedication is the invitation for you, as new parents, to enter a revised and enlarged covenant with God. You are asked to covenant with God to be **stewards** of the life now entrusted to your care. Normally, we do not apply the concept of stewardship to parenthood. We have heard frequently that our lives and our material possessions are not ours to do with as we please. We are trustworthy stewards of these gifts which are to be expended according to the will of the Owner; namely, God. Now, as stewards you have an added responsibility. You are challenged to dedicate yourselves to the arduous task of being faithful trustees of a new person. You offer your home as a school of Christian living, in which your child can gradually learn the Christian reality of life and love. Furthermore, as stewards, you relinquish the desire to possess your offspring, treating him as **you** please. Also, by entering this partnership with God in the task of parental care, you are confessing your faith in the adequacy of God to provide sufficient resources for the demands of parenthood.

Dedication of the Child

The Service of Dedication includes the dedication of your child to God. This act of consecration is essentially a prayer of intercession. Together as family and congregation we lift the potentiality of his life before God, asking that the child always may be at the center of God's purposes. We pray that your child, along with the other children of the congregation, will be open and responsive to the grace of God as mediated through our homes and church.

Also this act of dedication acknowledges the relationship of your child to the church. The ceremony does not itself change your child's status before God and the church, yet it does recognize that the child was born and will be reared within the sphere of the church. Your child is entering into this context of Christian community apart from any decision of his own.

Your child enters the life of this church as a "student" or "learner." The early church used the name "catechumen," meaning an unbaptized person who had been accepted by the church for instruction in the hope of a later confession of faith and baptism. This point of reference underscores two important truths about your child's relationship to our church.

1. As a "student," he is clearly within the church. In order for any student to learn, he must feel a part of the class. He listens, reacts, assimilates, rejects—but always feels himself to be a participant in the group. So it is with the child of a believing parent. He is neither an outsider, nor is he neutral, to the ministry of the church. By virtue of Christian parents and the concern of the church, your child is brought purposefully within the sphere of the church. As a vital participant in the Christian community, he will sing, pray, study, and serve. Influences of God's grace constantly will press upon his growing life through the relationships within the home and church.

2. Yet the status of "student" not only clarifies what your child is but also indicates what he is not. This Service of Dedication does not usher the child into the church as a full member. He comes as a candidate for Christian discipleship, participating in the process of nurture and instruction provided by the home and church. He is led to understand the meaningfulness of the Christian context into which you have placed him. Hopefully this growing religious awareness will reach its culmination as a young adult; namely, the appropriation for himself of the gift and demand of God's forgiving love shown most clearly in Jesus Christ.

Then baptism is the proper rite for this experience of conversion and commitment. It marks the apex of the child's training for discipleship and dramatizes his entrance into the responsible membership of the church.

Dedication of Congregation

Just as a person has been added to your family, so your child is an addition to the church family. The corporate life of this congregation will be affected for good or ill by the developing life of your child. Conversely, your child inevitably will be influenced by the quality of life he observes and experiences in this church.

Therefore, in placing him within the Christian community, you place upon this congregation an awesome responsibility to which it should respond with dedication.

In the Service of Dedication, the congregation assumes with you a responsibility for the Christian nurture of your child. The members vow to complement your parental influence by providing the most effective ministry possible for his religious development. In addition, the church seeks to expose you to the resources of worship, study, and fellowship so that you will be equipped to fulfill your ministry as Christian parents.

The key word throughout the Service of Dedication is **responsibility,** or broken into its component parts: **response—ability.** God has visited us in the gift of new life in Christ, and now in the new life of your child. The question remains: What will be your **response** to the graciousness of God? The Service of Dedication seeks to assist you and the congregation in the appropriate response of dedication.

Infant Baptism [13]

Churches of the Free Church tradition historically have insisted on adult baptism, rejected much that has been suggested in this chapter, and done so out of sincere belief. However, one of the bad side effects of the rejection of infant baptism has been an almost taboo-like fear of doing anything serious about the ministry to newborn infants and their parents.

A wholesome antidote to these bad side effects is found in the conviction expressed in the Presbyterian "household covenant" which is included in a formal statement in the Baptism of Infants. This service has *three* focii: the parent, the church, *and* the child existing as a living organism before God. This trinity of responsible participation is deleted in the much exaggerated individualism among Baptists and others who fear an ecclesiastical coronary if the baptism of infants is mentioned!

An inclusion of the following complete Presbyterian ceremony will serve as an informative study for reflective pastors of all Christian groups.[14]

Order For
The Administration of
The Sacrament of Baptism
To Infants

[13] This section has been appended by the editors.

[14] *The Book of Common Worship* (Philadelphia: The Board of Christian Education of the Presbyterian Church in the United States of America, 1946), pp. 121-125. Used by permission.

(While the Parents are bringing the Children to be baptized a Baptismal Hymn may be sung; or the following Sentences may be read by the Minister:)

The mercy of the Lord is from everlasting to everlasting upon them that fear Him, and His righteousness unto children's children;

To such as keep His covenant, and to those that remember His commandments to do them.

He shall feed His flock like a shepherd: He shall gather the lambs with His arm, and carry them in His bosom.

For the promise is unto you, and to your children, and to all that are afar off, even as many as the Lord our God shall call.

Glory be to the Father, and to the Son, and to the Holy Ghost; as it was in the beginning, is now, and ever shall be, world without end. **Amen**

(The Minister shall say:)

Dearly beloved, the Sacrament of Baptism is of divine ordinance. God our Father, who has redeemed us by the sacrifice of Christ, is also the God and Father of our children. They belong, with us who believe, to the membership of the Church through the covenant made in Christ, and confirmed to us by God in this sacrament, which is a sign and seal of our cleansing, of our engrafting into Christ, and of our welcome in the household of God. Our Lord Jesus said, Suffer the little children to come unto Me, and forbid them not, for of such is the kingdom of God. Verily I say unto you, Whosoever shall not receive the kingdom of God as a little child, he shall not enter therein. And He took them up in His arms, and put His hands upon them and blessed them. Saint Paul also declared that the children of believers are to be numbered with the holy people of God.

(The Minister shall say:)

In presenting your Child for baptism, do you confess your faith in Jesus Christ as your Lord and Saviour; and do you promise, in dependence on the grace of God, to bring up your Child in the nurture and admonition of the Lord?

(The the answer is given:)

I do.

(Then the Minister shall say:)

Let us pray.

Most merciful and loving Father, we thank Thee for the Church of Thy dear Son, the ministry of Thy Word, and the sacraments of grace. We praise Thee that Thou hast given us so gracious promises concerning our children, and that in mercy Thou callest them to Thee, marking them with this Sacrament as a singular token and pledge of Thy love. Set apart this water from a common to a sacred use, and grant that what we now do on earth may be confirmed in heaven. As in humble faith we present **this child** to Thee, we beseech Thee to receive **him,** to endue **him** with Thy Holy Spirit, and to keep **him** ever as Thine own; through Jesus Christ our Lord. **Amen.**

(All present reverently standing, the Minister shall say:)

What is the Christian name of this Child?

(Then the Minister, taking the Child in his arms, or leaving it in the arms of the Parent, pronouncing the Christian name of the Child, shall pour or sprinkle water upon the head of the Child, saying:)

N., I BAPTIZE THEE IN THE NAME OF THE FATHER, AND OF THE SON, AND OF THE HOLY GHOST. **Amen.**

The blessing of God Almighty, Father, Son and Holy Ghost, descend upon thee, and dwell in thine heart for ever. **Amen.**

(Then the Minister shall say to the Congregation:)

This Child is now received into Christ's Church: And you the people of this congregation in receiving **this Child** promise with God's help to be **his** sponsor to the end that **he** may confess Christ as **his** Lord and Saviour and come at last to His eternal kingdom. Jesus said, Whoso shall receive one such little child in My name receiveth Me.

(Then the Minister shall say:)

Let us pray.

Almighty and everlasting God, who of Thine infinite mercy and goodness hast promised that Thou wilt be not only our God, but also the God and Father of our children: We humbly beseech Thee for **this Child,** that Thy Spirit may be upon **him,** and dwell in **him** for ever. Take **him,** we entreat Thee, under Thy Fatherly care and protection; guide **him** and sanctify **him** both in body and in soul. Grant **him** to grow in wisdom as in stature, and in favor with God and man. Abundantly enrich **him** with Thy heavenly grace: bring **him** safely through the perils of childhood, deliver **him** from the temptations of youth, and lead **him** to witness a good confession, and to persevere therein to the end.

O God our Father, give unto Thy servants to whom Thou hast committed this blessed trust, the assurance of Thine unfailing providence and care. Guide them with Thy counsel as they teach and train their child; and help them to lead their household into an ever-increasing knowledge of Christ, and a more steadfast obedience to His will.

We commend to Thy Fatherly care the children and families of this congregation. Help us in our homes to honor Thee, and by love to serve one another.

And to Thy name be all blessing and glory, through Jesus Christ our Lord. **Amen.**

And now, as our Saviour Christ hath taught us, we humbly pray:

Our Father, who art in heaven; Hallowed be Thy name. Thy kingdom come. Thy will be done; On earth as it is in heaven. Give us this day our daily bread. And forgive us our debts, As we forgive our debtors. And lead us not into temptation; But deliver us from evil; For Thine is the kingdom, and the power, and the glory, for ever. Amen.

(Then the Minister shall say:)

The grace of the Lord Jesus Christ, and the love of God, and the communion of the Holy Spirit, be with you all. Amen.

SUGGESTIONS FOR FURTHER READING

Bell, Bernard Iddings, *The Parent, the Child and God.* Valatie, N. Y.: Holy Cross Press, n.d.

Blish, C. B., *Alice in Motherland.* Wilmington, Del.: Delaware State Society for Mental Hygiene, 1949.

Brenneman, Helen Good, *Meditations for the New Mother.* Scottdale, Pa.: Herald Press, 1953.

Carson, Ruth, *Your New Baby.* Public Affairs Pamphlet No. 353. New York: Public Affairs Committee, Inc., 1963.

Castallo, Mario A., *Getting Ready for Parenthood.* New York: The Macmillan Company, 1957.

Cressman, Rhoda Garber, *So You're Going to Be Parents.* Scottdale, Pa.: Herald Press, 1968.

Genne, Elizabeth and William, *The Ministry of Parents.* Nashville: The Upper Room, 1964.

Genne, William H., *Husbands and Pregnancy: the Handbook for Expectant Fathers.* New York: Association Press, 1956.

Link, Helen, ed., *A New Child in the Family.* Philadelphia: Board of Christian Education, The United Presbyterian Church, U.S.A., 1962.

Messages to Cradle Roll Parents. Series One: "Your Baby-to-Be." Series Two: "Infant Items." Nashville: Baptist Sunday School Board, 1958.

Nursery Packet #1, This Child of Ours, Ruth Guy. St. Louis: Bethany Press, 1964; *Nursery Packet #2,* Doris A. Younger. Valley Forge: The Judson Press, 1965.

Rowland, Lloyd W., *Pierre the Pelican Bulletins.* New York: The National Association for Mental Health, Inc., 1953. (These materials are obtained by writing the local Mental Health Association.)

Stopes, Marie, *Radiant Motherhood.* 9th ed. New York: G. P. Putnam's Sons, 1949.

Winnicott, D. W., *Mother and Child, A Primer of First Relationships.* New York: Basic Books, 1957.

Younger, Joan, *The Stork and You.* Philadelphia: The Westminster Press, 1952.

Mark S. Caldwell is a graduate of Baylor University and Southern Baptist Theological Seminary. He has worked with young people in the inner city and has been chaplain in the Child Evaluation Center of Louisville, Kentucky.

3

PASTORAL CARE OF PARENTS OF MENTALLY RETARDED CHILDREN

Mark S. Caldwell

INTRODUCTION BY BERNARD WEISSKOPF, M.D.

Director, Child Evaluation Center, Associate Professor of Pediatrics, and Associate in Psychiatry, University of Louisville School of Medicine

The parents of a mentally retarded child often turn to their minister for help in dealing with religious, social, and emotional problems created by having a chronically handicapped child. If the minister is to help such families, he will need to have an understanding of the different aspects of the problem. He particularly will have to recognize that the parents of the mentally retarded have specific feelings, attitudes, and needs which they have to resolve and for which they will often seek the help of their minister. Professionals who do not fully understand these feelings, attitudes, and needs may find themselves uncomfortable and frustrated when confronted by such a family.

The Child Evaluation Center, Louisville, Kentucky, recognizing the contributions that can be made by the clergy to the mentally retarded and his family, has been providing students of the ministry with an opportunity to gain a deeper understanding of the problem and its effect upon the patient's family and his community. The author of this chapter spent several months interviewing parents who brought their children to the Center for an evaluation and exploring with them the role of religion in their endeavor to resolve certain of their feelings, attitudes, and needs. Chaplain Caldwell was particularly concerned with defining the role of the minister in our setting and the contributions he could make to these families as a mediator of hope.

This chapter will give the reader a better understanding of mental retardation and the challenging role of the minister in dealing with this most complex problem.

PASTORAL CARE OF PARENTS OF MENTALLY RETARDED CHILDREN

Mark S. Caldwell

The Child Evaluation Center in Louisville, Kentucky, provided an excellent setting for an investigation of the minister's role as mediator of hope to the parents of mentally retarded children. Under the direction of Bernard Weisskopf, M.D., the staff at the Center provides expert physical, psychological, and social evaluations of children believed to be mentally retarded.

Based upon work at the Center, this chapter will: (1) examine mental retardation and provide the minister with some medical facts concerning mental retardation, (2) provide clinical material on parental reactions to mental retardation, and (3) provide several guidelines which can aid in the mature acceptance of reality. Many ministers suffer from an inadequate understanding of mental retardation and, as a result, are helpless when confronted with it in their parishes. Parents respond to their retarded child in many ways. The effective minister can serve these parents best if he is aware of the most common forms of responses. As a "reality tester" the minister must support competent medical personnel and function in a supportive capacity by seeking to engender in parents those qualities productive of maximum realization. In so doing, the minister truly will become a mediator of hope to the parents of the mentally retarded.

WHAT IS MENTAL RETARDATION?

A pastor can deal constructively with the parents of a mentally retarded child only when he has a clear understanding of mental retardation itself. The incidence, definition, and causes of mental retardation are essential ingredients of this understanding.

The Incidence of Mental Retardation

According to most estimates, there are more than 5½ million people in the United States (3 percent of the total population) who should be identified as mentally retarded before they are fifteen years old. Between 100,000 to 200,000 of the babies born each year are likely to join this group. The National Association for Retarded Children has determined that by 1970 natural population growth is expected to increase the total number of retarded persons to 6½ million unless far-reaching preventive measures can be introduced. The chances are that most religious communities include some mentally retarded. Similarly, at least ten million adults in our country are parents of mentally retarded children. These parents should receive wise pastoral care in order to introduce mature hope in face of an apparently hopeless situation. Those who serve as pastors, priests, or rabbis must learn to deal effectively with this phenomenon. For many people — including quite a few clergy, unfortunately — mental retardation is something to be feared, not something to be dealt with. Even today some ministers, as soon as they discover a mentally retarded child in their parish, will admonish the parents to "put that kid away." Such a culturally superstitious approach is harmful both to the child himself and to the parents who are experiencing a variety of emotional responses such as guilt, anxiety, or hostility. The first prerequisite in ministering to the parents of the mentally retarded is a clear understanding of mental retardation.

Definition of Mental Retardation

Mental retardation is not a disease, but it can be the result of one disease or of several diseases. The 1959 definition used by the American Association on Mental Deficiency is as follows:

> Mental retardation refers to subaverage general intellectual functioning which originates during the developmental period and is associated with impairment in adaptive behavior.[1]

[1] Rick Heber, "Modification in the Manual on Terminology and Classification in Mental Retardation," *American Journal of Mental Deficiency*, January, 1961, p. 499.

Thus, mental retardation is not to be equated with mental illness or emotional instability. Whereas mental illness results from personality aberrations, mental retardation stems from inadequate intellectual ability. Not all of the mentally retarded are mentally ill in the sense that personality distortions are present. The mentally retarded person can be as emotionally stable as the person functioning at normal or above normal intelligence. The ability of the mentally retarded to effect a harmonious relationship to his environment and toward himself may be hampered by the unrealistic demands placed upon him; yet there is nothing inherent in mental retardation which implies emotional instability.

There are degrees of mental retardation. Not all of the mentally retarded are incapable of attending school; however, not all can hope realistically to learn a remunerative trade. Various attempts have been made to catalogue the levels of mental retardation. The Child Evaluation Center has adapted a scale based on I.Q. classifications. The concerned minister must be aware of the different degrees of mental retardation and that various mentally retarded persons may be expected to achieve certain levels of social integration and intellectual competence.

The Causes of Mental Retardation

At the present stage of medical knowledge only about one out of five cases of mental retardation can be traced to any certain cause or causes. The minister should be aware of the complexity involved in determining the origin of mental retardation. Factors which can lead to some form of mental retardation can be placed under three broad categories:

Prenatal factors. These are factors which occur prior to the actual birth of the child. They include: (1) infections, (2) metabolic disorders such as hypothyroidism and diabetes, (3) injury to the child as a result of maternal medications, (4) genetic factors, and (5) chromosomal disorders such as mongolism (Down's syndrome) due to a malformation of the all important chromosomes which determine the process of growth.

Natal factors. Natal factors are those which take place at birth, including: (1) anoxia or loss of vital oxygen supply to the brain, (2) mechanical injury, (3) prematurity, (4) postmaturity, and (5) adverse drug reactions.

Postnatal factors. These occur after the actual birth of the child. Infections, accidents, poisons, nutritional abnormalities, and even psychosocial factors, such as emotional or cultural deprivation, can cause mental retardation.

PARENTAL RESPONSES TO MENTAL RETARDATION

After the minister has familiarized himself with mental retardation, he must become aware of the variety of parental responses to it. Studies have indicated that various factors play decisive roles in determining what these reactions will be. This section will deal with social and religious elements which influence parental response and with mature and immature reactions on the part of parents.

Social and Religious Factors

The social class of the parents can play a significant role in determining how they confront the crisis of a mentally retarded child. Often, social class distinctions carry with them certain value standards which, in turn, influence expected behavior patterns. The religious orientation of the family also has a good deal to do with parental response. The minister cannot disregard either of these areas if he is to render valuable assistance.

Social factors. Bernard Farber has shown that parents in the lower socio-economic groups who have severely mentally retarded children confront the basic problem of role-organization — the problem of dealing effectively with the financial crisis which such a child precipitates. At times these families are not able to provide properly for the child.[2] The minister can mediate a great deal of hope in such cases by introducing the family to whatever community or church resources are available. Families in the higher socio-economic brackets usually face a different crisis — the "tragic crisis" or the "expectation crisis." As these families usually have higher aspirations for their children, they are frustrated by the birth of a child who is not able to meet their demands. Nevertheless, families of lower social groups might expect their child to elevate himself along the social ladder, and,

[2] Bernard Farber, "Effects of a Severely Mentally Retarded Child on the Family," *Readings on the Exceptional Child: Research and Theory,* E. Philip Trapp and Philip Himelstein, eds. (New York: Appleton-Century-Crofts, 1962), Chap. 17.

they too might be frustrated with a mentally retarded child who cannot perform the necessary intellectual skills. In such a situation, the child prevents the parents from fulfilling their hopes and goals.[3] The minister must warn the parents against the dangers of such ambitions for their child. Parents who are extremely conscious of the opinions and pressures of others are highly susceptible to the danger of pushing their retarded child beyond the limits of his ability. The pastor should be careful not to become just another pressuring agent in the situation. He should resist a temptation to be a representative of social class needs and prejudices rather than remaining a representative of the God who accepts persons with their own unique capabilities and limitations. Religious instruction should be geared to the ability of the child.

Religious factors. Roman Catholic families tend to have a more traditional view of the family; they see the importance of family durability and regard the children as God-ordained responsibilities. Stubblefield concluded that even socially the Catholic family has less difficulty accepting the birth of a retarded child.[4]

Farber has suggested that Roman Catholics have less difficulty with the birth of a retarded child due to the more supportive role of the family.[5] G. H. Zuk has concluded that the Roman Catholic teaching that parents should not feel guilty about having a retarded child but rather should accept the child as a special gift contributes to greater acceptance.[6]

Gerhard Lenski made a study of families in Detroit and discovered that Catholic mothers, in general, seemed to feel that children were less trouble than did Protestant mothers. Lenski noted that whereas 68 percent of the Catholic mothers regarded the experience of raising children either "pleasant" or "very pleasant"; only 51 percent of the Protestant mothers did so. Also, Lenski's study revealed that Protestants valued intellectual auton-

---

[3] *Ibid.*

[4] Harold W. Stubblefield, *The Church's Ministry in Mental Retardation* (Nashville: Broadman Press, 1965), p. 18.

[5] Farber, "Effects of a Severely Mentally Retarded Child on Family Integration," *Monographs of the Society for Research in Child Development*, Vol. 24, No. 2, pp. 24-25, 61-65, 79.

[6] G. H. Zuk, *et al.*, "Maternal Acceptance of Retarded Children: A Questionnaire Study of Attitudes and Religious Background," *Child Development* (September, 1961), pp. 525 ff.

omy in their children above obedience and that Protestant children were expected to take responsibility for themselves earlier than were Catholic children.[7]

There can be little doubt that Lenski's work shows the result in Protestant families of the impact of the Puritan ethic with its stress on the value of work. In our society work has been the royal road to wealth and social standing, and the Puritan ethic, derived from Calvinism, generally has underwritten the divine admonition to work. The mentally retarded child, unable to meet the demands of a strenuous work ethic, has been seen as less than truly human. Such a situation does little to foster hope for the parents of these children.

Mature and Immature Parental Responses

Parental responses to the retarded child have a great deal to do with the child's welfare. The mature responses will lead to the maximum possible social, intellectual, emotional, and religious development of the child. Immature responses, on the other hand, will retard even further the possibilities of progress. In effect the immature response of parents represents a roadblock to maximum total integration by the child.

Mature responses. In the mature response to their mentally retarded child, parents face the reality of whatever degree of mental retardation is present and adopt a constructive attitude which allows them to live with the situation without undue stress. These parents learn to mobilize their energy and that of the child for the attainment of realistic, specific goals. Yet, mature responses often come after an initial period of emotional disorganization in which the parents experience tremendous anxiety and use various defense mechanisms to help them cope with the stress. Defense mechanisms become increasingly apparent during the subsequent stage of reintegration. These defenses rarely prove effective in relieving distress. The mature parent learns to adapt to reality and moves beyond the need for defense mechanisms which evade reality and foster a fantasy world where hopes can never be realized.

[7] Gerhard Lenski, *The Religious Factor* (Garden City: Doubleday & Company, Inc., 1961), pp. 198-200.

The mature parent may be expected to move through a bereavement reaction which Wayne Oates has described in six phases as the shocking blow of the loss in itself, the numbing effect of the shock, the struggle between fantasy and reality, the breakthrough of a flood of grief, selective memory, and stabbing pain, the acceptance of the loss, and the affirmation of the value of life as it is in itself.[8] The parent of the retarded child, unlike one who has a corpse to mourn, experiences what has been called "chronic sorrow."[9] Much parental grief is anticipatory in nature — parents coming to an evaluation center usually have an idea that "something is wrong." The uncertainty of what to expect produces an anxiety unlike that of one faced with the accomplished fact of the death of a family member. Once an evaluation is made and accepted by the parent, the process of mature adaptation to the realities of life can begin.

Immature responses. The immature response of the parent in effect represents a fixation at the stage where fantasy vies with reality. The process of mature adaptation has been stultified at a particular point, and continued progress becomes difficult, if not impossible, until the fantasy-reality stage has been negotiated successfully. Immature, or maladaptive, reactions are characterized by the following attitudes which function as defense mechanisms calculated to inject hope, however unrealistic, into the situation.

The most obvious defense mechanism is usually *denial.* Many parents cling to the hope that their doctor is mistaken. At times they express their denial by claiming to "misunderstand" what the doctor has told them or by simply "forgetting" his instructions. The parent who denies the reality of mental retardation cannot face the adaptations which are necessary if maximum results are to be achieved. His refusal to accept sound medical advice is based upon his apparent inability to accept the fact that *his* child is retarded. This denial leads to the employment of other defense mechanisms which create a fantasy world where retardation is replaced with other less threatening phenomena.

Another mechanism closely related to denial is parents' tendency to *shop around* for a diagnosis which suits them, to have

[8] Wayne E. Oates, *Anxiety in Christian Experience* (Philadelphia: The Westminster Press, 1955), pp. 52-55.
[9] Stubblefield, *op. cit.,* p. 21.

more than one professional opinion; but parents often "shop" endlessly for a doctor who claims to have a miraculous cure or for one who will tell them that the child is normal and will "grow out of it." Such parents become the victims of quacks and charlatans. This shopping around is an obvious attempt to force reality to meet the demands of their wishes or fantasies and also represents a fixation at a premature level of acceptance.

Quite often parents will express the child's *physical limitations* rather than his mental retardation. For example, a couple who had been ready to accept a diagnosis of cerebral palsy for their daughter fought for years to deny mental retardation. When their case came up in conference, the staff recommended that the parents be referred to a counselor for help in the acceptance of the real situation. There seems to be less social stigma attached to physical handicaps than there is to mental handicaps. Some mentally retarded children have no physical difficulty whatsoever and are, therefore, expected to be quite normal. In like manner, because some mentally retarded persons are able to function at a normal social age, people expect them to be normal mentally. When the child cannot meet the expectations adults place before him, he might resort to unacceptable social behavior in order to distract attention from his feeling of inability. This unacceptable behavior without obvious physical causes makes it harder for the parent and society as a whole to accept the child with mental limitations. Also, parents feel that some physical abnormalities, if caught soon enough, can be treated effectively or will clear up with time.

Many parents cope with the hopeless situation by *rejection* of the child. This may take several forms. Some parents overtly reject the child and refuse to care for him or demand that he be put in an institution even though there is no real need for such drastic action. More often, however, parents seek to cover their rejection with a veneer of overprotection. They become quick to list the child's virtues and accomplishments and hide any frustration they might feel toward him. Such parents rarely allow the child to test his ability to deal with the normal world; they protect him from all harm and thus minimize his chances for adaptation. In extreme form this rejection takes the form of a death wish. Donald Hastings has commented:

I have seen several instances wherein unconscious wishes for the death of the defective child were covered by the blanket of extreme solicitude out of all proportion to that called for by the reality of the situation.[10]

Leo Kanner has isolated three ways in which parents demonstrate a *tendency to misplace the problem.* When parents first discover their child is not functioning properly in school, their first reaction is to locate the problem in the method of instruction. When this proves inadequate, they tend to find the culprit in the child's body. For instance, one pair of parents became convinced that if Johnny had his tonsils out he would do better in school. When this procedure failed, they gravitated to the third stage. In order to satisfy their need for prestige they began to pounce on Johnny himself. They decided that he was lazy; they scolded him, deprived him of privileges, and spent hours helping him with his homework. The child, unable to meet the unrealistic demands placed upon him, came to see himself as a wretched, miserable, ungrateful soul who was letting his parents down.[11]

The following are typical *guilt* responses of young mothers faced with the reality that their child is mentally retarded.

> Doctor, did I have something to do with it? Did I do something wrong? . . . Well — maybe before he was born — did I do something then? . . . If it isn't what I have *done,* maybe it's what I *am* that brought it about.[12]

Parental guilt can be seen behind such questions as, "Why did God do this to me?" or "Why did God allow this terrible thing to happen?" John J. Waterman has called the psychological threat to the parent the greatest obstacle to parental acceptance of the mentally retarded child.[13] Social worker Sylvia Schild has commented that

> part of the resistance of the person seeking help [and thus having hope] stems from his feeling of responsibility for the problem. When guilt is intensified, the resistance to help will be proportionately increased. Because of this, those endeavoring to help parents of retarded children

---

[10] Donald Hastings, "Some Psychiatric Problems of Mental Deficiency," *Counseling and Psychotherapy with the Mentally Retarded,* C. Stacey and M. DeMartino, eds. (Glencoe, Ill.: The Free Press, 1957), p. 412.

[11] Leo Kanner, "Parents' Feelings about Retarded Children," *American Journal of Mental Deficiency* (January, 1963), pp. 375-383.

[12] Cited in Kanner, *ibid.,* p. 378.

[13] John J. Waterman, "Psychogenic Factors in Parental Acceptance of Feebleminded Children," Stacey and DeMartino, *op. cit.,* p. 399.

must be aware that heightened resistance is usually due to the inwardly projected guilt of the parent.[14]

Thus, some parents will feel the need to atone for some real or imaginary sin and will seek out a minister, priest, or rabbi to hear their confession. Only when the deity has been satisfied can they have hope. The minister must beware lest he condone such attitudes by a harsh demeanor. The minister who accepts the child as he is, who exhibits love and concern for both parent and child will reflect in concrete form the love of God.

A number of couples cope with the birth of a retarded child by claiming that they have been *chosen by God* to care for this defective child because they are better equipped to do so. Studies by Farber [15] and Zuk [16] have shown that Roman Catholics take this attitude more often than Protestants or Jews. Such families try to find hope by following the ordained will of God without question. Donald Jolly, M.D., formerly director of an institution for the mentally retarded, in personal conversation with this writer said he felt this approach to be "a trifle neurotic itself." The theological weakness of this approach lies in a conception of God and the world that does not allow for accident in any respect.

The crisis of mental retardation calls forth a number of immature reactions on the part of parents. These defense mechanisms may be seen as tools for the production of artificial hope. Either they fly in the face of reality or they attempt to lessen the sting of reality. If these people are to have a more lasting, more productive hope, they must come to grips with the facts and relinquish their dependence on pseudo-hopes which are the results of their inability to deal realistically with their child's difficulty. They must refrain from a fixation on fantasy and move to a mature integration of fact and possibility.

PARENTAL NEEDS AND SELF-AFFIRMATION

Edward Albee has written a play entitled *The Delicate Balance.* The place of hope in the crisis of mental retardation lies

[14] Sylvia Schild, "Counseling with Parents of Retarded Children Living at Home," *Social Work,* Vol. 9, No. 1 (January, 1964), p. 87. Reprinted with permission of the National Association of Social Workers.

[15] Farber, "Effects of a Severely Mentally Retarded Child on Family Integration," *loc. cit.*

[16] Zuk, *loc. cit.*

within the "delicate balance" of the child's condition and the possibilities for his development. The parent who would have creative hope must be able to see these limits, to accept them, to explore them to their depths, and to affirm himself and his child as creatures of God.

Realistic Hope

Since this study focuses on the Christian minister as a mediator of hope, hope will be understood within the framework of the Christian gospel. Therefore, hope will imply the resolution of the paradox between possibility and necessity by means of personal encounter with God as Creator and oneself as creature. Thomas Colley, chief psychologist at the Child Evaluation Center, in conversation with this writer, suggested a helpful definition of hope in connection with mental retardation. According to Colley, parents faced with the crisis of a mentally retarded child find most hope in the mobilization of energy for the attainment of *realistic specific* goals. For example, parents who are uncertain as to what the future holds are given a great deal of hope when they learn from competent medical personnel that their child might be toilet trained at age five, or that he could be expected to attend school and possibly learn a trade. Such information gives structure to the future and removes the ambiguity of the situation. Where there exists the realistic eventuality for progress, hope is present. Such parents, freed from the paralyzing uncertainty which was predominant prior to a sound medical diagnosis, can mobilize their energy for the task ahead.

Self-affirmation

According to a mother of one mentally retarded child, "the greatest single need of parents of these children is constructive professional counseling . . . which will enable the parents to find reasonably satisfying answers to their own problems at various stages in the child's life." This mother continued:

> We need guidance from someone who can help us to see that this thing which has happened to us, even though it may be a life-shaking experience, does not of necessity have to be a *life-breaking* one.[17]

[17] Mrs. Max A. Murray, "Needs of Parents of Mentally Retarded Children," *American Journal of Mental Deficiency*, Vol. 63, No. 6 (May, 1959), p. 1084.

Glib ministerial jargon about "God's will" or how "beautiful Johnny will be when he gets to heaven" fails to supply the constructive warmth the parents desperately need. Sentimentality and genuine human understanding are poles apart. As the apostle Paul says, love grows in knowledge and perception (Colossians 1:9-11). Leo Kanner's advice to physicians needs to be heard by ministers:

> What most [parents of mentally retarded children] hope to hear is indeed not so much a piece of etiological wisdom in words of Greek or Latin origin as an authoritative and sympathetic endorsement of themselves, of their human and parental competence, of their right not to blame themselves for what has happened.[18]

The following are attitudes which help meet parental needs.

Patience. Mental retardation is a long term affair. Parental ability to be patient influences parental hope. Whatever hope the future holds will require years of hard work and countless adjustments. Therefore, parents who are impatient will not be able to cope with the thought of year after year of the often tedious care which must be given their child. Thoughts from the Psalms may help both parents and pastor (Psalms 31:24; 33:18-22). The minister who becomes involved with the family can mediate hope through his own patient willingness to rejoice in even the most minute progress which the child makes while not expecting or demanding that the progress be rapid. Often hopeless parents can see only *one* path of action; a hope-inspiring pastor can enable them to see other alternatives. The minister who communicates an unhealthy sense of urgency in every aspect of his ministry will make the task of the parent of the mentally retarded more difficult.

A willingness to live with the mystery of life. Stubblefield has noted:

> Mental retardation, like all other manifestations of natural evil, must be regarded as both under God's sovereignty and as a mystery which cannot be explained. Limitations, pain, and suffering are woven into the fabric of human existence and cannot be understood as coming directly from the hand of God.[19]

Thus, parents who would have hope must be able to live with-

---

[18] Kanner, *op cit.*, p. 375.
[19] Stubblefield, *op. cit.*, p. 43.

out many of the often trite explanations as to why their child is mentally retarded. In fact, they may see through the clichés, react hostilely to the minister, and withdraw from him. The minister who is threatened by uncertainty or who feels that as a "man of God" he has all the answers to even the most puzzling human tragedies will most likely do more harm than good. The pastor who is clearly as perplexed by the evil in the world as the parents themselves will avoid the dangers of oversimplification. Even the apostle Paul admitted to being "perplexed, but not driven to despair" (2 Corinthians 4:8).

In a counseling conference for the parents of an eight-year-old boy who was functioning at a mental age of five years nine months and a social age of eight years five months, this writer learned that the parents' minister had told the family that their child had an "emotional block" which he could correct. This diagnosis was in direct opposition to that of the Child Evaluation Center. The staff recommended that since the child was mildly mentally retarded he should be placed in special education classes. The minister revealed in a private conversation with this writer that he was going to undermine the medical recommendations and launch an all-out attempt to cure the child. The minister's denial of the depths of the problem fed that of the parents. Previously they had come to the point where they could begin to deal realistically with their child's difficulty. The pastor's own need to succeed single-handedly denied him the joy of fellowship with other helping professions and a larger meaning of Christian community. He laid the groundwork for his own rejection later by the parents.

In the face of God's seeming arbitrariness, elusiveness, and inhumanity, Job refused to be satisfied with the trite explanations of evil proposed by his "friends." Apparently stripped of all hope, Job came to a startling realization. Neither life nor God can be explained to the fullest, but the man who is willing to strip himself of undue intellectual pride and to take his place as a part of a world racked with pain and filled with uncontrollable accidents comes closest to understanding what life is all about.

An ability to see God as a loving father rather than as a harsh judge. Israel Zwerling undertook to analyze the impact of initial counseling of parents with mentally retarded children. Parents contributed letters in which they recounted their experiences.

The positive role of religion was stressed in twenty-two of the eighty-five letters received. One letter contained the following:

> It was really through the church that I gained two important insights: one that we looked at things as punishment which might be our own guilt feelings . . . two, in connection with the Bible story of the man born blind, that these things were not a reflection on the parents, but could be used as a means of helpful endeavor.[20]

The parent who sees his retarded child as a punishment placed on him by God will be less able to undertake proper treatment for the child. Rather, he will tend to reject the child who remains as a constant reminder of some real or imagined sin. The pastor who does not refuse to come near a retarded child but who takes the child in his arms as he would a normal baby can communicate God's love in a most graphic fashion. Christ's compassionate admonition, "Let the children come to me, and do not hinder them" (Matthew 19:14), when followed by a concerned pastor, will be of help to insecure and often embarrassed parents; and it will serve as an example for other parishioners whose concern is vital to parents of the mentally retarded.

A willingness to deny personal omnipotence. Few people who have not come to understand their own limitations and the limitations of the entire human situation can cope with the tragedy of having a mentally retarded child. Since mental retardation casts into bold relief the imperfections built into this world, the parent who would adopt a healthy attitude toward it must be one who does not make man the measure of all things. The person who believes himself to be godlike and who has part in the birth of a retarded child has difficulty reconciling his own feelings of omnipotence with his participation in imperfection. However, the abnegation of personal omnipotence does not entail a fatalistic attitude which refuses to take action. Authentic hope is connected with an active participation, not a passive expectation which waits on other men or on God to do the job. Although man is not the Creator, at least he participates in the creation and has some responsibility for making the best of whatever situation arises.

A sense of community. Life is often too harsh for man to "go

---

[20] Cited by Israel Zwerling, "Initial Counseling of Parents with Mentally Retarded Children," *The Journal of Pediatrics,* Vol. 44, No. 4 (April, 1954), p. 474.

it" alone. The hope of the parent of the mentally retarded is vitally bound up with his ability to relate to a community. Parents must relate on a very deep level as husband and wife. Often the birth of a retarded child will precipitate family conflicts in which one member blames the other for the child's handicap. Also, parents must be able to benefit from the reconciling ministry of the church. The congregation which isolates the family of the mentally retarded does the family and also itself a disservice. They miss an opportunity to discover fresh meanings of the Christian faith. Some congregations can provide adequate teaching situations for the retarded. Many could make available a volunteer group to care for retarded children in the homes while the parents have an evening out. Some churches have organized discussion groups composed of parents of the mentally retarded. The dangers of parental isolation have been shown dramatically by Weingold and Hormuth:

> Group pressures basically had forced the family of a retarded child to withdraw from normal social contacts and isolate itself with the child. In turn, the family's attention was focused more sharply on every action of the child; the resulting frustration accentuated not only the personality difficulties of the parents, but to a large extent created feelings of guilt, shame, rejection and overprotection of the retarded child.[21]

The family who has little if any social or religious activity tends to view the child as the center of the family instead of as a member of it. Theologically such a situation leads to idolatry in which the child is worshiped as a god. This attitude leads to a neurotic overlay on top of the retardation problem.

Eschatological hope. The Christian minister cannot remain oblivious to the hope of a resurrection. The hope of a better life after the present one is a vital part of the way in which man copes with the suffering he faces in this world. True, not all men feel the need of this hope in order to live constructive, healthy lives; however, the hope of an end to suffering and pain plays a part in the faith of many Christians. This hope need not be for golden streets and pearly gates; it rests in the Christian conviction that man will be perfected as a "total being." God is working to reconcile the world unto himself; all of nature is

[21] Joseph T. Weingold and Rudolf P. Hormuth, "Group Guidance of Parents of Mentally Retarded Children," *Journal of Clinical Psychology*, Vol. 9 (April, 1953), p. 119.

groaning after a sense of fullness and wholeness, and the Christian has hope that the pain and imperfection of this world will be ultimately defeated.

However, ministers dealing with parents of the mentally retarded must guard against using this hope in the extreme. Faith in the future wholeness of their child should not keep them from meeting their child's needs now. As mentioned above, the hope which is a mere passive acceptance stultifies cooperative action.

THE MINISTER AS MEDIATOR OF HOPE

As a mediator of hope to the parents of the mentally retarded, the minister can help parents resolve the paradox between the necessity of accepting the retardation as a lifelong matter and the possibility of their child's achieving the maximum levels of intellectual and social integration of which he is capable. In order to accomplish this, the minister stresses the importance of a personal acceptance of the reality of God as Creator and the self as creature. This understanding puts the reality of mental retardation in the proper perspective. Imperfection is "built in" throughout the natural order; the world is a "fallen world," yet God is working to redeem the world. Life does not lend itself to easy solutions; the minister does not, out of some compulsion to please, make imponderable questions seem easy when parents ask, "Why did this happen to us?" Rather, the effective minister stresses those attitudes which produce realistic hope. He helps parents mobilize their energy for the attainment of realistic goals.

The minister's basic task in mental retardation is neither diagnostic nor therapeutic; it is supportive and creative. He participates in the struggles of the parents. He celebrates with them the joys which they experience with their child as he progresses. The minister communicates patience, understanding, concern, a willingness to live with the mysteries of life, and a sense of man's limitations in the face of adversity. He does not forsake them. From him the parents gain a stability which guards them against inaction or excessive zeal and helps them to develop a realistic estimate of the future. The minister functions as a "reality tester." He supports the medical diagnosis. He helps the parents guard against the idolatry of placing the child in the center of the family. He offers himself to parents as one who confronts denial mechanisms with the realities of the situation but also as one willing to help carry the parents' load of suffering. Through him they can confide in and become confident of God's love for their child. In him they find a friend who is willing to share their pain and frustration, if he does his work well. The minister who seeks to involve the retarded in the life of the church will communicate hope to the parents who may feel that their child is doomed to constant isolation. To the parents who have been advised to seek placement for their child in an institution, the minister has a responsibility to lessen the pain of separation and the guilt which placement brings.

The task of the minister as a mediator of hope to the parents of the mentally retarded is captured sensitively in this anonymous prayer:

> Almighty and Merciful God, we who are the parents and friends of the least of your little ones ask guidance and help in our efforts to brighten their life, that we will become reconciled to their affliction. Grant that we may not despair as those who have no hope, but rather give us the grace to know your wisdom and the courage to accept it nobly. Amen.

SUGGESTIONS FOR FURTHER READING

Doll, Edgar A., "Counseling Parents of Severely Mentally Retarded Children, *Journal of Clinical Psychology*, April, 1953, pp. 114-117.

Kemp, Charles, *The Church: The Gifted and the Retarded Child.* St. Louis: The Bethany Press, 1957.

Mental Retardation: A Handbook for the Primary Physician. A Report of the American Medical Association Conference on Mental Retardation, April 9-11, 1964. Chicago: American Medical Association, 1965.

Murray, Dorothy G., "A Parent Speaks to Pastors on Mental Retardation," *Pastoral Psychology*, Vol. XIII (September, 1962), pp. 23-30.

Perske, Robert, "The Pastoral Care and Counseling of Families of the Mentally Retarded," *Pastoral Psychology*, Vol. XIX (November, 1968), pp. 21-28.

Rheingold, Harriet L., "Interpreting Mental Retardation to Parents," *Counseling and Psychotherapy with the Mentally Retarded*, Stacey and DeMartino, eds. Glencoe, Ill.: The Free Press, 1957, pp. 390-398.

Sheino, S. L., "Problems in Helping Parents of Mentally Defective and Handicapped Children," in Stacey and DeMartino, *op. cit.*, pp. 403-410.

Stone, Marguerite M., "Parental Attitudes to Retardation," in Stacey and DeMartino, *op. cit.*, pp. 414-420.

Stubblefield, Harold W., *The Church's Ministry in Mental Retardation.* Nashville: Broadman Press, 1965.

Zuk, Gerald H., *et al.*, "Maternal Acceptance of Retarded Children: A Questionnaire Study of Attitudes and Religious Backgrounds," *Child Development*, September, 1961, pp. 525 ff.

J. Thomas Meigs, pastor of the Chaplin Fork Baptist Church in Chaplin, Kentucky, is a graduate of Carson Newman College and Southern Baptist Theological Seminary. In addition to pastoral work, he has been a high school teacher and a part-time chaplain at the Children's Hospital in Louisville, Kentucky.

4

PASTORAL CARE OF PARENTS OF CHILDREN WITH CANCER

J. Thomas Meigs

INTRODUCTION BY DONALD R. KMETZ, M.D.

Head Pathologist, and Director of Laboratories, Children's Hospital, Louisville, Kentucky; and Assistant Professor of Pathology, University of Louisville School of Medicine

In the following chapter, the attitudes of parents who face the potential loss of a child are accurately described and critically analyzed. Each of the parents interviewed had a child suffering from cancer or a serious blood disorder. The study considers potential methods of coping, the process of grief, and possible religious resources. Although the specific role of pastoral care in the support of these families is still not well established, there is convincing evidence presented which indicates that the minister can contribute significantly to the total scope of parental support. Studies like this provide greater insight into the problem.

As a physician responsible for the care of children with life-threatening and sometimes fatal disorders, I am personally grateful for this attempt to better understand parental attitudes toward a child's impending death. A physician must constantly be concerned not only with medical decisions, but must accept the responsibility of relating to the family in a meaningful way. The minister may well provide a mechanism by which greater insight into this complex family situation can be obtained.

Total care of the child must include parental support: at the time of diagnosis, throughout the period of hope, and during the period of grief. There is no doubt that continued cooperation and communication between the minister and the professional medical staff will ultimately lead to a better method of providing this total patient care.

PASTORAL CARE OF PARENTS OF CHILDREN WITH CANCER

J. Thomas Meigs

In recent years, leukemia, a form of cancer, has emerged as the leading killer of children, according to Beatrice Lampkin, M.D., an assistant professor of pediatrics in hematology at the University of Cincinnati. In 1965 cancer in children was second only to accidents in causing death. She stated that cancer continues to baffle both scientists and doctors.[1] If cancer in children baffles scientists and doctors, it is the cause of profound grief and heartache on the part of the families of the children. In such a situation parents resort to a variety of forms of coping behavior and expressions of grief.

This chapter will discuss the reactions of parents who brought their children to the Tumor and Hematology Clinic of the Out-Patient Services of Children's Hospital in Louisville, Kentucky, in the light of research which has been carried on in this field of pediatrics. Thus, both case studies and expert opinion will be used to develop guidelines by which pastors may minister more effectively to parents who find themselves in this crucial situation. The chapter will deal with coping behavior, the grief process, religious resources, and the implication for pastoral care. This is not a definitive study, but it is a presentation of several related aspects of the problem for a continuing and growing ministry to parents whose child has cancer.

COPING BEHAVIOR

The parent of a child with a life-threatening disease, such as cancer, must adapt in his own way to the threatened loss. There

---

[1] Beatrice Lampkin, "Leukemia Still Baffles Scientists," *The Courier-Journal* (Louisville), July 9, 1968, p. 15.

will be a spectrum of reactions, particularly to the initial diagnosis, by the parents. The threatened loss of a child and the later actual loss through death have different meanings to parents. The nature of the parents' adjustment to the diagnosis that their child has cancer will bring out among other things: (1) the parents' mode of coping with past crises; (2) their previous experiences with illness, hospitalization, and death; and (3) the "idiosyncratic meaning" the particular child may have to them.[2]

The term "coping behavior" refers to an adaptive mechanism which relates to the defenses a person employs to serve the function of helping the person in dealing with *stress*. These defenses would include denial, projection, or even social behavior. Healthy coping behavior is the channel used by a person to meet successfully a significant threat to his emotional stability. It also enables the person to function effectively. The stress that evokes such coping reactions in the situation under discussion involves the totality of events associated with being the parent of a child with a life-threatening disease. This includes both the external events and the inner conflicts, such as guilt.

Successful adaptive behavior tends to protect the parent of a child with cancer from being overwhelmed. It can enable the parent to move through and function effectively as a *parent*. An earlier study[3] found that most parents accepted medical treatment for the child in hope of preventing the loss. It is necessary to distinguish between *remission* and *relapse*. A remission tends to suspend the immediate threat of loss, but a relapse, by contrast, revives the fear that the threatened loss is becoming an actuality. A threatened loss, such as a relapse, mobilizes resources and activity that has the definite goal of preventing death. Two vignettes are illustrative of the parents' feelings of the child in remission and in relapse.

The Hosmiths are the parents of a seven-year-old son, Jim. Jim's leukemia has been in remission for 2½ years. This is a lengthy remission which has kept suspended a feeling of an immediate loss, especially since Jim seems to be as active and "healthy" as

[2] Stanford Friedman, "Care of the Family of the Child with Cancer," Supplement to *Pediatrics*, Vol. 40, No. 3, Part II (September, 1967), p. 498.
[3] Mary Bozeman, Charles Orbach, and Arthur Sutherland, "The Adaptation of Mothers to the Threatened Loss of Their Children through Leukemia: Part I," *Cancer*, Vol. 8, No. 1 (January-February, 1955), p. 1.

other children his age. Mrs. Hosmith wrote me: "It has been two and a half years since Jim was diagnosed and in that time the torment my heart knew has been erased with time and the little boy is each day very much a little boy."

By contrast, Mr. Kennal has a son, John, who is also seven years of age. John has had one relapse since he was diagnosed as having leukemia last September (1967). Mr. Kennal explained that he had a "stirred up" fear that his son was "going" when the relapse occurred.

The Family in Stress

Reuben Hill's study of the family under stress presents a conceptual framework to begin understanding the coping behavior of parents. There are three parts involved in this framework: (1) "the family as an interacting and transacting organization," (2) the stressor, or crisis-provoking event, and (3) "the meaning attached to the event." This last variable is the point at which the family defines the event as being stressful.

Hill proposes a formula that enhances the above three parts: "A (the event) ➔ *interacting* with B (the family's crisis-meeting resources) ➔ *interacting* with C (the definition of meaning the family gives to the event) ➔ produces X (the crisis)." The second and third elements (family resources and the meaning and interpretation of the event) are hidden within the family's style and values. The first element, the event itself with its hardships and difficulties lies outside the family.

The family's definition of the illness reflects several background components: the value system adhered to by the parents, their previous experience in coping with other crises, and the mechanisms used in other definitions of events. This is the *meaning* or the *interpretation* dimension of the crisis.

The adjustment to the crisis of illness presents this profile: "crisis ➔ disorganization ➔ recovery ➔ reorganization." (This seems to parallel the process of grief: disbelief, numbness, mourning, trial-and-error adjustments, renewal of routines, recovery.) Hill diagrams the adjustment by the pattern which is outlined on the next page.[4]

---

[4] Reuben Hill, "Generic Features of Families Under Stress," *Crisis Intervention: Selected Readings,* Howard J. Parad, ed. (New York: Family Service Association of America, 1965), pp. 32-52.

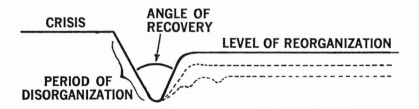

"The total impact of the crisis," according to LeMasters, "will depend upon several variables: (1) the nature of the crisis event; (2) the state of organization or disorganization of the family at the time of impact; (3) the resources of the family; and (4) its previous experiences with crisis." [5]

Learning the Diagnosis

Without exception, all parents interviewed by this author expressed a sense of shock or of being stunned when the definitive diagnosis was given to them by the doctor. Generally it took several days before this report "sank in." The experience of receiving this kind of report is probably too traumatic for parents to comprehend fully and to feel the impact of the initial presentation of the diagnosis. Indeed, a grief process is underway. Two examples are included at this point.

> Mr. Claypool, a Baptist minister, whose daughter, Laura, eight years of age, was examined by her physician and diagnosed as having leukemia, verbalized his feelings through a sermon that was both preached to his congregation and printed for distribution. This sermon was delivered on the Sunday following the news that previous week that Laura had leukemia. The father expressed the feeling that he and his wife had experienced shock and numbness at that first disclosure. He confessed that he is realizing that they are called now "of learning to care for her and learning to live with a degree of normalcy in the shadow of such an enormity. Needless to say, all of this has not come easily, and there are still areas of this experience about which I cannot speak." [6]

[5] E. E. LeMasters, "Parenthood as Crisis," Parad, *op. cit.*, pp. 111-117.
[6] John R. Claypool, "The Basis of Hope," *Crescent Hill Sermons*, Vol. V, No. 18 (July 7, 1968), p. 1. This sermon is an important case study and is included at the close of the chapter. The reference to Dr. Claypool is the only nonfictional name used in the chapter case studies.

Don Jones is a fifteen-year-old Negro. He has competed in football and basketball as a gifted sophomore at Crosspike High School. Don experienced a torn ligament in his right knee during a high school basketball game in February, 1968. While in the hospital, routine tests were run in which something keyed the doctors into checking the knee more thoroughly with additional tests. A bone marrow test was done. With complete and unexpected surprise, Don was diagnosed as having a rapidly-spreading cancer which necessitated an amputation. Within a week of this discovery, Don had undergone a mid-thigh amputation of the right leg for osteosarcoma, a type of cancer. This was performed in February at Kosair Hospital in Louisville. Don was admitted to Children's Hospital on June 27, 1968. Don has been a member of a singing gospel group called "The Spiritual Youths," which is affiliated with the Baptist church to which he belongs. Don's parents were "totally stunned" on receiving the news about his leg, especially since he had gone to the hospital only for what is considered a common athletic injury. Both parents expressed the feeling that they were "dazed" for days.

Bozeman, Orbach, and Sutherland reported in their study that the initial diagnosis was so traumatic to the mothers that many of them described their initial reaction in terms of *physical injury* to themselves, such as "an iron safe dropped on me," "it was a blow in the face," or "I felt as if I had been crushed." Two other mothers expressed the feeling that the diagnosis had no meaning when first told to them. One mother said, "It wasn't so much that I couldn't believe it, as it just didn't sink in." Another reported: "I knew, of course, that leukemia was fatal, but I didn't connect that with my child till afterwards, until one of the doctors said, 'Of course, it is fatal.' "[7]

Friedman *et al.* found in their study of the behavioral observations of forty-six parents of children with a neoplastic disease (tumorous condition) that generally the parents stated that they had some prior knowledge about leukemia and therefore suspected that their particular child might have leukemia before actually hearing it from the doctor. Thus they somewhat anticipated hearing the diagnosis. However, all parents remembered having stunned feelings on hearing the definitive diagnosis.[8]

[7] Bozeman, Orbach, and Sutherland, *op. cit.*, p. 4.

[8] Stanford Friedman, Paul Chodoff, John Mason, and David Hamburg, "Behavioral Observations of Parents Anticipating the Death of a Child," *Pediatrics*, Vol. 32, No. 4 (October, 1963), pp. 610-613.

Denial is one coping adaptation. It is the intellectual disclaiming of a painful or stressful event or feeling. Bozeman *et al.* stated that every mother of the twenty interviewed attempted to deny, in one way or another, the diagnosis or the implications of the diagnosis. Two basic methods of denial were focused in an attempt to withstand the stress brought on by the threatened loss of a child. One method tried to screen out the reality of the situation. The other method was an effort to reverse the diagnosis. Bozeman, *et al.*, reported:

> Although all mothers attempted to deny or disprove the validity of the diagnosis, this did not extend to the fact of the child's illness. There was no question about the existence of the illness; it was the hopelessness of the prognosis that mothers were compelled to deny or fight.[9]

Friedman concluded that parents are increasingly suspecting the seriousness of the diagnosis even prior to learning it from the doctor. For one thing, this reflects the "relative sophistication of the general population regarding medical matters," especially diseases associated with various community drives. Secondly, parents are apt to be vigilant for clues that might confirm their worst fears by observing the medical staff. [10]

At times, this pattern of behavior by denial may interfere with the parent's ability to give realistic care. The following case illustrates this:

> Mrs. Summers is the mother of a nineteen-year-old Negro girl. The daughter, Aileen, has a "metabolic abnormality" which gives the appearance of being physically retarded. Aileen recently had a cancerous spleen removed by surgery. Mrs. Summers lives in a small town about 120 miles from Louisville. Aileen was admitted to Children's Hospital on June 10, 1968. She had been in the Muhlenberg County Hospital for four days in May for a severe nosebleed. She had been transfused three times before coming to Children's Hospital. She was referred to Louisville by the Commission for Handicapped Children. Aileen's mother, Mrs. Summers, whose husband had left her, expressed a **style of denial** by telling Aileen's friends, neighbors, and others that Aileen had come to live in Louisville with her "auntie." She would not admit to them that Aileen was being hospitalized. Mrs. Summers refused at first to come for Aileen's surgery. She finally came while the surgery was being performed and left before Aileen had awakened in the recovery room.

[9] Bozeman, Orbach, and Sutherland, *op. cit.*, p. 4.
[10] Friedman, *op. cit.*, p. 499.

Denial tends to protect the parent from a sense of being over-whelmed. But this often contributes to the parent's inability to understand and participate in the care of the child. Friedman illustrates this:

> Mr. B became totally disorganized when he learned that his eighteen-year-old son had leukemia, in that he could not partake in any way in the care of his boy or assume any of his family responsibilities for a matter of some days. This behavior was soon replaced by massive denial that his boy had a fatal illness, and he spent many hours with the boy planning for his college education. This made it extremely difficult for the physician to discuss any aspect of the disease with the patient. In-creasingly, Mr. B questioned the necessity of medical procedures and therapy, maintaining that his boy was getting better and that the diag-nosis was in error. This eventually led to Mr. B's insisting that his boy be discharged.[11]

Interrelated to the pattern of denial is the matter of *false hope*. Friedman's studies point to the fact "that it is unwise to build any hope that the diagnosis is in question, unless, of course, this is the case." For an example, the referral of children to large medical centers for treatment might be an even more painful experience for parents if they have been led to think that the diagnosis might be changed. The unclarified referral usually re-flects the doctor's own anxiety. Some parents have referred to this as the experience of learning the diagnosis twice, instead of once.[12]

The dynamics of *anger and hostility* are commonly voiced in the parents of children with a life-threatening disease. These dynamics are important in the parent's struggle to reverse the diagnosis. Quite often these are focused and projected on the physicians. A common refrain echoes forth: "Why did this have to happen to us?" Often this anger and hostility is God-directed, as well as to others.

> Mr. Hosmith, according to Mrs. Hosmith's interpretation, reacted to the hearing of the diagnosis that their 5½-year-old son had leukemia by "rebellion." He cursed God, and even verbalized strongly that "there is no God." Mrs. Hosmith later wrote that "I feel in some ways perhaps I have failed my husband for he some-times doubts God." Mrs. Hosmith said that she responds to friends who ask, "Why your child? Why does it have to be Jim?" with "Why not? Why is our child anymore privileged than any-

[11] *Ibid.*, pp. 498-499.
[12] *Ibid.*, pp. 499-500.

body else's?" Jim has been in remission for 2½ years. Mrs. Hosmith did not hint or admit any anger from her own feelings when Jim was diagnosed. She did write: "There may be a day when I will not be able to understand that a certain way is best, and I would rather have things to go my way rather than the way of the Lord. I may be angry, but I pray that I will always remember that He is my Father and I am His child as also Jim is His child and for both of us and for my entire family He has an infinite plan." Her husband is a late comer into the church. One wonders how much protection she feels for her husband in not opening out her possible feelings of doubt and anger.

Mr. Claypool, the minister, honestly confessed that when he first heard the diagnosis, he went alone to cry. He questioned with deep feeling: "Why has this happened? Why do little girls get leukemia? Why is there leukemia at all? Why is there sickness and suffering and pain and death in a world that is supposed to be the creation of an all good and an all powerful God?" In an interview, he said that some feelings had surfaced very agonizingly and there was some "second guessing" on his part. He realized that friends mean everything in a time like this, and yet do not mean anything.

Mrs. Jones expressed her hostility about her son's amputation following the discovery of cancer: "I don't understand why this is happening to him. He's such a good boy." The father, who is divorced from Mrs. Jones, said: "What in the hell is going on? He was so healthy!"

Mr. Kennal expressed firm feelings of anger to the medical personnel when within a two-week period his son's diagnosis had radically shifted from a "fine" to leukemia. "What in the world were they doing? Don't they know what they're doing? I don't understand it." He also wrote to me: "The first question we asked was why? Why did something like this **happen to us** and to our child? But after you have had time to stop and think, you know that God has a reason for everything he does. There is also another question that you ask, especially if you have other children, you ask if maybe that child will have it too."

These are a few illustrations of the conflictual feelings that dynamically intermingle with each other in a person, although a parent may not recognize his feeling as anger. This is not to imply that anger and hostility can be easily disentangled and isolated individually from other feelings, such as anxiety.

Anxiety, as it is defined by Wayne Oates, is common among parents whose children have cancer:

Anxiety is a reaction of tension to threats to the selfhood of an individual or to the groups [for our purpose also, the family] to which he belongs and for which he feels responsible. It manifests itself at different levels of meanings in terms of the way it becomes conscious to him in his attempts to identify and deal with his painful uneasiness of mind.[13]

One clinical study of forty-eight children with leukemia and other neoplastic diseases suggested that parents had anxieties concerning their parental responsibilities for the development of the illness. Coupled with this is the feeling of guilt. This study proceeds to find that the emotional basis of this anxiety is revealed by the fact that questions arise in spite of the fact that intellectually most parents know better. The parents' questions ranged from "whether it would have been different if we had called the doctor earlier" to "do you think my spanking him may have brought this on?" However, this questioning has at least three significant aspects: (1) ventilation of anxieties gives therapeutic value; (2) reassurance is needed; and (3) a feeling of emptiness is filled.[14]

Separation anxiety is one pole of reaction. Much of the anxiety centers on separation and its irreversibility. Richmond and Waisman put it:

> The rearing of children represents a series of steps in separation from the birth process to the grave. When death comes prematurely, the blow is considerably more potent.[15]

Aspirations and developing plans are temporarily or permanently shattered. After all, what parent has not dreamed what his child will grow up to be? It becomes a dream deferred.

> The parents of Don Jones, the 15-year-old amputee, wanted him to go to college one day. He would have been the first in his family. Don expressed his ambivalent feelings about what is ahead for him. Even though his parents and the doctors have not and do not plan to tell him he is literally "sick unto death," Don is deeply aware of it. He told me of his plans to go to college and get his education, but added: "Just about the time I get started,

---

[13] Wayne E. Oates, *Anxiety in Christian Experience* (Philadelphia: The Westminster Press, © 1955, by W. L. Jenkins), pp. 9-10. Used by permission. Also cf. Seward Hiltner and Karl Menninger, eds., *Constructive Aspects of Anxiety* (New York: Abingdon Press, 1963).

[14] Julius B. Richmond and Harvey A. Waisman, "Psychologic Aspects of Management of Children with Malignant Diseases," *American Journal of Diseases of Children*, Vol. 89, No. 1 (January, 1955), pp. 42-47.

[15] *Ibid.*, p. 44.

I have to stop." It was in connection with Don that the pathologist at Children's Hospital confessed his own anxiety when he said: "This is going to be a hard case to manage. Don is a sharply alert boy. He's at an age where he knows what's going on." The parents suffered through more anxiety when they were told in July that Don had another malignant tumor that was causing extreme pressure on the left eye. Don found out in some way at the radiation treatment center that he was going to die. But the parents would not confirm it with him. Mrs. Jones, his mother, said: "What would anybody want to do that for? That's not right. It may be true, but we didn't want him told."

The manner in which the parents are informed and whether the physician holds out any hope for recovery or not are important factors in the handling of anxiety.[16]

The "event of hospitalization"[17] brought the experience of anxiety in parents, especially the mothers. Hospitalization necessarily implies separation. Bozeman *et al.* added:

> For mothers, hospitalization held not only the reality of an immediate and hoped-for temporary separation but also the implication of probable later permanent separation. "I hold my girl in my arms in the wards wondering if she will die tonight. How can I tell whether she will die tomorrow or not?" This ever-present fear of final separation was manifested by frantic clinging to the child during most of the visiting time and an insistence upon close bodily contact. It was as though mothers believed that they could prevent the feared loss by an intensified unity with their children.[18]

An interesting report during W. W. II shows that a child could take the threat of bombs better than his parents leaving him.

> It was not so much the fact of separation to which the child reacts abnormally as the form in which the separation takes place. The child experiences shock when it is suddenly and without preparation exposed to dangers with which it cannot cope emotionally. In the case of evacuation the danger is represented by the sudden disappearance of all the people whom it knows and loves.[19]

[16] Bozeman, Orbach, and Sutherland, *op. cit.*, p. 5.

[17] Expression used by Melvin Lewis, "The Management of Parents of Acutely Ill Children in the Hospital," *American Journal of Orthopsychiatry*, Vol. 32, No. 1 (January, 1962), p. 60. He relates that occasionally this event brings into sharp focus other areas of difficulty in the mother, such as marital difficulties.

[18] Bozeman, Orbach, and Sutherland, *op. cit.*, pp. 5-6.

[19] Anna Freud and Dorothy Burlingham, *War and Children* (New York: Medical War Books, 1943), p. 84.

One pattern of anxiety is seen in the repeated questions by the parents when the child will be discharged from the hospital. The diagnosis had not "sunk in." Also the event of hospitalization brings out conflictual feelings and meanings: both a possible cure or promise of preventive treatment and the reality of disease.

Quite often parents feel *guilt* about their possible role in "causing" the child's disease. Self-reproach is a part of the general search to understand the cancer's causation. The parents wonder whether the child would not have had a better chance of responding to treatment if the diagnosis had been made sooner. Mrs. Brock implied in her question that God might have been punishing them for their sins. Guilt is interrelated and becomes a manifestation of anxiety and stress.

Friedman *et al.* found in their study that guilt was not a prolonged and exaggerated feeling of wrongdoing. It was more a transient something. However, some did display a persistent self-blame for the child's illness, because of "my sins." Sometimes the parent blamed himself for not having been more appreciative of the child before the diagnosis. For example, the parent might feel that more things could have been done together, or perhaps that the child had been disciplined too harshly. This attitude often led to an overindulging and overprotecting pattern.[20]

A subtle and hidden tendency to blame parents for involvement in their child's disease was uncovered by Orbach *et al.* The Thematic Apperception Test was given to obtain information about emotional conflicts in the mothers who faced a threatened loss of child. One of the most significant and surprising points in these studies was the failure of most maternal grandmothers to give essential emotional support to their daughters when the daughter (the mother of the sick child) obviously thirsted for a supportive relationship. The grandmothers simply did not fulfill the stereotype role of the "good mother."[21]

Most parents tend to accept reassurance from the physician and from the chaplain that they as parents have not neglected the child, that as far as medical science is aware at this point, the child's life-threatening disease is beyond their control.

[20] Friedman, Chodoff, Mason, and Hamburg, *op. cit.*, pp. 613-614.

[21] Charles Orbach, Arthur Sutherland, and Mary Bozeman, "The Adaptation of Mothers to the Threatened Loss of Their Children Through Leukemia: Part II," *Cancer*, Vol. 8, No. 1 (January-February, 1955), pp. 20, 25-26.

THE GRIEF PROCESS

The grief process in most parents begins long before the child dies. Anticipatory grief is similar to the behavior observed in parents actually experiencing the loss through death. Erich Lindemann in his classic study contributed the emphasis that grief reactions are just one form of separation reaction. Death separates by irreversibility and finality. There are different causes for separation besides death. Lindemann found in his study a syndrome designated as *anticipatory grief.* The person feels under "the threat of death." The parent, for our purposes, is so concerned

> with her adjustment after the potential death of father or son that she goes through all the phases of grief — depression, heightened preoccupation with the departed, a review of all the forms of death which might befall him, and anticipation of the modes of readjustment which might be necessitated by it.[22]

The Element of Hope

Hope as it is used here refers to a favorable alteration of the expected and anticipated sequence of events. Friedman *et al.* concluded in their study that hope did not interfere with effective behavior. They also found that hope was compatible with an acceptance of reality. Hope actually helped to carry through the bad news of diagnosis. However, as the cancer progressed in the children, the parents tended to have a corresponding curtailment of hope.

At first the parents might hope for a curative drug to emerge. But as the child's illness increases, the hope might be concentrated on "just one more remission." Parents noted that they shifted more from long-range goals to a day-by-day perspective. This "narrowing of hope appeared inversely related to the increasing presence of what has been called anticipatory grief."[23]

Several parents were asked what the word "hope" meant to them. Here are some selective answers.

> Mrs. Hosmith, the mother of Jim, who has been in remission for 2½ years, wrote that "hope means better things to come . . . I have certainly learned that anything can happen, both the good and the bad."

[22] Erich Lindemann, "Symptomatology and Management of Acute Grief," *Crisis Intervention: Selected Readings,* pp. 19-20; reprinted from *American Journal of Psychiatry,* Vol. 101 (September, 1944), pp. 147-148.
[23] Friedman, Chodoff, Mason, and Hamburg, *op. cit.,* pp. 620-621.

Mrs. Daniel whose son Art, three years of age, was diagnosed as having leukemia, described the meaning of hope to her as "the cure for leukemia in the near future so that Art can benefit from it." And yet she wrote further, "as far as knowing what to expect in the future I don't know."

Mr. Kennal wrote that "we hope that a cure for the disease is found while our child is still here with us. If that is not possible, we are thankful for the medicine he is taking; that is helping him so much. Without hope and prayer there could be no future."

Mr. Claypool in his sermon explains his basis of hope. God "not only watched His child suffer and then understood; **He brought Him through it, even death!** He took the pain and gathered it up unto His purpose." Furthermore, "the twin events of Cross and Resurrection are the basis of hope in the face of evil. It cannot overcome God."

Anticipatory Grief

Grief gradually evolves as the disease progresses. If the child is hospitalized, anticipatory grief by the parent may be mirrored by some degree of emotional detachment from the child. Often there is a shifting interest in old family pastimes, or in family affairs, and possibly in other children. Parents may begin to relate more to other children on the ward. In a sense, parents have begun to rehearse how they will act.[24] This might be called a *rehearsal motif.*

Friedman *et al.* summarized the anticipatory grief process.

The signs and symptoms of this anticipatory mourning process were not as well defined as in an acute grief reaction. However, it was common for parents to complain of somatic symptoms, apathy, weakness, and preoccupation with thoughts of the ill child. Sighing was frequently observed, and many parents would occasionally cry at night and appear depressed. At other times there seemed to be an increase in motor activity and a tendency to talk for hours about the ill child.[25]

Anticipatory grief is diluted through time. If anticipatory grief has taken root, most parents have acted out a rehearsal of their feelings. (Mr. Kennal talked of his "not spending as much time as he should with John.") If parents have continually denied the diagnosis and its seriousness, the actual loss will come probably all at once.

Anna Freud presented some reactions to losing. These may be

---

[24] Friedman, *op. cit.*, p. 503.
[25] Friedman, Chodoff, Mason, and Hamburg, *op. cit.*, p. 621.

adapted here. She discussed the identification of the loser with the lost object (for our purposes the anticipated loss of the child). The parent feels deprived

> not necessarily because of the objective value of the lost item but more frequently because of its subjective value, as representative of an important body part . . . or an important love object. . . . On this basis all go through a period of detaching ourselves from it, almost as we do when *mourning* a dead person. Also, we feel *guilty*, as if we had not lost the thing unintentionally but discarded it in full consciousness.[26]

Veronica Tisza, M.D., Associate Director, Psychiatric Clinic, Children's Hospital of Pittsburgh, explains that instead of having a healthy child, the parents now have to relate to a sick child. They have to give up or postpone goals attached to a healthy child. New goals have to be developed. These goals must adjust to this changing reality of the disease and to the changing potentialities of the child. She suggests that parents can gain an appropriate adjustment in this new relationship: (1) "if they are able to release pre-illness goals," (2) if they are able to accept realistically the altered goals. This means that the parents have a real challenge before them in relationship. After all, that particular child was an embodiment of promise. Now that promise has either slipped away or at least is narrowed.[27]

Circumscribed Hope

Audrey Evans, M.D., assistant professor, Department of Pediatrics, the University of Chicago, revealed a "basis of circumscribed hope" by which parents may cling to the hope of recovery. In the first interview, the doctor may find that the parents have already explored their fears of the situation. Thus, the doctor can build a basis of circumscribed hope for the parents by emphasizing: (1) the possibility of remission, since the majority of those with acute leukemia achieve a remission; and, (2)

[26] Anna Freud, "About Losing and Being Lost," *The Psychoanalytic Study of the Child*, Ruth Eissler, Anna Freud, Heinz Hartmann, and Marianne Kris, eds., Vol. XXII (New York: International Universities Press, Inc., 1967), p. 13.

[27] Veronica Tisza, "Management of the Parents of the Chronically Ill Child," *American Journal of Orthopsychiatry*, Vol. 32, No. 1 (January, 1962), pp. 54-57. She says that the hospitalization period works in the service of denial. While the child was at home, he seemed to be healthy. But now he is desperately ill and in the hospital. This permits the fantasy, "Once he is discharged from the hospital and once he is at home again, he will be healthy."

the continuing research where there are advances, cooperative efforts, and undiscovered agents. Parents should be told of the difficult task facing them in treating the child normally and in not overindulging him.[28]

RELIGIOUS RESOURCES

Most of the parents that were interviewed expressed the feeling that their religious beliefs and resources were of comfort and help to them. These feelings ranged from "It helps us to be more accepting" to "Who knows about the great 'Not Yet' " and "Who knows what might open." Statements such as these seemed to be sincere reflections of the help that the parents received or were receiving from their religious resources. When they were with the doctor, they tended not to discuss the child's prognosis in terms of religion.

Some parents expressed a strong religious leaning for understanding the illness. Others expressed the illness in a religious context, such as "This is the Lord's way of protecting him from an even worse fate." However, some had doubts about "their previously unquestioned religious faith."[29]

Mrs. March talked of the inner resource of "wishful thinking." She later said in an interview: "I'm not much of a churchgoer. But there isn't a day that goes by I don't say a little prayer or something."

Mrs. Brock said that this experience had made her "faith" deeper. When asked "how" her faith had been deepened, she replied: "Well, I really can't explain it—I mean I know I trust God more. I just don't know how to put it in words."

Mrs. Hosmith wrote: "The inner or religious resource I rely on is very simply my faith in Jesus Christ." She quoted in this letter a lengthy prayer from her Lutheran prayer book which has been meaningful to her. She added that she had put "all things into God's hands. His will be done. Whatever happens is the best way."

Mrs. Turner, whose son has been treated in Los Angeles, Cincinnati, and now here, wrote interestingly about her feeling. "We didn't go to the Bible for our answer. We both feel that Pat's being

[28] Audrey E. Evans, "If a Child Must Die . . .," *The New England Journal of Medicine*, Vol. 278, No. 3 (January 18, 1968), pp. 138-142. The possibility of remission as a basis for hope applies mainly to leukemia patients and not to all cancer patients.

[29] Friedman, Chodoff, Mason, and Hamburg, *op. cit.*, p. 620.

> sick is God's will and if He wants us to know why He will let us know. We do both feel that we should learn something special from his being sick. Pat is one of God's special children as are all of those who are seriously ill. He is here for a special purpose."

Several parents were asked what the biggest temptation was that they faced as a parent in relation to that sick child.

> Mr. Kennal wrote that the "greatest temptation to us is wanting to have the child around us all the time, not wanting him out of your sight but that is not the right thing to do. You have to let him do all the things that he can do and let him lead as normal a life as he can."

> Mrs. Turner wrote that their greatest temptation is to favor Pat over his brother (four years of age) and his sister (fifteen months). "It is hard to discipline him like we do them but we see it has to be done."

> Mrs. Hosmith wrote that her greatest temptation "is not being proud of my ability thus far in handling this situation. When people come and say it is marvelous for me to be able to laugh and enjoy life and to be able to treat Jim as a normal child, the idea that all this is my doing would be very easy. But the ability I have to do this is not my own ability, it is the strength I receive from Jesus."

The question was asked concerning what they expected the church to be to them, particularly in relation to this crisis of a life-threatening disease. Two answers are cited.

> Mrs. Turner said: "I don't know what to expect of a church in this matter because we have not been going regularly for a long time. We do know it is the place to go for spiritual and mental peace of mind that we need." She had written: "That God will help us to be the best parents we can for Pat and also that He will give us the strength that we need to keep going in the crisis are other resources we believe."

> Mrs. Hosmith answered "I expect my church, particularly the group I am most associated with, to pray for my family and I am confident they are doing this."

PASTORAL CARE FOR FAMILIES

The pastor can have an *instructive* role in leading small groups on: (1) the nature of stress, and (2) ways of coping with it. This may include community resources such as a psychologist or a doctor. Stress for one thing involves coping with the elusive unknown. Thus, cancer is a style of mystery. Learning more about the facts insofar as they can be known is one step toward relieving the sense of mystery. However, this learning process may relieve stress but also focus anxiety. This educative approach with small groups may generate motivation for "keeping on" and for others besides the pastor to be representative of God in care to these families whose children have cancer. For instance, prayer can also be offered for the efforts of medical research to discover more about cancer. In this sense, their work is a style of prayer. This recaptures the sacramental concept of the Monks of Cluny: *Laborare est orare:* To work is to pray.

Studying the Process of Grief

Another perspective which the pastor can initiate is the education of his people in the process of grief. In this way they could identify some of their emotions and feelings and cooperate with the process. After all, this process of grief involves a community of faith as well as individuals. The anxiety of grief covers both significant losses that occur and the apprehension over the threat or the anticipation of such a loss. Grief is a tearing kind of feeling. It shuts off a person from the fulfillment of hopes and dreams. Some books on the subject would include: Wayne E. Oates, *Anxiety in Christian Experience* (Philadelphia: The Westminster Press, 1955); Charles Bachmann, *Ministering to the Grief Sufferer* (Englewood Cliffs, N. J.: Prentice-Hall, Inc., 1964); Edgar N. Jackson, *Understanding Grief* (Nashville: Abingdon Press, 1957), and *You and Your Grief* (New York: Channel Press, 1961); Granger E. Westberg, *Good Grief* (Philadelphia: Fortress Press, 1962).

Child's Concept of Death

The pastor can lead in a discussion of the child's concept of death, but he will need to know something of developmental steps and perspectives. The discovery of death by a child is a gradual crystallization. Especially is such a pastoral ministry helpful in the care of brothers and sisters of a child cancer victim. The course of cancer defines to a great extent the exact feelings and problems the parents may have in caring for the child. Parents and child tend to change a great deal as the disease progresses. The pastor needs to be aware of this changing relationship. Some helpful books would include: Earl A. Grollman, ed., *Explaining Death to Children* (Boston: Beacon Press, 1967); Edgar N. Jackson, *Telling a Child About Death* (New York: Channel Press, 1965); and Herman Feifel, ed., *The Meaning of Death* (New York: McGraw-Hill Book Company, 1959).

Channeling Grief Energies

Since cancer among children is a growing problem, most pastors will have a relationship with at least one family who has a child with it. The pastor can train a group of people experienced in the actual loss of a child to help others now facing it. Keen insight and judgment would have to be used in this. Grief energies could begin to be channeled by substitute relationships in the case of an actual loss. For example, a family can take an interest in a neglected child in the church similar to the one they lost if they examine carefully their motives and temptations.

The church often wears out the stricken family with questions of "what can I do"? This puts pressure on the family, for they are up against their own helplessness. A statement such as "If there is anything I can do, let me know" is a superficial involvement and a real pain to the family. The pastor can for himself explore the validity of the following *principles:*

Availability. What are some of the needs of the parents, or the problems as we see them? The pastor can be aware that sometimes the child is treated away from home in another city. Transportation to the clinic may be a problem whether within the hometown or to another city. How will the child get to the clinic and with whom? Does the mother drive? Will the father jeopardize his job by having to go each time? Are there church members or friends that can be enlisted to help drive, or baby sit while the parents are away? The pastor can be of real encouragement and support if the parents know he is available when the need arises. This will be based greatly on a faithful, durable relationship to them. Another perspective to this is, What kind of "grapevine" communication is open so that information is relayed to the pastor as to how and when to be available?

Continuity of Care. The value of a continuing relationship both to the parents and the child, and to the other children, if there are others, must not be overlooked. The total family must be remembered. There is a spirit of therapy in a consistent, durable, and faithful relationship, even when the parents seem hostile, anxious, or even overly hopeful. If the pastor is only "concerned" when the child goes routinely to the clinic, or if he pinpoints all of his concern on the event of hospitalization, the parents soon catch on to this piecemeal concern and hesitate to share their fears and troublesome questions.

The diagnosis of leukemia brings on the strong possibility of a remission. Thus a pastor needs to be aware of the different dynamics at work with the hospitalized child and how the parents react to this, as well as the periods of "normalcy." By a cumulative relationship in the periods of both the "ups" and "downs," the pastor will be expressing care to the family and providing an opening for bringing up their fears and burdensome questions.

Patience is a necessary ingredient to a continuity of care. The pastor will be dealing with anticipatory grief. For some parents this will be a life-tearing experience as if there were already an actual loss. The pastor can lead a family through the process of grief and help them to affirm that God does care. This crisis of illness has stirred up many thoughts, old and new. If the pastor is "too much in a hurry," patience is neglected and lost. The pastor can be a mediating channel of hope through his own patience.

Personalized Care. Attentiveness to such things as the child's birthday helps to unfold sensitivity and responsiveness to the parents' needs. This also means alertness to their feelings. For an example, "You seem to be somewhat discouraged today." The pastor can find out and converse about the particular interests of the child — sports, pets, hobbies, etc. He can develop an understanding of the fearful reactions that may come because of new or painful procedures to the child. The parents suffer in their own ways also. The parents can be alerted that the child interprets their facial expressions, especially if there are tears from crying.

A pastor can be a guide for parents at the time of hospitalization of the child by discussing with them or referring them to a helpful book such as *Children Going to the Hospital* by Harold Geist and Morse P. Manson. (This is available for $2.25 through the Western Psychological Services, 12031 Wilshire Boulevard, Los Angeles, California 90025.) The pastor can serve as a support for the medical personnel who ought to rehearse with the parents what, how, and who is to tell the child about the illness, or what questions to expect and how to respond.

The pastor can make some basic preparations in light of the hospitalization of the child. Does the hospital have a chapel or some private room that is available in preparation for the worst or in hope for the best? Parents have much pressure on them in a public setting where there are wondering and staring eyes. Parents tend to be reluctant to express their feelings in a room with strangers. Privacy is appreciated, especially if there develops grief because of death.

Reality Presenter. The pastor faces a somewhat ambiguous situation with a family whose child has leukemia. Leukemics will most likely have at least one remission. The pastor stands somewhat apart from the family to represent reality to them. The problem for parents is to treat this child as being healthy during the remission without neglecting the other children, if there are others, or overplaying their loyalty to the sick child now apparently healthy.

Pain and suffering, even for children, are interwoven into human existence. There is mystery in life, and the pastor does not have all the solutions and answers. He must see the overarching framework of cancer if he is to give realistic guidance and support. Besides supportive encouragement that God cares and knows well what they are going through, he can firmly stress, without unwarranted reassurances, that the doctors are giving their best attention and resources to the child's care. If the pastor permits himself to be engulfed and completely overwhelmed by the family's crisis, he will be on the defensive and helpless. To protect his own feelings he may have to be somewhat impersonal.

CONCLUSION

This chapter has attempted to study several related aspects of the feelings and attitudes of parents whose child has a life-threatening disease. A survey study of anticipatory grief with its rehearsal motif, coping behavior, and religious resources has been introduced. The materials available on pastoral care to these families are very limited.

The physician who has to diagnose and then establish treatment for children with cancer must understand that he is involved in a human experience of suffering unto death. A life-threatening disease is never merely a "therapeutic challenge or problem in management." Few other human experiences involve more anguish and suffering than the threatened loss and eventually the actual loss of the child.

The interval following the bad news of diagnosis is a time of intense parental anxiety. This anxiety may be seen by hostility toward doctors or God, failure to understand fully and to absorb the new information given, perhaps acute and heightened feelings of personal responsibility for the illness, disruption in parental functioning, and separation fears.

These sharp reactions and attitudes may abate shortly, but they may also continue for a longer time. These directions are dependent upon: (1) the dynamic or idiosyncratic meaning the threatened loss has to the parents, (2) the resources and mode of coping for adaptation, (3) previous experience with illness, hospitalization, and death, and (4) the emotional support that the parent receives. Stress is not going to be eliminated. However, much can be initiated to enable the parents to integrate the experience so that they may carry through and function without lasting disorganization.[30]

[30] See Orbach, Sutherland, and Bozeman, *op. cit.*, p. 29. Data from the National Cancer Institute tells us that physicians are oriented primarily to cure illness. For them to handle the meaning of death is an antithesis to their basic orientation. Thus, a parent participation program was initiated. See Joel Vernick and Myron Karon, "Who's Afraid of Death on a Leukemia Ward?" *American Journal of Diseases of Children*, Vol. 109 (May, 1965), pp. 393-397.

"The Basis of Hope," A Sermon by John R. Claypool

(This sermon was delivered at Crescent Hill Baptist Church, Louisville, Kentucky, July 7, 1968. Used by permission of Dr. John R. Claypool.)

SCRIPTURE REFERENCE: Romans 8:28-39

It is never what you might call "easy" for me to stand in this place and try to preach a sermon, but this morning I must confess to you that it is doubly difficult. As many of you know, the last two weeks have been full of trauma for me and my family. During these days my eight-year-old daughter was diagnosed as having leukemia, and we have been called upon to shift very swiftly from the shock and numbness that first comes with such a disclosure to the task of learning to care for her and learning to live with a degree of normalcy in the shadow of such an enormity. Needless to say, all of this has not come easily, and there are still great areas of this experience about which I cannot speak. It has been hard to concentrate or even think much in these last few days, and thus the prospect of preaching a sermon is rather foreboding. However, all of this is only one side of the picture. Long before this happened to me, I had come to the conclusion that it was the nature of God to speak to us in the language of events, and it was the nature of the Church for men to share with each other what they thought they had heard God say in the things that had happened to them. There is no evading the fact that I have just been through a dark place, but it has not been totally black or without its flashes of light. Therefore, difficult as it may be, there is something I want to share with you, my brothers and sisters in Christ. Please do not expect any great homiletical masterpiece. Do not look for any tightly reasoned, original creation. Rather, see me this morning as your burdened and broken brother, limping back into the family circle to tell you something of what I learned out there in the darkness.

The first thing I have to share may surprise you a bit, but I must in all honesty confess it, and it is that I have found no answer to the deepest question of this experience. When I first heard this diagnosis and went out alone to cry, I raised the question anyone would ask; namely, "Why has this happened? Why do little girls get leukemia? Why is there leukemia at all? Why is there sickness and suffering and pain and death in a world that is supposed to be the creation of an all good and an all powerful God?" These are age-old questions, and I searched the pages of the Bible and my books of theology and my memory and my Christian experience, and I found no neat and tidy answer to lay such a question to rest. I am already familiar with most of the attempted solutions to this mystery of evil and pain, and every one of them left something to be desired and left the question right where it had started; namely, a dark mystery for which there is no satisfactory explanation. Therefore, let me say at the very beginning that if you expect me to share an *answer* to this problem of pain, or give you some explanation of how this sort of thing happens and why, you are in for a disappointment. Up to this moment, in the Bible, in theology, in my experience — nowhere have I found an answer that settles all the questions or accounts for all the nuances of this tragic occurrence.

The name of honesty demands that I make this confession to you. I would be untrue to myself if I did not admit to what I have not found; namely, the answer that encompasses this whole problem. However, to stop with that would also be untrue to my experience. The same honesty that prompts me not to overclaim, prompts me not to underclaim, and while I have not found a total answer in the Bible and my Christian faith, I have found there three things that have been of tremendous value to me in the last two weeks.

One of these is the challenge to go on living even though I have no answer or any complete explanation. The Bible always arranges life and thought in just that sequence; namely, we are first called on to live passionately and openly, and then to use our minds to try to understand and interpret what we have experienced. In this way life moves on and whatever insight is possible is born. However, if we turn it around and try to put understanding before the living of life, the whole process locks and we become immobilized.

I found this to be so true in the first hours after I heard the diagnosis. The ultimate question of "why?" leaped to my mind almost immediately, and as I indicated, I could find no ready and pat solution to this enigma. But alongside that question were also several concrete realities — a little girl who was sick and whose course of treatment needed to be decided on; a wife who needed to be comforted, and a son who needed to be reassured that he was important, too. I could have turned away from all of these immediate necessities and said, "Until I find an intellectual answer for all this, I will not move a step or do anything." But that would have been criminal neglect and also would have been closing off the one possibility I might have for gaining insight.

Harry Emerson Fosdick once wrote that "a man can put off making up his mind, but he can't put off making up his life," and this has all the realism of the Bible behind it. The business of making up one's life, concretely and directly, is more basic than intellectualizing abstractly about life. And not only that; this is the way we were meant to learn. This business of making up our minds does not happen before we experience anything of life; it comes as we experience it through experience, after experience. Centuries ago a philosopher named Descartes climbed into a stove and determined to think out life before he acted. He finally came to this conclusion: "I think, therefore I am," and set the whole direction of modern thought. However, it was a fatal conclusion, for he reversed the true relation of living and thinking and "got the cart before the horse." It was the same mistake that Adam and Eve made back in the story of the Garden of Eden. God set the whole creation before them like a banquet table and invited them to participate in it wholly and fully. They were to eat, drink, work, feel, multiply; namely, to live passionately. Yet, instead of immersing themselves in life, they turned rather to the tree of the knowledge of good and evil, the symbol of the Ultimate explanation of all things that was God's alone, and lusted after it. In other words, before they lived they wanted to know all the answers, whereas God had ordained that knowledge come through and by and after experience.

This is always a temptation — to want to think life rather than live it, and it is a dead-end street. Descartes should have jumped out of his stove and instead of saying, "I think, therefore I am," he should have said, "I am, therefore I think." This is the sequence in which life and thought should always be put. We do not first get all the answers and then live in light of our understanding. We must rather plunge into life — the concrete necessities of meeting what we have to meet and experiencing what we have to experience — and in the light of living we try to understand. If insight comes at all, it will not be before, but only through and after experience. This emphasis of the Bible really helped me move on last week in the deeps. Instead of sitting down to brood and question and refusing to budge until I had an answer, I plunged headlong into the experience and got on with the business of "making up life," with the hope that out of this the making up of the mind might later come. The Bible, then, gave me no answer, but it gave me the challenge to face up to the situation and move on out into the darkness.

The second thing the Bible and my faith gave me was a stern warning to beware of superficiality and quick labeling and jumping to the wrong conclusions. If the Bible teaches anything about life, it teaches us that it is a deep and complex and mysterious affair. Just as icebergs show only a fraction of themselves above the surface, so events, according to the Bible, are always more than they appear to be at first glance. More is going on in every moment than meets the eye, and the Bible always cautions us against pronouncing too quickly: "This is all bad; this is all good; this is hopeless; this is the end."

I really needed this kind of safeguard in the past few weeks, for my first temptation was to conclude that all pain is evil, all sickness is totally bad, leukemia means certain death, and all is lost and at an end. The testimony of the Bible slowed me down here by saying: "Wait a moment. You can't always judge an event by its first appearance, any more than you can judge the content of a package by its wrapping. Be patient. Let events run their course. *God is not through with anything yet.* Who knows what might yet unfold out of all this mystery?"

I must admit the Old Testament story of Joseph and his traumatic life was of great comfort to my thought just here. All through this account there is what might be called "a double agenda" at work. The outward manifestation always seemed at first to be deceptive of the deeper realities that were moving. For example, as a lad Joseph was a cocky and spoiled favorite son of his father, and all his brothers could see in him and his dreaming was an intolerable arrogance. Yet Joseph had in him the potential to be a great leader of men, and what they mistook for something evil was actually the first appearing of these significant gifts. The brothers' hatred led them to sell Joseph into slavery and send him far away to Egypt, an act that bore every mark of sheer evil, yet look at what happened. The rigors of slavery in Egypt developed the character of Joseph in ways that never could have happened under the pampering of his senile old father, and what is more, this "evil" act catapulted Joseph into a position to save his family from starvation decades later. Reading this story always reminds me of the mysterious depth and patience of events, and causes me to put on the brakes when I rush out to define something as "good" or "bad" or "evil" or "hopeless." How do I know, finite as I am, the full import of events? For example, a few years ago I would have pronounced "good" the fortune of a lowly mechanic who won the Irish sweepstakes, and overnight became rich. Yet just the other day I read this man's tragic account of what instant wealth had done to his life. He had lost his desire to work, had become separated from his wife and alienated from his children, and said quite flatly: "I now look on the day I won that money as the darkest day in my life." By the same token I would always be tempted to judge a heart attack an evil and dreadful thing, full of darkness. Yet Jesse Stuart, the poet-teacher, wrote a whole book to proclaim that his coronary was the greatest blessing of an overcrowded life, and occasioned "the year of his rebirth."

My whole point is that the Bible is right in warning us against living on the surface or by appearance or too much into the future. It reminds us quite directly that *despair is always presumptuous,* for how do we know what lies in the "not yet," or how some present evil may not work itself out as a blessing in disguise? This has become my outlook as far as my little daughter is concerned. I have not embraced despair as to her future, or pronounced as hopeless her particular situation. After all, she might be the one on whom the long awaited cure for leukemia will be discovered. God may heal her, or even in taking her do something magnificent we can not now envision. At any rate, the Bible gives me a depth perspective as to events, and bids me wait on the Lord and be patient before I label any experience or close the door of hope. Despair is presumption, pure and simple, a going beyond the warrant of the evidence at hand. Who am I to say what lies hidden and yet real in "The Great Not Yet?"

This reminder of depth and mystery is a valuable gift indeed, but I must say the greatest gift of all out of the Bible is the vision of God it set forth, and the positive hope that streams from a nature such as His. I have just said that despair is presumption, for we have no evidence to conclude negatively about the future. However, the faith goes even farther than that — it depicts a God from whom something positive can be expected. Instead of just remaining neutral toward the possibilities of the future, there are grounds for hope in what He is.

Time will not permit a full application of theology to tragedy, but two facets of God's Being stand out. One is His acquaintance with evil and grief and suffering. The gods of other religions seem content to live on the other side of the sky, but not the God of the Bible. He comes again and again into the circle of the people in the Old Testament, and then in the fullness of time, He sent His Son, made in the image of man, to live totally and completely among us. That Son made no attempt to evade the horror and pain of life. In fact, the only verb used to describe His life in the Apostles' Creed is the verb "suffer." Between being "conceived by the Holy Spirit" and "born of the Virgin Mary," and being "crucified, dead, and buried," there is just one phrase: "He suffered under Pontius Pilate." Yes, the Son of God, "the Word made flesh," was a Man of sorrows and acquainted with grief, and this means God has drawn very close and understands from within the whole agony of life.

We do feel a certain kinship with those who have experienced what we are experiencing, and the God who came in Christ establishes just a kinship and a closeness. A minister was called once to a home during World War II just after word had arrived that an only son had been killed in battle. The father, half in grief and half in rage, blurted out as soon the minister arrived: "I want to know, where was God when my son was being killed?" The minister thought a long time and then replied softly: "I guess you would say He was right where He was while His Boy was being killed." This word had a revolutionary impact on the man, for it brought God from afar right into the circle as a grieving Companion. This has meant more to me than I can say in these last days. As I have stood and watched my child suffer, I have thought to my soul I could not stand it, and then I remembered, and suddenly I was not totally alone any longer, but companioned by Another who seemed to say: "I know, O how I know. For you see, I watched My Child suffer too. I understand." And believe me, out there in the darkness this companionship of understanding really helps.

The other thing about the Biblical God that is so significant is what He did about pain and evil. He not only watched His child suffer and then understood; *He brought Him through it, even death!* He took the pain and gathered it up unto His purpose! The raising of Christ Jesus from the dead is not only the greatest deed of the Bible; it is our basis of hope in the midst of tragedy. Here is what God can do with events that evil throws up against Him. He can bring us through it, raise us even from death, and then turn that evil inside out and transform it into something good. The killing of Jesus had many motives behind it, but only one purpose — and that was to defeat God. All the darkness of evil converged on that spot to do Him in; but what resulted? Jesus survived! Three days later He was back on earth as real as ever, and what is more, the Cross itself was gathered up and became the instrument of God instead of an instrument of evil. Just as in the Old Testament little David stunned Goliath and then used the giant's own sword finally to defeat him, so God stunned evil in the resurrection and then seized the cross from the scabbard of Calvary and now uses it as a power unto salvation instead of destruction. The twin events of Cross and Resurrection are the basis of hope in the face of evil. It cannot overcome God; He has overcome it, and not only overcome it, but so transformed it that it can become His instrument and be used of Him for good.

This is the bedrock of my own hope. If God could do this for His Boy in the midst of suffering, I dare to believe He will do this for my girl. I am staking my life on the belief that all of this will not end in darkness. She may suffer, she may even die, but God will bring her through, and us also, and out of this He will not be overcome but will somehow turn this evil to His purpose and in it all bring light out of darkness.

This, then, is what I have come to share with you as a burdened brother just in from the dark. I have no answer as to why this happened, or why such events should even be in the world, but out of the Bible and my faith I do have some things—a challenge to move forward courageously and not get locked in intellectualizing; a call to live in order to know rather than trying to know in order to live. I also have a warning against superficiality and concluding too quickly on first appearance. Reality is deep and slow and mysterious, and how can I yet pronounce good or evil or hopeless what lies in The Great Not Yet? Despair is presumption. But best of all: I have a vision of God, who has come close enough in His Son to understand, and who is powerful enough and resourceful enough to endure the worst that evil can do and then out of it bring His best. It is true; I do not have an answer that ties this all up in a neat and tidy package, but I have enough to move on and to give thanks and to form a basis of hope. And this is what I intend to do — by God's help and yours, to offer this whole experience up to God and wait upon Him and be patient. And I cannot believe I shall be disappointed.

I was deeply moved this week by an observation of Dr. George Buttrick's concerning the Dead Sea in Palestine. Again and again as a sermon illustration I have heard it compared unfavorably to the Sea of Galilee, which is fresh and sparkling and full of fish, while the Dead Sea is salty and no fish can live in it. The usual point is that the Jordan River flows *through* the Sea of Galilee, but only flows *into* the Dead Sea because there is no outlet. Dr. Buttrick concedes the truth of this point about life through giving, but then he goes on to point out another truth I had never thought of.

He claims the Dead Sea does have an outlet — the upward one, toward the sky. Across the centuries as it has surrendered itself to the sun, a residue of potash has built up and remains. Potash is a different form of life than water in which fish can live — it is a main ingredient of fertilizer. Engineers have estimated that if the potash around the Dead Sea could be mined and distributed, there would be enough there to fertilize the whole surface of the earth for at least five years.

The point is, life never comes to a complete dead end. When no outlet is open except surrender to the sky in helplessness, even this response is not without its positive residue, for out of it can come the miracle of a new form of life.

So this is my intention. I will do all I can, stay open and hopeful at all points, and finally surrender my burden to the sky. And surely, surely, out of that, some form of life, even if it is just potash, will mark the spot and something of good will remain to show for it.

John Bill Ratliff is chaplain of The Lincoln School in Simpsonville, Kentucky. He is a graduate of Colgate University, Yale University Divinity School, and Southern Baptist Theological Seminary and has done extensive clinical work with young people.

5

PASTORAL CARE OF EMOTIONALLY DISTURBED ADOLESCENTS

John Bill Ratliff

INTRODUCTION BY RAY H. HAYES, M.D.

Superintendent, Central State Hospital, Louisville, Kentucky

I believe that religious issues concerning life, death, guilt, and God can be very much a part of the struggles of a person who is emotionally ill. The resources of religion — in terms of a meaningful community, the insights gained from prayer and Scripture reading, and the establishment of a relationship of trust with a representative of God and the church — can also be important in the treatment of mentally ill patients and in their return to their community. As a result, the chaplain is an integral part of our healing community at the hospital. Pastoral care and pastoral counseling are long-established and vital dimensions to our treatment program. The chaplain works closely and in consultation with other staff.

Mr. Bill Ratliff was such a chaplain in our hospital for nine months. As the chaplain for our adolescents, he formed meaningful relationships with many and stood by them in their successes and failures, in joyful times and sad times. And he represented symbolically the concern of the whole Christian community for these troubled adolescents.

So a pastor has a definite place in dealing with troubled adolescents. He needs to take seriously their particular needs and problems. However, the pastor does not have to work as a chaplain in a mental hospital or be a specialist in pastoral counseling to be able to minister effectively to disturbed young people. Many young people who are in our communities are struggling with great problems, and most of them never get to the point of needing hospitalization. The care and concern of the church can be crucial at this point in their lives. If they are hospitalized, they need to know that the pastor and church have not abandoned them. The way the pastor treats them when they return home can be central in their reintegration into the community. So pastors have the potential to be effective and resourceful in caring for adolescents who may be frightened and confused. Perhaps this chapter can provide principles and guidelines by which pastors may channel their potential in ministering to young persons.

PASTORAL CARE OF EMOTIONALLY DISTURBED ADOLESCENTS

John Bill Ratliff

"Six thousand years ago an Egyptian priest carved on a stone, 'Our earth is degenerate. . . . Children no longer obey their parents.'" [1] The adolescent as a source of frustration and concern for people is not new. The church, as well, has found difficulty in ministering during the adolescent period in the life cycle of man. The pastor and the church have often been frustrated in knowing what is going on with the young people and what to do with them. The adolescent who becomes emotionally disturbed, and who may be institutionalized or placed under psychiatric treatment for a period of time, presents even more of a problem. By considering the problems of seriously disturbed adolescents, the pastor may be able to understand better other adolescents.

The content of this chapter is based on a year-long research study and experience as a chaplain on the adolescent unit of a mental hospital.[2] The writer worked in this role with the con-

[1] Silvano Arieti, ed., *American Handbook of Psychiatry*, (New York: Basic Books, Inc., Publishers, 1959), Vol. 1, p. 840.
[2] John Bill Ratliff, "The Pastoral Care of the Adolescent Unit at Midwestern State Hospital," Unpublished Master's thesis, The Southern Baptist Theological Seminary, Louisville, Kentucky, 1967.

viction that the Christian faith is relevant to the adolescent stage of development, especially as seen in its distorted form. In his identity crisis the adolescent is also determining who he is before God.

> An adolescent's religious background, and the teachings of his religion regarding the nature and destiny of man, play an important role in determining his conception of who and what he is, and what he should aspire to be.[3]

The understanding which the writer gained while functioning as chaplain with the adolescents, and the ways in which he found to minister to them, can be applied to the pastor's own work with adolescents, especially with disturbed adolescents, in his church and in his community. Much of what the chaplain learned and did in the mental hospital setting can also be applied to the local church community. The difficulties of the emotionally disturbed adolescents which are dealt with in this chapter are different only in intensity, not in kind, from the difficulties of every adolescent in our culture. Many pastors are in a position to minister to an emotionally disturbed adolescent before, during, and after his psychiatric treatment.

ROLE OF CHAPLAIN AND PASTOR

The chaplain on the adolescent unit could have taken one of two routes. On the one hand, he could have set up a structured program of religious activities and programs and kept office hours. On the other hand, he could have simply been present on the unit, to talk with staff and adolescents, to minister at the moment when the need arose, and to define his role in the actual situation. The latter way was chosen.

The advantage of the former is that the structured program could give stability and a sense of continuity in the unstable and changing situation. The advantage of the latter is that the chaplain could adjust to the changing situation and be where the need was expressed. To have set up a structured program at the beginning might have resulted in the chaplain's being left out of what was going on. Also, the adolescents already had a very structured day. To have instituted a program would have clearly

[3] Adelaide Johnson, "Juvenile Delinquency," in Arthur T. Jersild, *The Psychology of Adolescence* (New York: The Macmillan Company, 1963), p. 373.

allied the chaplain with the staff and would have been too regimented.

In the local church the adolescents may long to have access to the pastor and to be near him without his having to get them all together for a formal meeting. The presence of the pastor, rather than a program, may be one way to begin to minister to young people on the level where they live and hurt.

On the adolescent unit the chaplain was not clearly identified with the staff. He was far enough removed from the staff difficulties that some of the staff felt free to talk with him. Likewise, because the chaplain was not clearly identified with the staff, the adolescents also felt free to confide in him when they might not have done so with the staff.

In a local church situation the adolescents may feel more free to come to the pastor or to be honest with him if they know that he is not too closely allied with their parents. If they can trust him to listen seriously to them and not necessarily side with his parents or with the establishment, they will want to confide in him when they are troubled. The pastor is an adult and may have a close relationship to the parents of the adolescent, but he does not have to defend the parents to the adolescent. He really should be a bridge between them, not a beachhead for either group.

IDENTITY CRISIS IN ADOLESCENCE

Erik H. Erikson and others have talked and written much about the problem of identity as the central psychosocial crisis of adolescence.[4] Adolescents are faced with the question "Who am I?" Out of this a host of corollary questions emerge, such as, "What am I to do?" "Whom shall I marry?" "To what shall I commit my life?" The sense of identity comes when one's own sense of sameness and continuity is matched with the way others see his sameness and continuity. A clear sense of identity results if the crisis

[4] Erik H. Erikson, *Identity and the Life Cycle* (New York: International Universities Press, Inc., 1959) in *Psychological Issues*. See also Gordon W. Bronson, "Identity Diffusion in Late Adolescents," *Journal of Abnormal and Social Psychology*, Vol. 59 (November, 1959), pp. 414-417; E. M. Duvall, "Adolescent Love as a Reflection of Teenagers' Search for Identity," *Journal of Marriage and the Family*, Vol. 26 (1964), pp. 226-229; Joanne J. Hood, "Consistency of Self Concept in Adolescence." Unpublished doctor's thesis, Ohio State University, 1962.

of adolescence is met and successfully worked through. When his sense of inner sameness and continuity is not matched by others, a diffusion of identity results.

The adolescents who ended up on the adolescent unit at the hospital had not successfully answered the question, "Who am I?" The pastor will often meet adolescents who are struggling with different aspects of this question and who are looking for help. Erik Erikson states that eight alternatives are present in this identity crisis.[5] In identity diffusion, the negative alternative in each case is chosen as part of the adolescent's life style. Let us look in detail at these negative alternatives, how they were present among adolescents at the hospital, how the chaplain ministered in that situation, and how the pastor can minister in his own situation.

Time Diffusion

In identity diffusion, basic mistrust of time is present. The future is feared and the past is repressed. The two basic manifestations of time diffusion are a sense of great urgency and a sense of standing still, resulting respectively in hyperactivity and in boredom. In more extreme cases, there is an attempt to halt all time by committing suicide.[6]

On the adolescent unit the adolescents feared the future. Some of them felt a great urgency to leave the unit. Yet they were afraid to leave because they had no plans for the future. They feared the future because they were not confident that they could function effectively when they left. They feared returning to their homes where much of their trouble had begun. They feared returning to school, where their trouble may have originally shown up in acute form. They were afraid of growing up.

The adolescents also tried to forget the past. They did not like to talk about their unpleasant experiences with their families and friends. Even recent events on the unit tended not to be remembered. They wanted to leave the past and live in the present.[7]

[5] Erikson, *op. cit.*, pp. 140f, 166.
[6] *Ibid.*, pp. 126-127, 141-142.
[7] See also Robert J. Barndt and Donald M. Johnson, "Time Orientation in Delinquents," in *The Adolescent: A Book of Readings*, Jerome M. Seidman, ed. (New York: Holt, Rinehart & Winston, Inc., 1953, 1960), pp. 477-481, for a statistical study that reveals a tendency for delinquent boys to live in the here and now.

Time passed very slowly for some. Especially on the weekends when there were few activities, time barely moved for some of them. Some of the adolescents slowed down also. At least two boys walked slowly and dragged their feet. One crippled girl used her handicap as reason for walking slowly, although she seemed to get from one place to another rapidly when she wanted to. One boy often had to be forcibly removed from his bed in the morning.

Attempted suicide was the final act of the adolescent who mistrusted time. Recurring reasons given for attempted suicide were "I am not going to ever get better." "I'm afraid that I'm going to turn out just like my mother." "There's no hope for me." The complex psychodynamics of attempted suicide includes the loss of faith in the healing process of time.[8]

The chaplain remained calm when an adolescent would approach him with a sense of great urgency. By being stable and by asking the adolescent to slow down and tell him what was wrong, the chaplain brought some order into the situation. If the chaplain had another appointment and if the problem was not of great urgency, the chaplain would make an appointment to see the adolescent later in the day. In the midst of the confusion, the adolescent could hang onto the appointment for hope. A fifteen-year-old obese girl on the adolescent unit had been talking with a thirty-year-old married man. She had had several conversations with the chaplain. One day she burst into the room and said that she had to talk with the chaplain. Tense and upset, she said that the other girls told her that the man was tired of seeing her. He had missed a breakfast appointment. She said she was going to see him at lunch and ask him if he wanted to drop her. The chaplain talked with her about how she really felt about him, how she was going to ask him the question, and what she would do if he really did want to drop her. The chaplain had to leave, but he made an appointment to see her in the afternoon, to see what happened. She left quieter and with more of an idea of what she was going to do.

[8] For a more extended discussion of attempted suicide in adolescence, see George J. Mohr and Marian A. Despres, *The Stormy Decade: Adolescence* (New York: Random House, Inc., 1958), pp. 194-208; H. I. Schneer, P. Kay and M. Brogovsky, "Events and Conscious Ideation Leading to Suicidal Behavior in Adolescence," *Psychiatric Quarterly*, Vol. 35 (1961), pp. 507-515.

In the case of a depressed adolescent who talked about how life is not worth living, the chaplain, at the end of the interview, would make a definite appointment for a future interview. This was done for the purpose of demonstrating that the adolescent had a future and that the chaplain had pledged himself to a relationship with the adolescent. It also gave the adolescent one small thing in the future to live for.

The chaplain also asked questions about the adolescent's past and future. In talking about that which was mistrusted, some of the fear was removed. Also, helping the person to formulate his plans lessened the fear of the unknown.

Perhaps more important than anything done or said was the presence of the chaplain. His presence and concern may have symbolized the presence and concern of God for the adolescent. The chaplain's faithfulness may have symbolized the faithfulness of God, who has all time in his control. As a result, some of the adolescents may have been able to trust time and see it as good.

The experienced pastor is no stranger to young people who are afraid of the future (especially with the current world conditions) and who try to forget the past. He also is probably no stranger to suicides among the young people of his community. The pastor, in ministering to an adolescent who mistrusts time and all that it stands for, can perhaps best help by remaining a source of calmness and strength to the disturbed or upset adolescent. By helping the young person work out his plans for the future, the pastor can lessen the fear of the unknown. By remaining faithful in his presence with and concern for the adolescent, the pastor symbolizes and mediates the faithfulness of God. Then, hope may be engendered in the adolescent, as he learns to trust the processes of time, to trust the pastor, and to trust God who created time.

Identity Consciousness

The adolescent with a diffused identity feels that he is exposed to the world, and so he is ashamed. To escape this shame and exposure, the adolescent takes refuge in conformity and uniformity with his peers.[9] Without a clear sense of identity the adoles-

---

[9] Erikson, *op. cit.*, pp. 142f. See also Helen Merrell Lynd, *On Shame and the Search for Identity* (New York: Science Editions, 1965).

cent feels unprotected from the searching and sometimes brutal eyes of the world. For protection he turns to others who are experiencing the same kind of fear.

Uniformity of dress, manners, habits, and attitudes was apparent on the unit. The boys in the in-group tended to wear faded blue-jeans and sneakers in the winter, bermudas and sneakers in the summer. In a period of crisis the adolescent would often dress entirely in black or dress very sloppily. Practically everyone on the unit smoked. Almost everyone had a current boyfriend or girlfriend. The following attitudes were prevalent: "Why should I cooperate on the unit?" "The whole hospital is against us." "The aides don't spend enough time with us." "Why should I do what someone else can do?" The boys often felt as though the girls ran the unit.

Fads were popular and tended to spring up and die out quickly. Playing solitaire, knitting (for the girls), dyeing one's hair, making fudge candy in the kitchen, playing a guitar, breaking windows, running away — all tended to be popular for a time.

When there were elections of officers in the unit meetings, the adolescents both wanted and did not want to be nominated for an office. They liked the approval of the group in electing them; yet their election set them apart from the group and gave them responsibilities which they were not sure they could perform. An eighteen-year-old male adolescent, who had been in trouble with the law and who skillfully manipulated the hospital staff to get what he wanted, was elected chairman of the unit meeting. He saw the chair as a source of power and prestige, so he accepted the position. In the first meeting at which he presided, he showed his ignorance of parliamentary procedure and was ashamed.

The attitude of the chaplain toward the desire for conformity on the unit was to accept the conformity as the expression of a need and yet to support each adolescent in developing his unique potential. The chaplain did not condemn the uniform dress or attitudes. He did compliment an adolescent when he appeared one day dressed neatly and with a clean shave and combed hair. He supported the adolescent who was painting a picture, taking piano lessons, playing the cello, doing handcraft, or presiding at the unit meeting.

The pastor is usually aware of the need of conformity among

the adolescents of his church and community. However, he may not be aware of the particular need which this behavior meets, mainly that of protection against shame and exposure. When the adolescent becomes more sure of himself and who he is, he will become willing to be who he is without excessive need to either conform or rebel against prevailing standards. The adolescent's unique personhood needs to be affirmed without denying his need for conformity.

This identity consciousness may also be present when an adolescent both wants and does not want an elected office in a church youth group, as shown within the unit meetings at the hospital. The adolescent may also fear taking any leadership role in the church, or any position where he stands out from his peers. One wonders if the adolescent who appears to revel in the attention which a church heaps on him may not also be reacting against his self-consciousness.

Negative Identity

A negative identity may be chosen in order to fulfill the unexpressed desires of the parents, to rebel against parental demands, or to escape the ambiguity of a diffused identity.

> . . . Many a late adolescent, if faced with continued diffusion, would rather *be nobody or somebody bad, or indeed, dead — and this totally and by free choice — than be not-quite-somebody.*[10]

A negative identity may be prematurely stamped on an adolescent by a society which too eagerly labels a person criminal or homosexual after his first misdeed.[11]

For the adolescents, the hospital served as a psychosocial moratorium,[12] a place where they could experiment with different kinds of behavior. They could act out by smoking, cursing, rebelling, and wearing old clothes. They could select from a wide variety of jobs and could change each six weeks. There were many things to make in occupational therapy. Some adolescents, who came from respectable homes, tried being hippies for a while.

One girl acted out the unconscious wishes of her mother who was continually putting her daughter in a position to get into

[10] Erikson, *op. cit.*, p. 132.
[11] *Ibid.*, pp. 129-132.
[12] *Ibid.*, p. 111.

trouble. The mother got the daughter a job at a drive-in restaurant as a car waitress. Also the mother married an alcoholic sociopath and left him at home on Sundays with her daughter while she went to church.

Another girl perceived the unexpressed feelings of her adopted mother toward her. She and her twin had been adopted at age nine. Her twin was the favorite of the adoptive mother, who in many ways rejected the girl. The girl expressed "fear" that she was going to be like her real mother, who had been a prostitute. She began to act like her and assumed her last name. After coming to the unit, she insisted for a long time that she had not been legally adopted, so that she had her mother's last name.

The attitude of the chaplain toward experimentation in the moratorium of the hospital was to accept behavior unless it was destructive of property or infringed on the rights of others. Support was given in those times when the adolescent would break out of his negative identity and would make a positive achievement. An attempt was also made to help the adolescent see that he was free to choose what he wanted to be. He did not *have* to choose a negative identity.

In reference to the girl who was acting out the unconscious wishes of her mother, the situation was handled administratively. A shift occurred from the shepherding perspective to the organizational perspective.[13] Contact was made with the pastor of the family. He had only heard the mother's side of the story. He was made aware of the way the girl was reacting and what might be causing it. He expressed his concern about the possibility of the new father's seducing the girl. He said he was going to talk straight with the father and tell him that if he bothered the girl, he would see that he went to court. The chaplain participated with the staff in deciding that the girl would be kept in the hospital so that she could not take the job at the drive-in. He also participated in the decision to stop permitting the girl to go home on weekends.

The church, sometimes implicitly and sometimes explicitly, has set definite standards of conduct, often according to the social class standards of the congregation. These standards of con-

[13] Seward Hiltner, *Preface to Pastoral Theology* (Nashville: Abingdon Press, 1958), pp. 61ff.

duct have given adolescents searching for an identity something against which to rebel, or something against which to try out their own standards. The tragedy is that the church may reject the adolescent when he transgresses their standards. An alternative is for the pastor and the church to embody "the Way" without throwing out or freezing out the young person who doubts "the Way." The church and the pastor can commit themselves to stand by the adolescent as he travels the road of experimentation.

Most churches at some time have within their fellowship a girl who becomes an unwed mother. The way that the members of the church treat her and what action they take will reveal the values of the church. If the church tries to understand what happened and to give support to the girl and the boy in whatever way they need it, then the church is probably saying that persons are of primary importance and that all the members are sinners before God. On the other hand, if the church censures the girl and boy and overtly or covertly excludes them from the fellowship, then the church is probably saying that morals are more important than persons and that one mistake cannot be understood or forgiven.

The church and the pastor have close contact with the adolescents in the church who attend church regularly and who assume leadership positions in the church program. This kind of adolescent usually is praised highly and rewarded for his good deeds. However, like the negative identity, this positive identity is also an experimentation. And the adolescent boy or girl who has appeared to be so upstanding in the church may suddenly begin to act very differently. Again, this is experimentation and needs to be understood as such. Even in the adolescent who consistently maintained his positive identity, the pastor can be aware of the fact that in addition to his positive acts, he has many negative or unacceptable thoughts, feelings, and fantasies. This adolescent needs to know that he is not bad or unchristian when he thinks or feels in this way.

Work Paralysis

In the case of identity diffusion, the person loses his ability to produce. This occurs either in the form of not being able to complete a task or in the form of preoccupation with only one activity, to the exclusion of all others.[14]

Almost every adolescent on the unit had had trouble in school. When educational classes began on the unit, a lot of anxiety was present. On the unit itself, the staff had great difficulty in getting the adolescents to keep their rooms clean, to clean up when they used the kitchen, and to do their assigned duties on the unit. The staff also had difficulty in seeing that the adolescents continued their industrial therapy assignments for six weeks. Many of the adolescents began a project in occupational therapy and then left it.

One of the major aims of occupational and industrial therapy was that the adolescent choose a job that was commensurate with his abilities and interest and that he carry it through to completion. Also, every adolescent, before he left the hospital, was helped to find a job in the community.

The attitude of the chaplain was to support the adolescents in their work. For example, an adolescent girl, who had feelings of inferiority and unworthiness, was working on a handcraft project. Some of the work was exacting. She asked the chaplain if he would do the difficult part for her. However, with encouragement and support, she found that she was able to complete the project by herself. She was very proud of the finished product.

Along with support has gone a willingness to listen to the fears and anxieties of the adolescents about work. A custom of the chaplain has been to eat lunch, or at least to talk alone, with an adolescent who was scheduled to leave the hospital and to begin working. These times together have been especially productive. On one such occasion, a fifteen-year-old obese girl who was leaving the hospital to enter business school had lunch with the chaplain and expressed to him her fear of not being able to make it at business school. Her admittance to the hospital had been precipitated by her refusal to go to school, where she had not been able to make friends. She was afraid that this would happen again. Also, most of the other students enrolled at the business school had graduated from high school, but she had not.

After she left, the chaplain called her pastor to find out how she was doing and to encourage the pastor to support her.

[14] Erikson, *op. cit.*, pp. 127-129.

The local pastor is probably familiar with adolescents in his church or in his community who have difficulty in school. As this difficulty is often seen as a matter of laziness and lack of motivation on the part of the young person, adults handled the situation with punitive measures. However, as indicated here, this difficulty with school may be a manifestation of a more deeply underlying problem having to do with the central issue of the adolescent's identity.

The pastor may also encounter adolescents in the church who hesitate to accept a position of responsibility; or, if they accept it, they fail to complete the task. The adolescent may not know who he is and especially whether he is a faithful churchgoing person. When this identity confusion is acted out, the pastor may sense a deeper problem than just the adolescent's being irresponsible, and he may take initiative in dealing with the deeper problem. A punitive approach toward the adolescent's irresponsible behavior misses what is really going on. Who the adolescent is may be partially hammered out through what he does. So the adolescent needs to have responsibilities in the church which are commensurate with his interests and abilities.

Bisexual Diffusion

". . . The development of psychosocial intimacy is not possible without a firm sense of identity." [15] When there is not a "firm sense of identity," bisexual diffusion occurs. This diffusion can be expressed in two ways: by concentrating on genital activity without intimacy and commitment and thus attempting to foreclose the adolescent stage; or by repressing all genital activity by emphasizing intellectual and cultural values.[16]

On the adolescent unit all the patients seemed to have problems with members of the opposite sex. It was popular to have a boyfriend or girl friend; yet there was a fear of closeness. The result was a series of broken courtships. One girl always went with the boy most recently admitted to the unit. When a more recent one arrived, she went for him. The courtship seldom lasted more than a few weeks.

Another way to avoid closeness was for the adolescent girl to choose an older, married man in the hospital. He was sup-

[15] *Ibid.*, p. 145.
[16] *Ibid.*

posedly safe to date. Some of the girls found less traditional ways to avoid closeness. One girl, when she began to get close to her boyfriend, would act out on the unit and thus be placed on restriction, or in seclusion. In either case, she was not allowed to see her boyfriend.

Girls were the first to be admitted to the adolescent unit. When the boys were introduced to the unit on a day-care basis, most of the adolescent girls reacted strongly. More acting out occurred when the boys first moved onto the unit. The unit meetings were even more stormy. There was one especially calm unit meeting during this time. Near the end of the meeting someone noted that no boys were present that day because of a group therapy session.

Many of the adolescents liked to talk about their sexual exploits. It became a matter of gamesmanship, especially after a holiday. This sometimes upset the staff. For a girl to announce that she was pregnant was an especially effective way to upset the staff.

There were also more unusual forms of sexual behavior. At least one girl had had incestuous relations with her father. During one period a "gay" (*i.e.* homosexual) fad occurred.

The chaplain found that the adolescents on the unit had had little effective sex education, and yet they were curious. Some of them ordered moralistic, religious publications on sex. The chaplain felt that part of their anxiety about the opposite sex may have been simply a lack of knowledge and a lack of freedom to talk about their fears. He suggested a sex education program, but it was never begun.

A favorite topic of conversation, especially with the girls, was their current "flame." Because many of their problems centered around boys, conversations often focused on that area. One girl told the chaplain about the horrible previous weekend when she spent all her time trying to see her man, who was older and married. She was mad at him for not keeping his date, and was wondering if she ought to forget him.

Chaplain: You're sort of torn then between wanting to drop him and yet wanting to stick by him and prove yourself.
Patient: There were lots of others before him. Since January there have been. . . . (She named about eight boys.)

The chaplain related to the adolescents as one sexual being

to another. His own sexual identity was important in some relationships. For example one boy had homosexual feelings which he feared. Consequently, he stayed at a distance from the chaplain, and the chaplain respected his need for distance. However, on the last day, when the boy knew that the chaplain was leaving, he took the initiative in meeting with the chaplain.

The church and especially the youth group meetings are places where adolescents learn to relate to each other and to members of the opposite sex. Some sexual experimentation — both heterosexual and homosexual — may occur in church camps, on outings, and on hayrides. Some adolescent girls who are in the church, or who are marginally attached to the church, may become pregnant. A boy in the church may become a father. These problems are complex and difficult, so that no simple answers can be given. However, two suggestions are offered.

First, the sexual experimentation may be just experimentation and no more. The person may get caught and be exposed to public shame, but the person should not be labeled homosexual or promiscuous by the church for one act. This labeling might well serve to give the adolescent a negative identity, which he may then seek to embody and act out. If the adolescent repeatedly gets into trouble, he may need psychiatric help.

Second, the church has a responsibility to teach adolescents the Christian attitude toward sex. Most adolescents know the facts about human sexuality from films and courses in school, but they may be puzzled as to how they are to feel about themselves and their new urges and how they are to handle them. The prohibition against having premarital intercourse can no longer be enforced by fear of pregnancy, because of modern means of contraception. But many fears and anxieties swarm around the area of sex for the adolescent, and these fears need to be handled from a Christian perspective. Christian education in sex has proved to be very helpful when planned carefully in conjunction with local professional people and in cooperation with the adults in the church.[17]

[17] For bibliography on sex education, write to SIECUS, 1855 Broadway, New York 10023; also write to Order Section, American Medical Association, 535 N. Dearborn Street, Chicago, Illinois 60610; and see Isadore Rubin and Luther A. Kirkendall, eds., *Sex in the Adolescent Years: New Directions in Guiding and Teaching Youth* (New York: Association Press, 1968).

Authority Diffusion

In authority diffusion one would suppose that the adolescent had no clear authority in his life. Rather, there are many authorities, perhaps competing with each other. The young people on the adolescent unit appeared to be testing all authority; yet they expected the persons in positions of responsibility to use their authority in setting clear guidelines. Many were testing the authority of their parents, or indeed, the authority of any older person. Many of the parents (the first authority figures in the life of the adolescents) were divorced. Others often argued and drank excessively. In at least two cases, the father had died. Two mothers had been in a mental hospital several times. Another mother had a "nervous breakdown" in the spring. Most of the parents were inadequate.[18] In recognition of the importance of the family in the adolescent's recovery, the clinical psychologist, the social worker, and the consulting psychiatrist met weekly with the parents in group therapy.

The staff, in some sense, replaced the adolescent's parents while the adolescent was on the unit.[19] The staff numbered more than two, a fact which confused the adolescent, especially when the chain of authority among the staff was unclear. Because of the adolescent's problem of authority diffusion, it became even more imperative for the staff to speak with one voice. When they did not, the adolescent felt free to manipulate one side against the other.

A common practice was for an adolescent to make his request to the aide. If the aide refused, he would go to the licensed practical nurse, then to the registered nurse, then to the clinical psychologist, and finally to the unit director. He would never tell one that he had seen another previously. If his request was granted, he would stop before he got to the top. Needless to say, only open communication among staff members could prevent this kind of manipulation.

[18] For research on the effect of family patterns on child behavior, see Shirley Gehrke and Martin Kirschenbaum, "Survival Patterns in Family Conjoint Therapy," *Family Process*, Vol. 6 (March, 1967), pp. 67-80.

[19] The hospitalized adolescent's recovery is often dependent upon the way in which he settles the conflict of loyalty between his parents and the hospital. See D. B. Rinsley and D. D. Hall, "Psychiatric Hospital Treatment of Adolescents," *Archives of General Psychiatry*, Vol. 7 (October, 1962), pp. 286-294.

The unit meetings were often anxious times for the adolescents, because the staff was present but did not dominate the meeting. The unit meeting was the responsibility of the adolescents although the staff would vote and help to carry out decisions made at the meeting. When the young people could not reach an agreement on an issue, some of the adolescents would turn to the staff and demand that they resolve the matter in some way.

The chaplain represented the authority of the church and of God for most adolescents. For adolescents who were rebelling against the religion of their parents or of their childhood they rejected the chaplain without knowing him. For others who had experienced a good relationship to the church, or who had identified with religion, they accepted the chaplain before they knew him. There were fewer of the latter type.

The chaplain also represented the authority of previous ministers known by the adolescents. An adolescent girl, who had been born in Italy to an American soldier and an Italian woman, had recently arrived on the unit. During one of the first conversations with her, the following incident occurred:

Patient: I was a Catholic in Italy. Everyone in Italy is Catholic. But when I came here, a missionary talked with me, and I saw that it is wrong for a Catholic to confess his sins and then go out and smoke and drink. I learned that I had to believe in my heart.

Chaplain: But you don't believe now?

Patient: Well, when I first got sick, I . . . I know it's wrong . . . but I blamed God.

Chaplain: Do you still blame God?

Patient: (She glanced at me angrily and then continued her handcraft.) Well, sorta'.

Chaplain: Why did you look at me like that, M.?

Patient: I know what you are doing.

Chaplain: What am I doing, M.?

Patient: Well, I don't really know, but I think you're trying to push me back to God. (Her voice rose.) But you can't push me back.

Chaplain: Let me tell you what I was doing. Fair enough?

Patient: Okay.

Chaplain: M., I am trying to understand you and see why you.
. . .

Patient: (She interrupts.) Oh God, it has been horrible. I never had a family or a home. My mother was sick, and I stayed with many relatives. I came to the U.S. and found my father an alcoholic. He beat me.

She later told the chaplain that she had avoided him at first because she thought he would make her talk about God, as the missionary of her story had done, and she didn't want to do that.

The chaplain also was identified with morality and with the superego by some adolescents. Although they had previously related warmly to the chaplain, several adolescents would avoid him after they had done something wrong. A number of the boys would stop in the middle of telling a joke and others would quit singing a bawdy song.

The pastor is seen by adolescents in the church and in the community as an authority. As with the chaplain on the adolescent unit, the pastor will often meet either wholesale acceptance or wholesale rejection on the part of many adolescents before they even know him. In all cases the adolescents in a church to which a pastor has just moved will test the pastor to see what kind of person he is. They want to know if he is phony or if he can be trusted. The temptation of the pastor is either to become one with the adolescents in an attempt to bridge the generation gap, or to withdraw into his other duties and let a lay person deal with the youth. The first alternative misses the need of the adolescent for the authority to be an authority and to set clear guidelines against which the adolescent can try out his own ideas. The second alternative misses the need of the adolescent to learn to trust and relate to persons in authority and to have a model for his own life. The middle path is for the pastor to be patient and firm, caring and demanding, listening and asking. In this way the pastor teaches the adolescent something about God and about the gospel which embodies both love and demand.

The local pastor has many opportunities to see his congregation, including the adolescents, in a social setting. The pastor can relax and enter into the festive occasions with a full spirit of participation. The adolescents may especially appreciate knowing that the pastor is not a "stuffed shirt" or someone who never has fun. On the other hand, to try to imitate the actions, language, or dress of adolescents may make the adolescents and the pastor uncomfortable. He may try too hard to shed his religious identity. He must remain the pastor, although a warm, friendly pastor.

Diffusion of Ideals

An ideology, which is between a theory and a religion, is necessary to a growing ego, for it synthesizes the past and the future. Part of the task of adolescence is precisely this synthesis, so that ". . . identity and ideology are two aspects of the same process." [20] When there is identity diffusion, there is also ideological diffusion.

Wayne E. Oates has noted that the religious ideas of a mentally ill patient tend to symbolize the self-estimate and the difficulties in interpersonal living the patient himself has.[21] Since the adolescents had diffused identities, they also did not have a clearly focused ideology or religion. They did not know what to believe although they were concerned about life, death, God, and guilt. The adolescent's religion expressed his level of maturity and his current problems and crises. It revealed in every case a lack of a clear sense of identity for God and for the adolescent himself. In no case did the adolescent have a model after whom he wanted to pattern his own life.

Institutional religion had little meaning for most of them. One girl had been confirmed in an Episcopal Church about a year ago. The chaplain made arrangements with the priest of her church for her to attend the Sunday evening youth group while she was in the hospital. She went a few times when she was home for weekend visits. However, she told the chaplain that she did not like the youth group. After she had been discharged for a few months, the priest informed the chaplain that she had quit coming to the youth group. Another girl, after a home visit one weekend, said that she was never going back to church. She said that the people "looked at her" and were cold.

Sections of the Draper Religious Inventory were used to discover and evaluate the religious maturity of the adolescents.[22] The verbalized religious beliefs of the adolescents tended toward two paths. One was the path of intellectualization, as in the case of a sixteen-year-old, intelligent boy who was admitted

[20] Erikson, *op. cit.*, p. 157.
[21] Wayne E. Oates, *Religious Factors in Mental Illness* (New York: Association Press, 1955), pp. 59ff.
[22] Edgar Draper, *et al.*, "On the Diagnostic Value of Religious Ideation," *Archives of General Psychiatry*, Vol. 13 (September, 1965), pp. 202-207.

to the hospital. Glue-sniffing had precipitated his admittance. During an initial interview he said his favorite song was "Where am I going?" because he did not know either who he was or what he wanted to be. His esthetic intellectualism showed up in the following ways: He had so many talents and interests that he could not decide which one to follow; as a child, he liked a minister because he noticed the large words that he used; his favorite passage of the Bible was a poetic one; his three greatest wishes in life were for love, entertainment, and eternity. In the interview the following conversation occurred:

> Chaplain: What does prayer mean to you, M.?
> M.: It has meant a lot to me. I have prayed more in the last year than I ever have. I pray when I sniff glue, and that often helps me to stop.
> Chaplain: How does it help you?
> M.: Well, I pray for help for myself. I never pray for anyone else. That's egotistical and not good, I know.
> Chaplain: M., if God were a person, what would he look like?
> M.: Well I'm not sure if he would be a man or a woman. . . .

Religion was used by the boy as an esthetic enjoyment. He also tried to use religion to help control his impulse to sniff glue. A function of this "sick" religion was for self-preservation and for controlling anxiety.[23] The adolescent boy's tendency to intellectualize all of life was also revealed in his religious beliefs. His own sexual confusion also was symbolized in his confusion as to the sexual identity of God.

The second form of verbalized religious beliefs of the adolescent tends to follow the legalistic path. For example, the girl who was born into the Roman Catholic Church in Italy, but later was converted to a fundamentalistic Protestantism, said that she knew that God did not want her to smoke. She said that she had been happy in her religion until she began to get sick. She prayed that God would help her to get better. When she got worse, she blamed God and stopped going to church. After she had been on the adolescent unit for several weeks, she approached the chaplain one day and asked him what the Bible said about punishment. She then told how the idea had occurred to her that perhaps God had a purpose in her presence in the hospital. She was scared that God would punish her for

---

[23] Oates, *Religious Factors* . . ., pp. 59ff.

blaming him. This girl had received almost no love in her life. She tended to see God as a distant judge, who handed out punishments and rewards. Her religion tended to be legalistic. She had a great deal of hostility, which she had internalized at times in suicidal attempts and in physical illness. She also projected some of this hostility onto God, who then was angry with her. She felt that God was angry because she had blamed him, because of an unacceptable impulse in herself.

Pastoral care was given in terms of the findings of the Draper Religious Inventory which helped to locate where the adolescents were in their religious development. However, the Inventory also served to stimulate the adolescent's own interest and concern about his personal religion. Several adolescents expressed their appreciation to the chaplain for helping them to think through what they believed. They said that they had never done that before.

The chaplain tried to help the adolescents to discern the important from the unimportant, the significant from the insignificant. He tried to help them find out what they really wanted to do in life, what they wanted to live for. The result in some instances was a clarification of the adolescent's ideals.

The local pastor must realize that the unsureness of the adolescent as to who he is extends to an unsureness of what he believes. To expect an adolescent who has recently joined the church to be clear about his religious convictions and to have no doubts is to expect more of him than he is capable of fulfilling. The church needs to accept him where he is with whatever motivations he has in coming to church and move with him as he struggles to clarify his beliefs about such matters as God, the Bible, and the nature of sin and suffering. If he finds the church community meaningful in his pilgrimage, he will want to be a part of it.

The local pastor may find religion in the life of the adolescent based on a kind of esthetic enjoyment or childish pietism. If the adolescent is interested in religion and if the church is willing to commit itself to the adolescent, then this kind of religion can be used as a starting point on which to mold a mature faith that can be integrated into his whole life-style. The need for mature guidance and the freedom to search are two indispensable poles for the adolescent. If he gets both from the church, the adolescent will find the church and the Christian faith to be meaningful as he grows, and he will want to participate in the caring community.

The validity of giving this kind of support is demonstrated by the experience of one boy in high school who began to have doubts about his faith and later became an atheist. In college he expressed his atheism openly and vocally. However, he was very much interested in religion and served on the campus church board. This church gave him the freedom to express his views honestly and yet stayed by him. Later in life he joined a church and was an active church member. The church community had meant something to him during his struggles with his own religious beliefs, and he wanted to be a part of it and help others.

THEOLOGICAL MOTIFS IN CARE OF ADOLESCENTS

This section is an attempt to use the incarnation and the resurrection of Christ as theological motifs that illumine and give perspective to the kind of pastoral care which was extended to the adolescents on the unit.

The correlations between the life and work of Christ and the life and work of the chaplain are not intended to imply an identification between the chaplain and Christ. Rather, Christ is seen as the motive and the example for pastoral care.

Incarnation

"And the Word became flesh and dwelt among us . . ." (John 1:14a). As Jesus Christ assumed the limits of time and humanity to be with man, so the chaplain adopted the limits of the adolescent unit and the role of chaplain to be with the adolescents. Tension, confusion, and crises often occurred on the unit and between the unit and the hospital. The situation was by no means perfect. However, given that situation with its difficulties and limitations, the chaplain chose to work in it.

The local pastor always has a less than perfect situation in which to work. If he is to minister effectively in that situation, he has to assume the limits and ambiguities of that time and place. His role as pastor also has limits and ambiguities as well as advantages, but the pastor has chosen his role. If he assumes these limits, the adolescents will sense his genuineness and thus will be ready to listen and to respond when he speaks of the love of God for them. They have experienced the pastor's love as acted out toward them in any particular situation.

". . . *Those who are well have no need of a physician, but those who are sick*" (Mark 2:17). Jesus came to minister to the sick, the poor, the criminal, and the disinherited. He lived and ate with them. The chaplain went to the emotionally disturbed adolescents. He did not ask them to come to him. He lived a part of his life with them and ate with them. As was mentioned above, some of the chaplain's most productive moments with the staff occurred when they were washing dishes, ironing or folding clothes, while talking with him. With the adolescents, an invitation to go to the canteen, to take a walk, to eat lunch together, or to play ping-pong together often resulted in a dialogue and resulting insight.

If the pastor has had a continuous relationship with an adolescent, he is often in a better position to sense what is going on in the adolescent's life than any other professional person in the community. The pastor may have known the adolescent since he was a child. When the adolescent begins to show signs of maladjustment or illness, the pastor can be sensitive to these signs. On the other side, the adolescent hopefully trusts the pastor, and thus feels free to talk to him when the need arises. The adolescent needs a pastor, or someone in the church, who he feels will accept him even when he tells that person his deepest secret or fear.

In the words of the Apostles' Creed, "*He descended into Hell.*" Jesus suffered on behalf of man. He lived and suffered with and for man. One adolescent said that the hospital was hell for him. It was a place of real suffering for him and for many of the adolescents. The chaplain went to that place. As he listened to them, he shared part of their troubles. It was easy to withdraw from the agony of the situation and to remain aloof. But there were times that the chaplain suffered with the adolescents. In such occasions, the adolescent felt a sense of refuge and comfort in the chaplain.

The pastor may find that working with the sick is not very pleasant or even rewarding. Associating with nice, socially acceptable people may be more enjoyable. But he evades involvement with the sick and distressed only at the risk of losing part of his unique ministry as a Christian pastor. The hell of loneliness in an adolescent boy who is afraid to ask a girl for a date, of grief in an adolescent whose best chum has moved out of town, of anxiety in an adolescent girl when her boyfriend begins to want to go further in their physical relationship than she feels is appropriate, of fear in an adolescent that he is not normal — this hell of theirs does not have to be borne alone. Christ has entered their hell, and the pastor, as Christ's representative, enters that hell.

". . . I have not come to bring peace, but a sword" (Matthew 10:34b). Jesus brought judgment and condemnation as well as refuge and comfort. He challenged the Pharisees, and he drove the money-changers from the Temple. The presence of the chaplain was also a judgment, in that it made the staff aware of the lack of organization on the unit. He was a judgment to some of the staff members who would have preferred not to think about their real feelings toward the adolescents. He was a judgment to those adolescents who had been acting out and who knew that their actions were not right. In showing some of the adolescents a more mature way of life, he was a judgment on their old way of life. In making the adolescents in the unit meeting aware of what they were really doing, he was judging their inadequate way of seeing things.

The local pastor, in his commitment and maturity, stands in judgment on the lack of commitment and the immaturity of adolescents. Whether this judgment comes in the form of an accepting relationship as mediated through the Good News of Jesus Christ or in the form of harsh legalism is the responsibility of the pastor. The pastor serves as a model to the adolescent, and in the adolescent's patterning his life after the pastor's the adolescent is testifying to his own personal lack. For some adolescents the pastor serves as a sword-bearer with whom they want to battle.

As a bringer of the sword, the pastor is committed to speak the truth with love, even if the truth is painful. As such, he may be called to speak the truth to the parents of adolescents. The parent may need to hear that he is expecting too much of his son or daughter, or that he needs to spend more time with his son, or that the adolescent needs to have more freedom in order to grow up. The pastor earns the right to speak the truth in love when he is faithful to God and to the people in his church.

"I have come in my Father's name . . ." (John 5:43a). Jesus came as the Son of God. As such, he represented his Father. He was the messenger, the ambassador of his Father. The chaplain symbolized Jesus Christ to some of the adolescents and staff. The chaplain came in the name of Jesus. Thus he represented, although he did not fully embody, Jesus Christ. His very title, "Chaplain," by which he was called on the unit, set him apart from the other staff members.

The local pastor also comes in the name of God and the church. The pastor is not a social worker, poverty program worker, psychologist, or just a buddy. He is a man called from God. The pastor begins, carries through, and ends his task with a firm grounding in theology. The pastor lives and ministers out of his commitment to God, and that, more than anything else, is what the adolescent needs to see.

Resurrection

The resurrection of Jesus Christ gives man the hope that relationships will continue. Death cannot destroy relationships forever. The theme of the resurrection was present in the work of the chaplain in the fact that he formed a continuing relationship with some of the staff and adolescents. In the midst of tension and change, the chaplain maintained a durable relationship with these people. He kept his commitments and appointments.

The local pastor can do no more important thing with the adolescents in his church than to keep his promises to them. If he promises them to get a particular speaker, or that they can have a hayride, or that he will meet one of them in the church to talk, then he ought to follow through. If he cannot fulfill his commitment, he needs to inform the adolescent in a responsible way.

The local pastor is in the unusual position of being able to form a relationship with a person who is still very young and to follow the person much of the rest of his life. This is true even though the pastor may leave the church to which the other person belongs. The pastor can act out the faithfulness of God to the adolescent by not abandoning him, no matter where he goes — to juvenile court, to an unwed mother's home, to a psychiatrist, or to a mental hospital. Other professional people may be primarily responsible for the adolescent in these situations, but they cannot take the place of the presence of the caring community of the church. In the above sense the pastor through his continuing and faithful relationships to the adolescent embodies the meaning of the resurrection for the adolescent.

Paul says that one of the hopes of the resurrection is the hope of perfection (1 Corinthians 15:42-44). In the resurrection there is hope that man's body and relationships will be made complete. On the adolescent unit the chaplain has the hope that the emotions and the lives of the adolescents will be made mature. He has the hope that broken relationships in the community of staff will be restored, although perhaps not in the forseeable future.

The local pastor lives also in the hope and conviction that the adolescents in his church and community will grow to maturity. He knows that he does not have to take total responsibility for the adolescents, because he is not God. That fact in itself produces hope. In his faithful ministry which enables the adolescents to experience his help and hope, the hope of completeness or maturity is also engendered in the adolescent.

SUGGESTIONS FOR FURTHER READING

Blees, Robert A., *et al.*, *Counseling with Teen-Agers*. Englewood Cliffs, N.J.: Prentice-Hall, 1965.

Erikson, Erik H., *Identity and the Life Cycle*. New York: International Universities Press, Inc., 1959.

_____, *Identity: Youth and Crisis*. New York: W. W. Norton & Company, Inc., 1968.

Gesell, Arnold, *et al.*, *Youth: The Years from Ten to Sixteen*. New York: Harper & Row, Publishers, Inc., 1956.

Golburgh, Stephen, ed., *The Experience of Adolescence*. Cambridge, Mass.: Schenkman Publishing Co., Inc., 1965.

Miller, Haskell M., *Understanding and Preventing Juvenile Delinquency*. Nashville: Abingdon Press, 1958.

Muuss, Rolf, *Theories of Adolescence*. New York: Random House, Inc., 1962.

Rubin, Theodore Isaac, *Coming Out*. New York: Pocket Books, 1968.

_____, *Lisa and David*. New York: The Macmillan Company, 1961.

Stewart, Charles William, *Adolescent Religion*. Nashville: Abingdon Press, 1967.

Stone, L. Joseph and Church, Joseph, *Childhood and Adolescence*. New York: Random House, Inc., 1957.

Boyd S. McLocklin is Director of the Pastoral Counseling Center in Louisville, Kentucky. He has also served as a hospital chaplain and a pastor. A graduate of the University of Georgia and Southern Baptist Theological Seminary, he is accredited as a hospital chaplain by the College of Chaplains of the American Protestant Hospital Association.

6
PASTORAL CARE OF AN EMOTIONALLY DISTURBED ADULT

Boyd S. McLocklin and Andrew D. Lester

INTRODUCTION BY ROBERT A. CLARY, M.D.

Medical Arts Building, Louisville, Kentucky

A case like that of "Mrs. Jones" as presented by Chaplain McLocklin offers a special opportunity for the chaplain-pastor and psychiatrist to complement each other in rendering service to a deeply troubled and emotionally disturbed young woman. It is inconceivable to imagine this patient receiving help from any source without deep involvement in her religious conflicts. This patient, as well as many others, cannot be adequately counseled by the chaplain-pastor who is cautiously avoiding stepping on the toes of the psychiatrist. Neither can the psychiatrist adequately prescribe treatment if he is apprehensively avoiding the religious aspects of the patient's illness.

This particular patient had a very involved and positive relationship with the chaplain-pastor prior to her transfer to my care. The question of alliances was dealt with in a simple, direct manner. She was told unequivocally to continue with her pastoral care, and a direct and immediate phone call by me to the chaplain-pastor relieved the patient's anxiety and established a line of communication, when needed, between the pastor and psychiatrist. It is my opinion that both have been able to work effectively with this patient.

The chaplain's most difficult and complex interaction with the patient comes from the obvious fact that he is the living and concrete symbol of much of the patient's psychopathology. He was initially the symbolic ambassador of a frightening and destructive God. The chaplain-pastor's capacity literally to endure this hostile projection of the patient has been a vital factor in her increasing ability to reach out tentatively again for deeper meaning in her religious life. In this particular case the chaplain-pastor and psychiatrist have attempted to offer the patient the specialized and unique contributions of two modalities that seek to relieve human suffering. It should be the hope — and purpose — of this book and this chapter to demonstrate to the minister that he be less fearful of involvement in dealing with the patient's mental symptoms, as psychiatrists should be less apprehensive in dealing more directly with the religious aspects of the patient's illness. Thus, the minister and the psychiatrist can work together more closely.

PASTORAL CARE OF AN EMOTIONALLY DISTURBED ADULT

Boyd S. McLocklin

The following case is presented as an illustration of some ways in which a pastor might be meaningful to a person who is undergoing severe emotional stress and who is under the care of a psychiatrist. The pastoral management of this situation is not presented as an ideal but rather as one chaplain's attempts, some of which succeeded and some of which failed, to minister in such a situation. It is hoped that the presentation of this case will illustrate some of the basic principles of pastoral care, especially those of durability and faithfulness, to which all pastors should be attentive. Many of the insights in this situation came as hindsight rather than foresight. Throughout the relationship the chaplain found himself groping and uncertain about what was taking place and how he needed to respond. The relationship with Mrs. Jones began with a routine pastoral visit in a general hospital and has lasted, to date, for twenty-five months. The account of this relationship, as it is presented in this chapter, will be interspersed with comments upon its meaning for the pastoral care of other disturbed persons by Andrew Lester.

BIOGRAPHICAL SKETCH

Mrs. Jones is a twenty-nine-year-old married Caucasian with three children. She was raised in rural Appalachia and now lives in an urban area. Her father was a rigid man with no formal education. He became a Baptist minister in his late twenties. Mrs. Jones has very fond memories of her father from her earliest memory until approximately her tenth or eleventh year. These memories include such experiences as riding to church with him on the front seat of the car and quietly talking together on Sunday afternoons while sitting with him on a large rock located near their home. Although she has pleasant memories of these early childhood years, she also remembers him as being very stern.

During adolescence the relationship to her father became a very trying one, and she found herself constantly at odds with him. There were four events around which her struggles seemed to revolve: (1) At age thirteen Mrs. Jones decided to join the church during a revival meeting in which a young pastor was preaching. Her father restrained her from joining at that time, expressing his fear that her felt need to become a Christian might instead be some sort of sexual attraction to the young minister. (2) At age fifteen Mrs. Jones became quite involved with a young man in her community who was three years her senior and a devout Roman Catholic. From all indications her relationship with him was quite wholesome, and there was no sexual experimentation. About the middle of her fifteenth year this young man proposed marriage to Mrs. Jones, and she accepted. Her father, upon hearing this news, took the ring from her, called the young man to his house, returned the ring, treated him very rudely, and forbade him to see Mrs. Jones again. (3) At about the middle of her sixteenth year, Mrs. Jones had a whirlwind relationship with a twenty-two-year-old man just home from service in Korea. She married him against her father's wishes, and her family refused to come to her wedding. (4) During her twentieth year, Mrs. Jones' father had a sudden stroke and died. His death occurred one week after she experienced a violent disagreement with him, which in her opinion hurt him deeply and stirred him tremendously.

Mrs. Jones' mother was a passive person and quite astute at exercising power by the creation of guilt and shame. Mrs. Jones has very few early memories of her mother, and those few are quite benign. During the troublesome teen-age years the mother voiced her opinion in favor of neither the father nor Mrs. Jones. But in the eyes of Mrs. Jones her mother agreed with and supported the views of the father.

Mrs. Jones is the youngest of seven siblings and the only girl. The six boys were quite vehement in their rebellion against their father's rigid, puritanical views. Throughout their teen-age years they were well known in their community for their roughness, drunkenness, and cursing. Mrs. Jones shared in this rebellion and now experiences a great deal of guilt over her participation. Throughout her childhood she identified with her brothers, participated in masculine activities, and became known in her hometown as a tomboy.

Mr. Jones is large and overweight. His strongest defense mechanisms are repression and suppression enabling him to avoid almost any conflictual situation. Over the years he has expressed some negative feelings to his wife, berating her emotional problems; but, primarily, he has been a supporting factor to her. They have three children: a twelve-year-old daughter and two sons, ages eight and three. Although at certain times Mrs. Jones undergoes extreme emotional stress, she remains throughout a devoted mother and one who is able to provide a substantial degree of emotional support for her children. She has not experienced any major problems with them to date. At the present time her daughter is beginning to struggle with her own femininity, and Mrs. Jones is responding to this in a surprisingly concerned and effective way.

During her teen-age years Mrs. Jones seemed to be quite popular in school even though she was undergoing extreme emotional stress. She was an elected cheerleader and was involved in other social activities until she dropped out of school to marry. Between the time of her father's death when she was twenty years old and the initial encounter with this minister when she was twenty-six, Mrs. Jones had suffered six "nervous breakdowns," had attempted suicide four times in three different cities, and had been treated by four different psychiatrists.

INITIAL ENCOUNTER

At the time of the initial encounter with Mrs. Jones, the minister was serving as chaplain in an urban, middle-class, denominational hospital. Mrs. Jones was encountered on a medical floor during routine ward visitation. The first meeting took the following form:

> Chaplain: Hello, I'm Chaplain McLocklin.
> Mrs. Jones: Who?
> Chaplain: I'm Chaplain McLocklin.
> Mrs. Jones: Who did you say?
> Chaplain: I am the preacher here in the hospital.
> Mrs. Jones: (At this point Mrs. Jones develops a frightened and somewhat angry look. She slowly draws into a fetal position with her back to the chaplain and pulls the cover up around her neck.)
> Chaplain: (After a few moments of silence.) Mrs. Jones, I am the minister here. I gather that you would rather not talk now. Unless you have some objection, I am going to sit here silently beside your bed for a few minutes, and then I will leave. (After a three-minute silence the chaplain excuses himself indicating that he will return the following day.)

Immediately upon leaving the room the chaplain consulted Mrs. Jones' physician, who was a local psychiatrist, and read her medical chart. She had been admitted to the hospital because of a severe depression with the concomitant threat of suicide. In consultation with Mrs. Jones' doctor, it was decided that the chaplain should make a daily visit to her in a supportive role as a pastor but leave the initiative for the relationship, as much as possible, upon her.

The second and third visits were very similar to the first with Mrs. Jones remaining extremely quiet and the chaplain sitting briefly by the bed. Toward the end of the fourth visit the following exchange took place.

> Mrs. Jones: (After about a three-minute silence with her back turned to the chaplain, suddenly she turns toward him with a somewhat fearful, yet angry, expression.) Why the hell do you come in here every day, anyway?
> Chaplain: I would like to get to know you, to become acquainted with you, and to share with you as another person; however, if that is impossible at the present time, it seems that the least I can do is come and sit with you. (Mrs. Jones has a very puzzled look on her face as if she is trying to figure something out. Suddenly she turns her back, pulls herself into a fetal position, and

pulls the sheet up around her shoulders. After a few minutes of silence, the chaplain responds.) Mrs. Jones, even though I would like to get to know you, it could be that my presence is causing you some unnecessary stress. If it is your desire that I not return tomorrow, I want you to know that I will honor that request.

Mrs. Jones: (She turns in the bed very fast, leans on one elbow, and says in a very apologetic way.) I did not mean to offend you. I like for you to come. I want you to come. I hope I did not hurt your feelings.

Chaplain: No, you did not hurt my feelings, but I wanted to be sensitive to you. If it is your desire that I return tomorrow, I shall come back at approximately the same time. (Mrs. Jones nods with a slight smile to indicate that this would be acceptable. He excuses himself and leaves the room.)

Principles of Pastoral Care

The most obvious lesson in this initial encounter concerns the meaning of "presence." Human beings usually underestimate the importance of "presence" in interpersonal relationships. Ministers represent certain ideas and thoughts to people by their physical presence, whether or not they speak. Pastors are familiar, for example, with the change in tone and content that often takes place when they enter a conversation. The minister represents — for good or bad — God, religion, conscience, and the church. He often polarizes a number of attitudes and dated emotions. As this chaplain was to find out later, he represented God to this patient, polarizing her attitudes and emotions of affection, hate, and guilt. The positive aspect of this representation and polarization is that the pastor's presence alone can confront a person with his or her unresolved personal conflicts and hidden religious struggles. This confrontation may open the door for a meaningful pastoral relationship, as in the case under consideration. In this particular clinical encounter it is obvious that the chaplain's presence precipitated significant responses from the patient.

A second lesson from this clinical situation concerns the creative use of silence. Most ministers are expected, by both themselves and others, to verbalize in any situation. When gaps develop in pastoral conversation, the pastor usually assumes it is his job to fill the vacuum. Silence is very threatening. Pastors often become anxious for fear that the other person thinks he has nothing to say. In our culture, where "doing" and "acting" are paramount to success, silence represents failure.

Silence, however, can stimulate "creative brooding." Silence gave this emotionally disturbed patient opportunity to think about the unthinkable past and gently pushed her to concretize her feelings. When visiting with an emotionally disturbed parishioner, a minister's anxiety may cause him to react even more strongly than usual to silence. However, if he can remain calm and secure in his "presence," he will allow the person ample time to gather loose, scattered thoughts, and participate with him in meaningful pastoral conversation.

Silence in this clinical situation communicated concern, interest, and acceptance on the part of the chaplain, which finally enabled the patient to respond. Emotionally disturbed persons feel more secure when they sense that the pastor is at ease with silence. They do not feel compelled, then, to talk about superficial thoughts just to make social conversation.

Thirdly, we learn from this chaplain to take seriously the Christian belief in the freedom of man. Although he persistently made himself available and opened himself to a relationship, he never infringed upon her rights as a person under God to refuse his offer. As recorded in the biographical sketch, the most influential person in the patient's past, her minister-father, continually usurped her freedom during adolescence. The chaplain demonstrated to her that he was different.

The reader should note that this woman's freedom was never threatened by the chaplain-pastor. Her willingness both to begin and to continue the relationship could be basically attributed to this fact. The pastor must remember that emotionally ill people often feel the perimeters of their personhood to be preciously small and threatened on all sides. The pastor who concretely recognizes and respects their freedom as individuals — and, therefore, their worth — will find a much more open response.

INTIMACY AND AGITATION

Following the fourth visit the chaplain's relationship to Mrs. Jones began to develop. As a degree of intimacy entered into the relationship, Mrs. Jones began to experience more and more agitation. During the chaplain's visits her conversation became more flighty. Between visits she went to the rooms of other patients in the hospital talking for long periods of time and, occasionally, in an obnoxious manner. The chaplain began to receive anonymous phone calls at his home from a party who would neither speak nor give her name. Because of the reports from other patients and personnel on the ward, the chaplain was quite sure that the phone calls were coming from Mrs. Jones; but when confronted with this possibility, Mrs. Jones denied the claim and became quite evasive. Her psychiatrist hypothesized that Mrs. Jones was forming strong erotic feelings toward the chaplain and that her agitated behavior was an attempt to deal with these feelings. Toward the end of the second week of Mrs. Jones' hospitalization, the chaplain found himself struggling with his own angry feelings toward her for the continuing anonymous phone calls and for her agitation on the ward. He was tempted to break off the relationship in hope that she would be able to settle into her treatment plan. After struggling with these emotions for several days, and in consultation with the psychiatrist, he decided to confront her honestly and straight-forwardly in an attempt to "clear the air."

Principles of Pastoral Care

If the pastor is going to minister effectively to persons, he must be sensitive to the interpersonal dynamics which affect his relationships. Psychoanalysis identifies these dynamics as transferences or projections onto the therapist of feelings and emotions from the person's past. Pastors can educate themselves to some degree by acquainting themselves with the literature in pastoral psychology. They can also seek clinical training experiences as part of their continuing education. Trained colleagues and professional people in the community can provide assistance in interpreting relationships that are either confusing or threatening. It would be impossible here to point out all of the potential dynamics that a pastor might encounter. However, pastors who are oblivious to these patterns of relationship are endangering their ministry. In the relationship under consideration the chaplain and the psychiatrist identified the erotic pattern of relationship and established appropriate structures in which it could be handled.

We learn from this chaplain the importance of the pastor's awareness of his own feelings. The hostility which the chaplain felt toward this patient could have seriously affected his efforts to minister to her if he had not appropriately expressed it. How could it have affected the relationship? If the chaplain had been afraid of his angry feelings, for example, or had been excessively influenced by cultural taboos concerning the expression of anger, he might have consciously or unconsciously broken the relationship. Breaking a relationship is one method of ridding oneself of feelings which are considered "sinful" or "unchristian." The chaplain recognized this temptation and rejected it. Actually, when a pastor does break a relationship, he sins against the parishioner by rejecting him either because of his own immaturity (fear of angry feelings) or because of his poor theology (believing that Christian faith and anger are incompatible).

Another possibility would have been for the chaplain to continue his relationship with Mrs. Jones but refuse to acknowledge his hostility. Hostility, however, is a strong emotion, and sooner or later it would have leaked out in some inappropriate way. Sarcasm, displays of temper, and defense mechanisms, such as displacement and projection, are several ways in which bottled up hostility spills over in interpersonal relationships.

This chaplain, however, took seriously Paul's admonition, "Be angry but do not sin . . ." (Ephesians 4:26). He realized that having hostile feelings does not make a man sinful any more than the anger felt by Jesus of Nazareth (Mark 3:5; Matthew 23:23-28; John 2:13-17). It is not the possession of angry feelings but the use of them which is decisive. Whether or not a man handles his angry feelings responsibly and within the context of love indicates whether or not he is being Christlike. Pastors must respond to the biblical injunctions concerning the Christian's responsibility for personal growth and development. The writer to the Hebrews counsels his readers to ". . . go on to maturity" (Hebrews 6:1). This maturity must include learning how to express responsibly emotions of both affection and hostility. This chaplain was not afraid of his feelings and by expressing his hostility openly, honestly, and appropriately, he kept from sinning with his anger.

CONFRONTATION AND CONFESSION

Upon being confronted with the chaplain's feelings, Mrs. Jones became quite anxious but not immobilized. She attempted to explain her unusual behavior during the previous week. She indicated that there was one situation from her past life that had caused her great concern and hurt over the past few years. She had been unable to reveal this episode, or her feelings about it, to anyone. As her relationship with the chaplain deepened, she felt a sense of trust and openness that left her with a desire to share with him the events of her past life. Along with this desire to share, however, she experienced the fear that her confession would engender rejection and condemnation from the chaplain. Thus she attempted to keep her conversations with the chaplain on a very superficial level as a means of concealing her past. At times she felt that she could share her past life if she did not have to face him physically. This is why she made the phone calls to his home. Before each attempt to call him she had fully intended to share the details of her past life, but upon hearing his voice she had found herself unable to speak. After expressing her deep regret about the inconveniences which she had placed upon him and his family, she went on to reveal the nature of her confession.

Her marriage had been an act of hostility against her father. When he retaliated by not attending her wedding, she "hardened her heart" against him and became belligerent in her expression of anger toward him. During the following two years, she engineered situations and conversations in such a way as to either expose or take cuts at her father. One week before her father's death she and her family were visiting her parents' home. As they were preparing to leave, she went to each member of her family and said goodbye with a hug and a kiss. When she came to her father, she looked at him with scorn and disgust, turned her back upon him, and walked away. Three days later she received word that he had suffered a stroke. The following day he died. At the time of his funeral she was overtaken by grief and guilt. In an attempt to console her, many of her father's friends came to tell her how much her father had loved her; they illustrated this by telling how much he had been hurt by her rejection. These statements confirmed in her mind that she had undoubtedly killed her father by rejecting him, that he had died without forgiving her, and that her behavior had been so despicable that she was really an unforgivable person.

After hearing Mrs. Jones' confession and helping her clarify some of the issues she had discussed, the chaplain asked if she would like for them to pray together. She replied that since the time of the death of her father she had been totally unable to pray but would be very grateful if someone could help her regain some contact with God. At the present time she was too ashamed even to attempt to face God. The chaplain indicated that he would like to pray with her. The prayer was short and simple. It expressed to God her feelings of separateness, guilt, fear, her inability to forgive herself, and her fear that her sins were unforgivable. It acknowledged the biblical testimony that God had dealt with difficult situations in the past and asked that his will be done in this chaotic life-situation. At the conclusion of the prayer a brief silence was broken by Mrs. Jones. "Do you really believe God could forgive my sins?" After a pause the chaplain replied, "Mrs. Jones, do you believe that I could forgive your sins?" A sudden look of shock came over Mrs. Jones' face. Her expression became cold and stone-hard. There was a three- to five-minute silence broken only by Mrs. Jones' attempts to speak.

When unable to speak she fell silent for a few more minutes and then said that she felt cold and tingly all over. She asked in a very puzzled tone, "What happened to me?" The chaplain indicated that he did not know and asked if she could interpret to him what she had felt. At first she was confused, but then she began to articulate the fact that his statement had suddenly caused her to realize two things simultaneously: (1) Her fear that if she ever revealed her secret to anyone she would be rejected; and (2) the fact that the chaplain had in no way appeared to respond in a judgmental or rejecting manner. His question had caused her to feel that there was someone who could forgive her. The chaplain wondered with her if these strange physical sensations that she had experienced might not be the liberating experience of forgiveness. At this point she bowed her head and mumbled, "Thank you, God."

The chaplain expressed to Mrs. Jones that as it had been a trying day and she needed some rest, he would be leaving. He asked if she would prefer that he contact her psychiatrist concerning what had happened. She expressed anxiety over the psychiatrist's knowing about her past life. After some discussion she indicated that she would take the responsibility of telling him about these events.

In the following three days Mrs. Jones became a model patient from both a nursing and a psychiatric point of view. She was open, cooperative, and helpful. Her psychiatrist decided after the third day that she could be dismissed from the hospital. During this time the chaplain visited her daily to aid her in her quest for understanding of what had taken place in her life.

In consultation with the psychiatrist, it was decided that the chaplain would do two things upon Mrs. Jones' leaving the hospital: (1) Emphasize his availability to her in the future if she felt the need to talk to him; and (2) refer her to the pastor of the Baptist church near her home. The doctor and chaplain felt that a relationship with a local pastor could be the first step toward developing a community relationship which could give her the kind of support and fellowship she needed. However, in the event that this referral might be too threatening, the assurance of the chaplain's availability would give her someone to fall back upon in an emergency. The chaplain took the initiative to call the local pastor, with Mrs. Jones' consent, and gave him the pertinent facts about her situation.

Principles of Pastoral Care

The ministry of confession has been misused through the years. Roman Catholics have institutionalized it and made it compulsory, while Protestants have individualized it to the point of extinction. The need that people have for unburdening themselves of guilt, however, is still a major problem. Pastors have historically served their parishioners as confessors. When persons are involved in actions and attitudes which are less than ideal and which result in heavy loads of guilt, many still turn toward the pastor. In recent years the dialogue between psychology and religion has created a new interest in confession. Depth psychology has revealed the destructive potential of private guilt. Catharsis, which refers to the release and cleansing of hidden emotions, has become an important dynamic in both psychotherapy and ministry.

One result of guilt is the experience of isolation. People who experience feelings of shame and unworthiness often retreat from human relationships because they feel "unclean" or worry that they will be "discovered." Confession is the method by which such a person can move back into the human community.

With the emotionally disturbed individual, who is probably isolated to a greater degree than normal, it is especially important to help him socialize his existence. Confession, when heard and responded to with warmth and acceptance, can help a person reidentify with humanity. It helps him to realize that his particular expression of finiteness does not make him different in kind from his fellow human beings. When Jesus listened carefully to the confessions of the woman at the well, she felt free to go back into her community and talk with the people. She could feel free and human again. Mrs. Jones learned from the chaplain's response to her confession that having acted and thought in sub-human and sub-Christian ways did not separate her from humanity but actually underlined her participation in the human dilemma. Now she could move out of her isolation and into a community.

One of the relationships which usually suffers from brokenness as a result of guilt is the person's relationship with God. Feelings of guilt, failure, or inadequacy make a person feel unworthy of God's interest and attention. The existential result of this emotional response is the assumption that communication is also broken. Prayers become exercises in futility. Feelings of alienation and estrangement dominate the parishioner's religious thoughts.

In this situation the wise pastor will not immediately argue the technical theological aspects of a "hindered prayer life" but will seek to understand the parishioner's total life-situation. The result of a careful "exploration of the inner world" will usually reveal the hidden concerns, whether external or internal, which are prohibiting him from activating his religious faith and practice at that particular time. By becoming an intercessor the pastor may help the parishioner reestablish his faith in God's loving kindness and eagerness to hear him regardless of his present life-situation.

In the Hebrew religion, as in other religions, there have always been persons whose identity and function involved mediation between man and God. The Christian tradition acknowledges Jesus Christ as the High Priest who represents man's concerns before God. The New Testament goes even further to suggest that every Christian is a member of the royal priesthood. The Christian pastor's identity must include his willingness to represent the concerns of individuals who, for whatever reasons, are ashamed, embarrassed, or frightened to approach God by themselves.

The validity of intercessory prayer may be debated theologically; but, practically, in the crucible of human crises it is a reality. The priestly function of this chaplain is evident in his readiness to gather up the multiple concerns, thoughts, fears, and guilts of Mrs. Jones and express them to God for her. Pastors must explore and listen carefully so they can faithfully relate the parishioner's concerns in his prayer. The difference between this chaplain's prayer and the prayers of some pastors is its emphasis on honest representation. He did not "preach at her" with his prayer nor include peripheral platitudes. He simply verbalized in the vertical, Godward dimension her life-situation as she had revealed it to him in the horizontal, manward dimension.

The wonderful result of confession, prayer, and acceptance is the realization of forgiveness. Again we see the chaplain representing God at some crucial juncture. Here he represents God the forgiver. Because the chaplain demonstrates forgiveness in the context of their relationship, Mrs. Jones can begin to believe that maybe she is a forgivable person.

Many pastors, however, by their preaching, teaching, and interpersonal relationships, actually represent a God of harsh judgments, moralistic expectations, and strict discipline. It is difficult for an emotionally disturbed individual to respond positively to either a wrathful, rejecting pastor, or to the God whom he serves. The life of an emotionally disturbed person is already burdened down with defeat and rejection. Pastors should help to "set the captives free."

REESTABLISHING THE RELATIONSHIP

After leaving the hospital Mrs. Jones made some initial gains toward establishing a community and attaining meaningful dialogue with those around her, but later she began to relapse into her old patterns of depression and isolation. About three months after her dismissal from the hospital she called the chaplain late one afternoon in a very depressed mood, reminding him that she had once promised to notify him if she ever began to think of suicide. She informed him that during the past week she had been contemplating suicide and had been unable to remove the idea from her mind. She felt that she could not call her psychiatrist. The chaplain used the time on the phone to reestablish his relationship and rapport with Mrs. Jones and began to point her in the direction of her psychiatrist. She was able to accept his advice at this point, and within two hours she was in touch with her doctor. They set an appointment for the following day.

In consultation with her psychiatrist Mrs. Jones decided to ask the chaplain for an appointment to discuss her present situation. The psychiatrist contacted the chaplain and indicated that he felt it would be advisable for her to enter into structured pastoral counseling with the chaplain. This recommendation was based on the psychiatrist's interpretation of the trust and rapport established between Mrs. Jones and the chaplain. He felt that the chaplain could provide the kind of support and encouragement that she needed to sustain her and could give her the security that she needed to begin to work through some of her problems. Mrs. Jones was open to this recommendation, and a structured counseling relationship with the chaplain was started.

Principles of Pastoral Care

The chaplain and the psychiatrist had agreed that the chaplain should emphasize his continued interest and availability to the patient in case of future needs. Now we see that when she ran into further emotional stress, she did call the chaplain. Such a response did not occur just because of his verbalized concern. His availability was a reality in her mind because of the faithfulness which the chaplain had already demonstrated. He had cared enough in the beginning to weather the storm of her rejection. He had treated her as an adult with adult freedom. Honest feelings of affection and hostility had been communicated so that a trusting, secure relationship had been established. He had been admitted into the secret closets of her life and had represented her struggles before God. She turned again to this chaplain-pastor because of these accumulated experiences within the context of a warm, human relationship. The lesson should be obvious.

The art of referral is a difficult one to master. The pastor must educate himself to identify the types of emotional stress which he is not trained to handle. If he has established the type of trustworthy relationship described above, his referrals will probably be acceptable to his parishioners.

Communication between the pastor and the psychiatrist is extremely important. The psychiatrist is the individual primarily responsible for the emotional health of his patient. The chaplain-psychiatrist relationship described here is ideal for providing the most complete ministry and therapy. When a pastor demonstrates his care for emotionally ill persons and practices the basic principles established by pastoral psychology, he need not be surprised if a doctor asks him to participate in the care of his patients.

SEARCH FOR COMMUNITY

Both the chaplain and the doctor felt that one of the crucial tasks for Mrs. Jones was the development of a community around her. As her condition slowly improved, she began to develop more interest in outside relationships. While the therapist began to move her toward the idea of group therapy, the chaplain was discussing with her the meaning of her religious faith and the nature of her commitment to God, Christ, and especially a local church. She rejected the idea of group therapy but became more open to the idea of involvement in a local church. The chaplain and psychiatrist in working together on the matter of involvement agreed several months after she had decided against group therapy that she had not been ready for a group and, therefore, had made a valid decision.

Three primary factors seemed to be inhibiting her participation in the life of her church:

(1) Her guilt about "killing her father" was almost paralyzing.

(2) The forceful, dogmatic attitude of the local pastor "put her in mind of her father." Therefore, when he preached she found herself constantly fantasizing that the pastor was her father.

(3) The period in Mrs. Jones' life in which the church had been most meaningful was around her fifteenth year when she was dating the young Roman Catholic boy and regularly attending both her own Baptist church and his Catholic church. Now, while sitting in a church service, she found herself thinking about him and fantasizing that she was sitting with him at

church. The fantasies about both her father and the young man caused her a great deal of guilt. Bringing these factors into the open and discussing them freely seemed to rob them of some of their power.

About ten months after the beginning of her relationship with the chaplain, Mrs. Jones made a public confession of faith in Jesus Christ and joined the church. She was surprised when she realized her husband was joining with her.

Mrs. Jones' concept of baptism held many magical ideas. Many hours were devoted to discussing the meanings that she had attached to baptism. Although some of the magical connotations began to drop away, the sense of wonder and awe over baptism was never altered. Of special significance to her concerning the baptismal service was whether or not her mother and brothers would attend the service. For years she had the feeling that her family was against her and secretly hated her. The strength of this feeling was enhanced by the lack of closeness between family members and the presence of constant bickering. Symbolically, her family's attendance at this service would indicate their acceptance of her as a person. With little concern and no understanding of the significance of this event, her family notified her one week before the service that none of them would be present. This was a tremendous shock and an almost unbearable setback.

Two months before this time, immediately after having made her confession of faith, Mrs. Jones had asked the chaplain if he would attend her baptismal service. He had unequivocally assured her that he would be present. The assurance of his presence offered a thread of hope that ran consistently through the other disappointments. Although she had a great deal of trust in the chaplain, she feared that he, too, would not show up at the service. On the night of the service she was quite elated to find the chaplain, his wife, and children at the service. After the service she took pride in introducing them to her new friends.

In the weeks following her baptismal service it became evident to her that, although she had accepted Christ one year before her baptismal service and had exercised some dependence upon God during that year, her primary dependence had been upon the chaplain. She began to see the baptismal service as a slight shift toward placing more of her dependence upon God.

Principles of Pastoral Care

One of the pastor's regular functions is leading worship, which includes his preaching ministry. This function can either subtract from, or add to, his ministry to mentally ill parishioners. Mrs. Jones had a difficult time in her attempts to worship because of her intense guilt and because of her experiences with authoritarian religion.

Many emotionally disturbed people, particularly those with a religious orientation such as Mrs. Jones has, carry heavy burdens of guilt. Worship services in churches where legalism and perfectionistic doctrines are of primary importance often aim at creating a sense of guilt within the congregation. Where guilt is engendered without the context of Christian love, mercy, and forgiveness, the needs of the individual are not met; and the anxiety of guilt is increased. If the pastor keeps the total Christian faith in view as he leads in worship, he will minister more effectively to his mentally distressed parishioners.

The chaplain's attendance at a meaningful "rite of passage" in Mrs. Jones' spiritual pilgrimage illustrates the extent of his commitment to the people under his care. Is it any wonder that Mrs. Jones continues to struggle with her illness and to find continued hope in living?

DESPAIR, THOUGHTS OF SUICIDE, AND COMMITMENT TO LIFE

During the fifteenth month of counseling, Mrs. Jones' mother became severely ill with malignant cancer. In addition to this stress, Mr. Jones decided to take on a part-time job in addition to his regular full-time employment. As a result of these two situations, her sense of isolation began to increase, and depression began to creep upon her once more. As the situation became acute, persistent thoughts of suicide began to increase. She reported that on one particular evening her desire to kill herself became so strong that she gathered all of the tranquilizing drugs she had accumulated from her psychiatrists and prepared to place them in her mouth. Suddenly she felt the actual physical presence of the chaplain. According to her report, the chaplain physically restrained her from placing drugs in her mouth and reminded her of the things she had to live for.

During the discussion of her feelings concerning this event, she indicated that she had accumulated quite a number of pills from her physicians over the years. Her temptation had been to take them all at once; whereas, at other times she felt that she would like to throw them all away. The chaplain explained that he saw this as her own struggle between her fear of living and her desire to commit herself to life. It was suggested that it might be good if she could symbolically commit herself to life by literally throwing all the pills away. Three weeks later, in the middle of her counseling session and after her depression had lifted, she reached into her purse, removed several bottles of pills, and handed them to the chaplain, saying, "I wanted to make a formal, religious commitment to life; so, I decided to bring them to you." The chaplain took the pills and supported her in her commitment, but he indicated that this commitment would have to be reaffirmed each day of her life. Furthermore, as her counselor he would not dispose of the pills but would hold them for her in case she ever decided to reverse her commitment.

During the most acute phase of the crisis just discussed, Mrs. Jones changed psychiatrists. Several factors contributed to this decision, but the precipitating cause was her need for help at a time when her psychiatrist was on vacation. Fortunately, she was able to settle into a good therapeutic relationship with another psychiatrist.

Principles of Pastoral Care

Attention is called again to the significance of the relationship which existed between Mrs. Jones and the chaplain. The strength of his commitments to her and to life influenced her at a time of ultimate choice. Pastors represent many things to their parishioners, as already stated above. In the section prior to this, the local pastor represented Mrs. Jones' father and his dogmatic beliefs. The chaplain, however, represented the possibility of growth.

Symbolic acts are very meaningful to mentally ill persons. When people are of a divided mind, it is often helpful to communicate nonverbally. Mrs. Jones wanted to concretize her commitment to life by surrendering the tempters of death, the pills. Pastors have as part of their tradition numerous symbols and rites which can provide an unusual method of communication for the mentally ill. We have already seen the importance which Mrs. Jones placed on her baptismal service.

Consideration of Mrs. Jones' freedom was evident again in the chaplain's willingness to symbolize the day-to-day necessity of commitments by keeping the pills rather than destroying them. Many people who make "once for all" commitments are disappointed when the same choices and decisions present themselves again. This can lead to frustration, self-devaluation, and despair. The pastor can help the emotionally ill person to realize the necessity for continual reaffirmation of commitments. Reality would dictate that patience with getting well is an important ingredient in recovering mental health. Unrealistic promises are more closely related to mental illness than to emotional health. Regular worship is one of the meaningful ways in which the Christian faith expresses this need for continuity and reaffirmation.

THE VIEW FROM HERE

Mrs. Jones is still under a great deal of emotional stress. Many of the problems with which she has struggled throughout her life are still present. The chaplain has not cured her. Even though he hoped that healing might come as a side effect of his ministry, it was not the primary goal. Her psychiatrists were in charge of her emotional growth and development. The chaplain attempted to be a minister — one who stands by, supports, offers the elements of faithfulness and durability in a relationship that allows a person to have a firm base from which to draw security and begin to move out toward the world. His ministry has not failed if it does not bring about a cure, for there is an intrinsic value in support itself.

Two intertwined questions that run like a thread throughout this relationship were: (1) Who is God for Mrs. Jones? (2) Wherein does her hope lie? At the time of the first meeting, Mrs. Jones' god was her father, and her hope lay completely in receiving from him the assurance that she had been forgiven for her sin against him. As the relationship with the minister developed, she vacillated between seeing the minister as god and seeing her father as god. During this period she held on to the fantasy that her hope lay in getting forgiveness from her father. Yet she was able to experience a degree of realistic hope in the minister who came representing One greater than himself with a relationship that offered acceptance and forgiveness. At present there seems to be a three-way struggle as to who God is: her father, the minister, or God. As the emphasis begins to shift more and more to God, her sense of realistic hope and her ability to trust the world increases.

The chaplain recently received a letter from Mrs. Jones in which she attempted to recount her perception of the events she has experienced during the last four years. An excerpt documents some of the statements above.

> At first, I had a nervous breakdown and took sleeping pills. I had lost my faith and felt I had nothing to live for. I have had five doctors in the last four years. When I went into the hospital the last time I wanted to die, but when I came out I had something to live for and I felt that I owed it all to you. Now there is another person in my life and that person is God. You are a part of God. I want to thank God for sending you to my room that day in the hospital.

Hope in Mrs. Jones' instance seemed to be able to take roots, grow, and flourish in the soil of durability and in a climate of faithfulness.

Principles of Pastoral Care

This summation demonstrates a different criterion for "success" in relationships than is often used by ministers. It is realistic in its realization that Mrs. Jones is not yet well and may never function at a completely healthy level. The chaplain measures his success by the faithfulness and durability manifested in the relationship. He believes in, and has represented to Mrs. Jones, a God whose love and acceptance is not conditioned by the mental health or unhealth of any individual. Nor is the chaplain functioning as if his ability to "cure" people were the only thrust of his ministry and the condition under which his self-esteem and fulfillment as a minister exists.

People suffering from mental illness are no different from other humans when they choose their own gods. From the Christian viewpoint this is idolatry. The pastor is a reality-tester for the emotionally ill person concerning the finitude and fickleness of idols. In their place he introduces the living God, Creator and Sustainer of the universe. As can be seen from Mrs. Jones' letter, the chaplain-pastor has the unique opportunity of representing

God amidst the suffering, despair, discouragement, guilt, and struggles of life. To the mentally disturbed he may be the incarnation which can help them transfer allegiances to an ultimate concern.

With the shift in loyalty from finite idols to the living God, hope becomes more realistic. The mentally ill person whose hope is in finite gods carries only a tentative hope which results in a basic insecurity. When introduced to God through relationships which exhibit realistic faith and meaningful love, that person can begin to comprehend, and place trust in, a hope which is transcendent and infinite. The result is a more secure base from which to encounter the world.

SUGGESTIONS FOR FURTHER READING

Boisen, Anton T., *The Exploration of the Inner World.* New York: Harper & Row, Publishers, Inc., 1936.

Bruder, Ernest E., *Ministering to Deeply Troubled People.* Englewood Cliffs, N.J.: Prentice-Hall, Inc., 1965.

Clinebell, Howard J., *Basic Types of Pastoral Counseling.* Nashville: Abingdon Press, 1966.

Draper, Edgar, *Psychiatry and Pastoral Care.* Englewood Cliffs, N.J.: Prentice-Hall, Inc., 1965.

France, Malcolm, *The Paradox of Guilt: A Christian Study of the Relief of Self-Hatred.* Philadelphia: United Church Press, 1967.

Hillman, James, *Insearch: Psychology and Religion.* New York: Charles Scribner's Sons, 1967.

Klink, Thomas W., *Depth Perspectives in Pastoral Work.* Englewood Cliffs, N.J.: Prentice-Hall, Inc., 1965.

Menninger, Karl, *et al.*, *The Vital Balance: The Life Process in Mental Health and Illness.* New York: The Viking Press, Inc., 1963.

Oates, Wayne E., *Religious Factors in Mental Illness.* New York: Association Press, 1955.

Franklin D. Duncan is the Chaplain at the Silver Crest Tuberculosis Hospital in New Albany, Indiana, and at the Rehabilitation Center in Louisville, Kentucky. He is an Acting Supervisor in the Association of Clinical Pastoral Education. In addition to his clinical experience and training, he has served as the pastor of a local church. He graduated from Baylor University and Southern Baptist Theological Seminary.

7

PASTORAL CARE OF DISABLED PERSONS

Franklin D. Duncan

INTRODUCTION BY ROBERT P. SMITH, M.D.

Medical Director, Rehabilitation Center, Louisville, Kentucky

The severely disabled individual faces a long and frustrating struggle if he is to return to some semblance of independence. For him to confront this prospect, battle off the severe discouragement and despair which threaten him on the way, and have the patience required to carry out a fairly prolonged and sometimes monotonous treatment program requires motivation. Life must have sufficient meaning and value to draw him on. We in rehabilitation can help him only if something leads him to want improvement. In simple terms, we make little progress until he has worked out strong reasons for wanting to struggle. In our Center we depend heavily on the chaplain to help the patient work through to a meaningful role in life.

Realistic and knowledgeable counseling are most comforting to patients who are suddenly wondering about their own value and a seemingly blighted role. Confronted with overwhelming reality, they are much like young soldiers in a war, seeking out a reason for all the evil which befell them. A chaplain can help recall the absolute values in such a moment of despair. Thus, the chaplain can help the patient develop a new perspective from which he can find meaning for his life once again.

Chaplain Duncan, who has explored this role in a most helpful and enlightening manner in our Center, outlines the means by which a pastor can help severely disabled people.

PASTORAL CARE OF DISABLED PERSONS

Franklin D. Duncan

The physically disabled person is not a person who is totally disabled. The Christian pastor should not overlook the fact that a physically disabled person is also a physically *abled* person. There are things that he *can* do as well as things that he *cannot* do. A person who is physically disabled, even if he is permanently disabled, is not *totally* disabled. Rather, he is first a person with many unspecified abilities, characteristics, and possibilities in addition to a particular disability. Beatrice A. Wright distinguishes between the terms "disability" and "handicap" in this fashion:

A disability is a condition of impairment, physical or mental, having an objective aspect that can usually be described by a physician. . . . A handicap is the cumulative result of the obstacles which disability interposes between the individual and his maximum functional level.[1]

A physical disability, therefore, is a physical handicap when the person sees it as a significant barrier to the accomplishment of attainable goals.

The pastoral care of physically disabled persons is a form of religious ministry which integrates the findings of behavioral studies on the process of adjustment to physical disability with Christian theology. It is an attempt to lead the disabled person beyond the barrier of a handicap to the attainment of his realistic possibilities and the development of a rich, full meaning in life under the Lordship of Jesus Christ. When the pastor ministers to the disabled person, he does so in order to bring into focus a calling, meaning, and hope out of the boredom, purposelessness, despair, and sin of human existence, thereby making it possible for a person to experience a life of hope in

[1] Beatrice A. Wright, *Physical Disability — A Psychological Approach* (New York: Harper & Row, Publishers, Inc., 1960), p. 9.

fellowship with God "through the forgiveness of sins made possible through faith in Christ."[2] Consequently, the pastoral care of physically disabled persons is understood as the establishing of durable and meaningful relationships by which the physically disabled person may be challenged to discover his calling in life, to participate in a true and mature fellowship with God and his fellowman, and to discover for himself a meaning of life.

EMOTIONAL DYNAMICS OF FACING DISABILITY

Since World War II, psychological research studies on disability have revealed that such factors in the disabled person's experience as heredity, physical and mental health, the family and community, cultural mores, religion, economy, education, and vocation are all important considerations for rehabilitation, but they find their proper place in human existence when they are integrated around those goals and values which represent a *positive reason for living*. Franklin C. Shontz states:

> It is not hard to justify the argument that the patient himself, particularly the patient with severe chronic illness, is not primarily concerned with physical health, home, job, *except* as these hold for him the prospect of furthering his deeper human wants. From his difficult position, the patient seeks for what might best be called a "meaning in life."[3]

Economically, society's goal of "independent living" for the permanently disabled is justifiable; but viewed existentially from the patient's point of view, such a goal cannot be so easily justified or achieved in a psychologically or spiritually meaningful way. The pastor must be aware that reinforcement of society's goal of economic independence and a return to society as "normal" as possible is not an answer to the problem of motivation for the disabled person. To support society's idolatry of financial self-sufficiency as a means of gaining self-respect would be to give priority to negative goals for living, such as becoming less burdensome to family or community. Too often the disabled are reminded that as long as they remain in any way dependent, they are costing taxpayers money.

[2] Wayne E. Oates, *The Christian Pastor* (rev. ed.; Philadelphia: The Westminster Press, 1964), p. 5.

[3] Franklin C. Shontz, "Severe Chronic Illness," in *Psychological Practices with the Physically Disabled,* James F. Garrett and Edna S. Levine, eds. (New York: Columbia University Press, 1962), p. 422.

What the permanently disabled person needs and seeks, even more than a sense of financial value to himself and to society, is a positive reason for living. Shontz adds, "This is what all persons with a disability seek, even when they select employment as a means to an end; and this is essentially what rehabilitation must help them find." [4] The task of the pastor, therefore, is to aid the disabled person, undergoing a process of adjustment or value change, to discover for himself a meaning in life in God's kingdom, and to commit himself through faith to a positive reason for living.

Research on the process of adjustment to disability has progressed since World War II. Dembo, Wright, Garrett, Barker, and others have contributed largely to a deeper understanding of conscious and unconscious factors affecting a person's acceptance of disability.[5] More recent research has been done by Stephen L. Fink and Nancy Kerr Cohn to form theoretical models of adjustment to disability.

Fink describes the processes of adjustment to disability in terms of four sequential phases: (1) *shock,* at which time the person experiences the psychological impact of the reality of the disability; (2) *defensive retreat,* the period during which the person activates a defense against the seemingly overwhelming implications of the disability; (3) *acknowledgment,* the period when the person faces the realities of his situation; and (4) *adaptation,* whereby the person actively accepts his condition in a constructive manner.[6]

Nancy Cohn designates five stages of adjustment to disability, which are based upon the thesis that there is a relationship between the patient's attitude toward himself as a disabled person and the quality of his physical or vocational rehabilitation. Through private interviews with orthopedic patients in a large rehabilitation center, she found marked similarities in

[4] *Ibid.,* p. 420.

[5] Tamara Dembo, Gloria Ladieu-Leviton, and Beatrice A. Wright, "Acceptance of Loss — Amputations," in *Psychological Aspects of Physical Disability,* James F. Garrett, ed., Rehabilitation Service Series No. 210 (Washington, D.C.: Department of Health, Education and Welfare, Office of Vocational Rehabilitation, 1953), pp. 80-96.

[6] Stephen L. Fink, "Crisis and Motivation: A Theoretical Model," *Archives of Physical Medicine and Rehabilitation,* Vol. XLVIII (November, 1967), p. 592.

the patients' progressive changes in attitude and behavior. Five stages were identified and described as follows:

1. *Shock* — "This isn't me."
2. *Expectancy of Recovery* — "I'm sick, but I'll get well."
3. *Mourning* — "All is lost."
4. *Defense* — A. (Healthy) "I'll go on in spite of it." B. (Neurotic) Marked use of defense mechanisms to deny the effects of the disability.
5. *Adjustment* — "It's different, but not 'bad.'" [7]

For our purposes we will follow the four phases designated by Fink, while utilizing pertinent material from Cohn, Wright, Dembo, Rusk, and others who have gathered material on the adjustment process.

Shock

This phase is observed early in the diagnostic and treatment period. The person cannot comprehend that his body is different, that is, that a change has occurred in his physique. Emotional numbness is experienced along with a sense of depersonalization. He shows no appropriate reaction; no constructive plan to cope with the situation is evident. He continues to see himself as a normal person in pursuit of the same goals and values he had prior to the disability.[8] Coordinated thinking is disrupted; the person feels confused, and he has great difficulty accepting those perceptions which conflict with his more complete body-image.

Change occurs with the process of time and as a result of the person's testing of reality. One specialist contends that the patient needs time to absorb the alterations in his bodily function and to integrate them into his new self-concept.[9] Reality testing by the person usually results in his gradual recognition of his condition; that is, he no longer can walk, use his hands, or sit up in bed.

[7] Nancy K. Cohn, "Understanding the Process of Adjustment to Disability," *Journal of Rehabilitation*, Vol. XXVII (November-December, 1961), p. 16.

[8] *Ibid.*

[9] H. R. Blank, "Psychoanalysis and Blindness," *Psychoanalytic Quarterly*, Vol. XXVI (1957), pp. 1-23.

Denial of Illness

The person may remain fixed in the symptomatology of the shock phase. This is not uncommon among disabled persons. Persistent denial is an unrealistic attempt by the person to preserve his pre-injury status and to maintain his pre-injury system of values. Denial is evident when the person explains that the best way to cope with his disability is to forget it. He feels that the more the injury is forgotten, the fewer difficulties he will have.

There are two primary reasons why a person will utilize denial as a means to cope with his disability. First, denial may provide him with much needed emotional relief, that is, a psychological moratorium.[10] Denial is an effort to keep the onslaught of reality from destroying the person's system of values and rendering total chaos to the unity of the personality. The disabled person reveals his denial reaction through "as if" behavior; that is, he acts "as if" he were not injured. A second reason for denial may be the person's need to cope with his unacceptable dependency needs. His feelings of inferiority, due to his bowing down before the idol of physical normalcy, are only augmented when external help is offered. Using every physical and psychological means possible, the person attempts to assure his independence and autonomy. To accept any help would be to admit his disability. In essence he says, "Do not help me, because a non-injured person would not require help in this situation."[11]

Defensive Retreat

In this phase the person becomes aware of his disability, but he interprets it as only temporary. Full recovery is idolized. All the person's energies and strivings are incorporated into this one, central goal. Whereas in denial the disabled person acts "as if" the disability did not exist, here the person acts "as if" he will gain back *all* that he has lost. Cohn says, "The assumption of a normal body is implicit in any discussion of future plans."[12] This phase, therefore, could be named a "preparation syndrome."

---

[10] Dembo, Ladieu-Leviton, and Wright, *op. cit.*, p. 81.

[11] *Ibid.*, p. 83.

[12] Cohn, *op. cit.*, p. 17.

In conversation with the person who is in the phase of defensive retreat, one may notice his relating of stories of people who had late, miraculous recoveries which were contradictory to the medical prognosis. In the form of religious ideation, the person may express interest in faith healing or ardently claim that a firm faith in God will result in full recovery. The underlying and sometimes conscious feeling is, "When all is right with my body, then all will be right with my world." He needs a whole body in order to attain those goals and values he held as a normal person.[13] In the stage of defensive retreat, therefore, one can see that the physically disabled person absolutizes two factors — normal physique and full recovery. Herein lie his hope and his ultimate concern.

Acknowledgment

Eventually the defenses begin to break down, for life does not return to its former state; hoped-for physical changes do not occur; and emotional support regarding unrealistic claims is withdrawn. The person experiences acute distress. He feels his loss in terms of both social and personal values now denied him. Attention is focused on lost values.[14] Valuable goals are seen as inaccessible to him. Motivation reaches a low ebb. The feelings in this state are ones of deep despair, not unlike those claimed by William F. Lynch to be the essence of hopelessness: (1) "the sense of the impossible," whereby whatever one does leads to failure and defeat; it is an "exitless" existence; (2) "the feeling of *too-muchness*," that is, life (or disability) is too big to cope with; and (3) the feeling of futility or apathy, wherein the person sees no goal, no sense or reason for life. Life becomes a type of death.[15] Thoughts of suicide, therefore, may occur at this time.

The pastor need not see the grief or mourning response in negative terms; rather it can be thought of as a favorable prog-

[13] Cf. Alfred A. Mueller, "Psychological Factors in Rehabilitation of Paraplegic Patients," *Archives of Physical Medicine and Rehabilitation,* Vol. XLIII (April, 1962), pp. 151ff.

[14] Wilbert E. Fordyce, "Psychologic Assessment and Management," *Handbook of Physical Medicine and Rehabilitation,* Frank H. Krusen, *et al.,* eds. (Philadelphia: W. B. Saunders Company, 1965), p. 141.

[15] William F. Lynch, *Images of Hope* (Baltimore: Helicon Press, Inc., 1965), p. 48.

nostic sign. If anything, it reveals that the person has recognized the reality of his situation. Denial has been removed. This is a period in which he compares his present state to his past one, but the comparison is necessary before he can shift to perceiving himself as a person with valuable values which still remain.[16]

Adaptation Phase

Change is now possible. The person has acknowledged his physical disability and has experienced the depths of hopelessness. Now, however, he begins to visualize goals that can be attained despite his being disabled.

At this stage value changes begin for the physically disabled person. The psychological barrier of the physical disability is pushed aside. He becomes aware of his ability to achieve certain goals which were accessible to him prior to becoming disabled.[17] The individual wants to find out what kind of person he is going to be, what he is going to be able to do, what life will be like as one who is physically disabled. Basically, he says to himself, "Maybe I am not, nor ever will be, quite the same person I was before, but basically I am still me, and there are ways in which I can be of value to the world around me." [18] In the adaptation phase, therefore, the disabled person's psychological and physical makeup "grow together." His energies are no longer centered on the past; rather his outlook is oriented toward the future. A positive assessment is made of his crisis; he has become more sensitive to the deeper values of life; he feels better prepared for future crises which may occur.[19]

THE SEARCH FOR MEANING

This discussion on the phases of adjustment to the impact of physical disability ought to reveal that the focus of pastoral care is not on the disability but on the person. The great task of pastoral care is not to refashion a man but to make him conscious of his own unique, God-given capacities and values and to help him to discover a meaning in life. In this, he is a man like

[16] Fordyce, *op. cit.*, p. 141.
[17] Cohn, *op. cit.*, p. 18.
[18] Fink, *op. cit.*, p. 595.
[19] Tamara Dembo, Gloria Ladieu-Leviton, and Beatrice A. Wright, "Adjustment to Misfortune — A Problem of Social Psychological Rehabilitation," *Artificial Limbs*, Vol. III (1956), pp. 4-62.

other men, all of whom are compensating for one lack or another. The greatest danger faced by the disabled person is not that he will lose his earning power or ability to function physically; rather, it is the possibility of his losing the awareness of his own worth and dignity as a human being. As Talbot says:

> The time is come when, if the work is to be fruitful, we must reach toward those intangible values that give life meaning and savor — toward a concept of rehabilitation that recognizes that man is, or is capable of becoming, a spiritual being.[20]

Religion, subjectively speaking, can be defined as an expression of man's desire for the ultimate meaning in life. All religious intention represents man's earnest longing for a meaning — a meaning which can provide unity of thought, feeling, and deed; which can challenge him constructively in his process of becoming; which can reconcile him to his work, to his fellowman, and to what he considers of eternal value. Viktor Frankl, creator of logotherapy, states that the original striving of man, his central longing, is his "will to meaning." Even more than our need for power or pleasure, therefore, is our need for a meaning in life. Frankl points out that life can be made meaningful through three distinct groups of values. First, life can be made purposeful through *creative values*. Each of us finds meaning in creative action — through what we give to life. Second, Frankl states that *experiential values* are realized through experiencing beauty or truth and through encounter with other persons; that is, in receptivity to the world. A third pathway by which we can still realize values is through our *attitudes*. Frankl states that meaning is found through the attitudes adopted toward unavoidable circumstances or the limiting factors of one's life. Life, therefore, has meaning to the last breath.[21] We can realize values by the very attitude we take when faced with unchangeable suffering.

Religion is a clear affirmation of attitudinal values. Frankl pointedly describes the value of religious belief:

> It is self-evident that belief in an overmeaning — whether as a metaphysical concept or in the religious sense of Providence — is of the foremost psychotherapeutic and psychohygienic importance. As a genuine faith

---

[20] Herbert S. Talbot, "A Concept of Rehabilitation," *Rehabilitation Literature*, Vol. XXII (December, 1961), p. 364.
[21] Viktor E. Frankl, *The Doctor and the Soul* (New York: Alfred A. Knopf, Inc., 1965), pp. 49-50.

springing from inner strength, such a belief adds immeasurably to human vitality. To such a faith there is, ultimately, nothing that is meaningless. Nothing appears "in vain"; "no act remains unaccounted for" (Wildgans). The world appears to manifest something akin to a law of the conservation of spiritual energy. No great idea can vanish, even if it never reaches public circulation, even if it has been "taken to the grave." In the light of such a law, the drama and tragedy of a man's inner life can never have unfolded in vain, even when played out in secret, unrecorded, uncelebrated by any novelist.[22]

Religious belief, therefore, is an expression of our desire to conserve all values which can provide a sense of the Eternal within our transitory existence. Paul Tillich expresses a similar approach to religion by supplying a formal definition of faith as "the state of being grasped by that toward which self-transcendence aspires, the ultimate in being and meaning." [23]

THE RELIGIOUS DYNAMICS OF THE DISABLED

As the Christian pastor ministers to the physically disabled person, he needs to develop a sensitivity toward the disabled person's ultimate concern and the order of his religious values. Based upon Viktor Frankl's claim that man's original striving is the "will to meaning" which he discovers through creative, experiential, and attitudinal values, the writer has formulated three categories or trends of religious ideation derived from the clinical data gathered from his interviewing and testing of inpatients of a rehabilitation center where he serves as a Protestant chaplain. The establishment of these categories does not mean that the religious thinking of any one person in the clinical sample can be totally described by only one category. Both positive and pathological religion can be found in every human being. The three religious categories — religion of works, religion of pleasure, and religion of faith — are meant as descriptions of what appears to be the overarching pattern of the religious ideas and values of disabled persons. These categories will help in understanding how religion affects the rehabilitation of these individuals.

Religion of Works

A person who tends toward a religion of works is one who

[22] *Ibid.*, pp. 37-38.
[23] Paul Tillich, *Life and the Spirit, History and the Kingdom of God*, Vol. III of *Systematic Theology* (3 vols.; Chicago: University of Chicago Press, 1963), p. 130.

gives primary emphasis to the functional goals of living. During times of great stress the person does not necessarily concern himself with the deeper meanings of his existence, but rather he focuses his energies on functioning. His ultimate concern is with physical or vocational activity as the prerequisite for a satisfactory life. His sense of personal worth as a person before God and man is closely tied to his ability to function. Not to be able to walk or to work, for example, would threaten the destruction of an image he has struggled so ardently to uphold. When disabled, he forges the idol of normal physical functioning and absolutizes creative values. Religion, therefore, is used as a means to an end, the end being his self-centered need for normalcy, independence, activity, and power. But the activity is not enjoyed for its own sake. No value is found in the process of the activity. He, therefore, isolates and buries the possibility of deriving experiential values from his daily routines and work. For example, one of the patients, a twenty-nine-year-old married engineer with a paraplegic condition, replied to a question concerning his family's attitude toward his being disabled in the following words:

> I am sure they are sad, sorry, and so forth. They have confidence like I do that I will make it, so we all feel it is a matter of time. I am sure my wife, although she comes every night, sometimes hates to come and see me this way. She has never said so. At first I objected to my little boy's coming in very often, because I did not want him to see me in bed all the time. He is in a very impressionable stage in his life, and I do not want him to form too strong an opinion of me as being unable to walk or something.

Evident here is the subject's fear of his son's seeing him totally inactive and confined to a bed. The absolutizing of normal physical functioning is implied by his tendency to overlook the experiential values possible in the intimate relationship of a father and son, regardless of any abnormal physical condition.

Even the person's conception of his religious faith and practices are expressed largely in terms of activity. Insight and depth of expression are lacking. His religious ideas and concerns are largely functional. Discussion is centered upon involvement with religious activities and services, but there is little evidence of any deep, warm relationships with the Christian community or God. The engineer stated how he felt his church saw him:

I think they see me as a reasonably **active** Christian. I feel that I am looked upon in a good way by the church people. I have never given any sermons or this sort of thing; but I feel they believe I am a Christian because of my **daily actions** and the way I live.

In a religion of works, limitations or finiteness tend to be denied. The limitations of freedom are denied the opportunity to come to consciousness. Consequently, the person becomes a slave to his own ambitions and idolatrous strivings. Power over oneself, one's world, and others must be accomplished at all costs. The end result is an unrecognized existential despair or vacuum. William Lynch points out that for many people this hopelessness is so intolerable and painful that they push it out of consciousness. "It becomes repressed or denied, and often appears under the guise of its opposites: overactivity, boastfulness, arrogance, even violence." [24]

The holder of a religion of works, therefore, lacks experiential values. He cannot receive from God or his world. Rather than working with his environment and the limitations of his existence, he acts upon them. Freedom as grace, God's gift to man, is foolishness to him.

Closely tied with his concept of freedom is the person's approach to the meaning of authority. He tends to deny the various authorities of his life. He sees God in an either/or category. God, the Ultimate Authority, is either wholly transcendent or wholly immanent, either of which really places the locale of authority in man rather than in God himself. God as wholly transcendent leads the person to adhere to a works theology stated as "God helps those who help themselves." God is seen as removed from the world and not to be called on or depended upon for those things that man must do on his own. God intervenes only when one does not "toe the line." God as wholly immanent results in a self-centered, power-centered religious orientation. Prayer, for example, is seen as communication with one's self or conscience. The locale of authority is within oneself. No help is needed from the outside.

Along with this concept of God, the person with a religion of works does not tolerate irresponsibility in himself or others, that is, irresponsibility defined in terms of inactivity, lack of con-

[24] Lynch, *op. cit.*, p. 32.

trol, and dependence. Rather than seeing responsibility as one's establishing a balance between authority and freedom, he approaches it as man taking hold of his destiny and making it what he wills. "If you think you can, you can," is the philosophy behind his actions. The result is a shallow, restricted religious outlook which is open to only a few of the various ways by which one can find meaning and fulfillment in life.

Within a religion of works one finds the phenomenon of the denial of suffering. Physical pain may be confessed, but not any existential or spiritual suffering. Denial, therefore, "handicaps" the person from participation in the despair of human existence wherein he becomes aware of the inner depths of his selfhood and his need for God. He is unaware of his existential suffering; therefore he is separated from himself, and "to be separated from one's self and not to know it means the possibility of freedom is remote."[25]

Guilt or sin is expressed both in terms of transgression of law and the failure to live up to one's own potentialities in functioning. The person is conscious of little guilt regarding irresponsibility in his relationship with friends, family, and God. Failure to achieve his autonomous or creative values tends to be the central source of guilt or the consciousness of sin for the person with a religion of works.

A person with a religion of works usually is cooperative with the rehabilitation team. He is highly motivated in physical therapy. He works hard on all assignments given to him by the physical therapist. However, difficulty arises when he insists on doing more than his muscles or bone structure can tolerate. Also, the time reference of this person lies so fully in the present that he tries to make everything happen now. He cannot wait creatively. He is impatient with himself and others when they place restrictions on him. He withdraws emotionally from others and is characterized by a rigid concentration on his physical progress. His only goal is physical normalcy. He feels that no adjustment is necessary in his case, for in the end he will eventually "overcome" it.

However, such a person feels guilty because he is not able to achieve all of the goals that he feels he should.

[25] James E. Loder, *Religious Pathology and Christian Faith* (Philadelphia: The Westminster Press, 1966), pp. 42-43.

Religion of Pleasure

This category of religious experience is grounded in the "pleasure principle of life." The person's ultimate concern is directed toward what life can give him without his having to encounter any unpleasant experiences. The pleasant experiences of life are absolutized: happiness, joy, sexual fulfillment, financial security, peace, and so forth. The person is much aware of the unpleasant aspects of life and the inevitability of death, pain, and guilt. But instead of denying their existence, he attempts to avoid them. A comparison of the religion-of-works category with the religion-of-pleasure category, therefore, reveals a perverted sense of responsibility and a denial of consciousness for the religion of works while in a religion of pleasure there is a perverted consciousness and an avoidance of responsibility. Neither one is both conscious and responsible.

One male patient, a fifty-eight-year-old married factory worker, openly expressed consciousness of an irresponsible life due to his wanting only to "enjoy life." He claimed that he had learned from his mistakes and wanted to live more responsibly before God. When he related why he wanted to join a church, however, the pleasure principle which had enslaved his life remained.

> Chaplain: How did you see God before your disability?
> Patient: I didn't. I just went out and enjoyed life. I didn't know exactly how life was. I found out who my friends were too. I got friends at church. These old drinking friends never come to see me. They don't care about me.
> Chaplain: What would you like for God to mean to you now?
> Patient: Give me a good life now and show me that I was wrong. Prove it to me that I was wrong.
> Chaplain: Is this why you want to join the church?
> Patient: Yes. **Everybody seems so happy when they go to church.** I could have been that way if I had went to church.

Along with an overemphasis on the pleasure principle of life, the person with a religion of pleasure reveals an imbalance between freedom and authority. He forfeits his freedom through the avoidance of his own authority. Rather than being unaware of the authorities of his life, he acknowledges them and becomes overly dependent upon them. He feels that he has no inner resources; therefore he is incapable of discovering the possibilities and limits of his freedom. God, his employer, his wife, a crisis, that is, anything or anyone outside of himself that represents a degree of authority, is depended upon — in some cases compelled — to define the nature and meaning of his existence. In other words, he cannot believe in his freedom. Because he can see no inner resources within himself, he feels tossed to and fro by external forces and powers; he feels controlled by the outside rather than seeing himself as the captain of his own soul. He panics and flees from his freedom. His existence is similar to that of an escapee from prison. He runs from the confines and limits of his existence in hope of finding happiness, freedom, and peace of mind. Instead, he reaps intense anxiety, loneliness, and a constant fear that sooner or later he will be caught, struck down, or returned to prison. The middle-aged factory worker responded to a question concerning the reason for his disability in the following manner:

> It is a funny feeling. Honest, it is hard to explain. I think it happened because of the way I have lived and because I have not thought there is a God. You have to be struck down sometime. You can't go on forever. You are bound to be stopped, and I have been stopped.

This fearful anticipation of punishment, whether by God or life, implies that the person with a religion of pleasure has a concept of God as wholly transcendent. However, God's immanence is revealed when punishment is rendered. Similar to a religion of works, a religion of pleasure views God as demand and punishment; but unlike the person who emphasizes works, he does not feel capable of any attempt to meet the demands. He flees from God and anticipates his inevitable punishment.

Because of the imbalance between authority and freedom, the individual is unable to accept responsibility. He has chosen the path of giving up his freedom in order "to overcome his aloneness by eliminating the gap that has arisen between his individual self and the world." This approach to life is termed by Erich Fromm as the "escape from freedom."[26] He is conscious of his responsibility, but he cannot act upon this consciousness. He retreats from decision-making. He seeks help to loosen the chains

[26] Erich Fromm, *Escape from Freedom* (New York: Holt, Rinehart & Winston, Inc., 1941), pp. 140-141. More extensive discussion on these religious categories may be found in a thesis written by the author: Franklin D. Duncan, "Logotherapy and the Pastoral Care of Physically Disabled Persons." Unpublished Master's thesis, The Southern Baptist Theological Seminary, Louisville, Kentucky, 1968.

that bind him to an irresponsible way of life, but he refuses authentic help when it is offered. Such help is too costly, involves too much suffering, and is too unpleasant. This is why one of the patients in the study finished an incomplete sentence by indicating that the most hopeless thing in the world is "to change."

The person with a religion of pleasure has not developed a responsible theology of suffering. He attempts to escape from suffering, to avoid anxiety and loneliness. Similarly, he runs from the inevitability of his mortality. Time robs him of the possibility of change. He wants to change, to be reborn, but he cannot bring himself to stand courageously before unchangeable suffering. He is always seeking a way out; he asks God to help him, to change him, to make him a new man. He cannot wait on God. The struggle, the suffering, the darkness are all too much for him. Therefore, the religion of pleasure provides no meaning or purpose to suffering, and it establishes feelings of hopelessness and defeat regarding the meaning of death. As suffering is contradictory to the pleasure principle, it is seen as an unjust phenomenon of life. When asked why he thought people suffered, the fifty-eight-year-old factory worker replied:

> That is another thing that I would like to know. Why? As good as some people are—Christian people—why do they suffer? **Why shouldn't you enjoy life instead of suffering?** I can't understand it. I can't explain it either.

However, when the person reflects on the meaning of his own suffering, he tends to approach it negatively. He interprets his suffering as a result of his irresponsible way of life. The factory worker expressed this attitude in the following interchange with the chaplain:

> Chaplain: Why do you suffer?
> Patient: Well, I feel like I have not lived right; that is why I am suffering. I did not give myself to the Lord like I should have.
> Chaplain: Would you prefer a world without suffering?
> Patient: No.
> Chaplain: Why not?
> Patient: I think anyone who doesn't do right should suffer before they die. It would prove to them that there is a God.

In a religion of pleasure, guilt is expressed qualitatively rather than quantitatively, as in a religion of works. The person is more conscious of the quality or lack of quality of his life than he is of his void of creative accomplishments and values. Guilt, therefore, is expressed in terms of irresponsibility in personal relationships. The person usually is excessively dependent upon one or two persons. He is aware that he borrows his selfhood from others. When asked about his experiences with forgiveness, one patient replied:

> I think that I have been forgiven for many things that I have done. However, I wonder if it is from my part. I don't think it is. I think it is due to my daughter. I think I depend on her instead of myself. I should be doing the praying instead of her.

The person's attitude toward his disability is that of despair and hopelessness. He has no goals or values which provide him with the challenge to fulfill his responsibilities. He will tend to blame others for his difficulties. Complaints are common, and in physical therapy he demonstrates little motivation. He asks nurses, aides, and family to perform tasks for him which he could easily do for himself. Sometimes this person leaves a rehabilitation center in worse condition than when he came.

Religion of Faith

The meaning and purpose of life is the ultimate concern of a religion of faith. Rather than restricting itself to the relative values of activity or pleasure, it seeks those religious values which are unconditional and give consistency to life. Creativity and receptivity are found together in a harmonious, balanced relationship, rather than being separated and opposed to one another. Therefore, the primary characteristic of this religious category is an unconditional commitment to unconditional values, that is, faith. But this commitment leads neither to an irresponsible conformity nor to fanaticism. Rather, it is characterized as a spirit of openness to life and the Spirit of God, a willingness to stand firm in one's encounter with the anxieties and sufferings of life, and a patient waiting for the grace and creative Spirit of God. In all the persons in this study whose religious experience can be described as a religion of faith, the focus of their commitment or faith was in the person of Jesus Christ.

The openness to God and others, the courageous stand before unavoidable suffering and anxiety, and the patient anticipation of help and grace are evident in Mrs. Lewis's feelings after she had been told three days previously that she had lung cancer.

> Well, at first I just thought I might as well give up. I have gone through enough, so just let it take its course. But I have gotten over that. I know how willing they are to help me around here. Then I thought: "Well, then, it is all up to me. The Lord would want me to avail myself of everything there is to help me and leave the rest to him." And that is the way I feel now.

For the religion of faith, meaningfulness is seen as a necessary goal of life. Mrs. Lewis could have retreated, given up, lived out the rest of her life in total emotional and physical dependency on others; but this would not have given her any meaning in her suffering, no hope for the future, and no sense of responsibility to God.

In the religion of faith there is a balance of freedom and authority. This kind of religion does not focus upon a one-dimensional approach to life. Various possibilities are seen, but they are not acknowledged without a realistic acceptance of the limitations of human existence. As Mrs. Lewis explained her attitude toward life as a disabled person:

> I used to feel both helpless and hopeless, but now I still feel somewhat helpless, but not hopeless. You can't get over an experience like this totally, but you have to realize that you will never be the same as before, that is, physically; but with the limitations, we can go on.

The balance of authority and freedom is found also in the person's conception of God. He sees God as both transcendent and immanent, not totally one or the other. This conception of God provides him with a conscious recognition of God's authority; yet it also reminds him of God's calling him to a life of responsibility. Thus, God is not seen as one who makes unrealistic demands and punishes when these demands are not met. *None of the subjects in this category of religion indicated that they felt God punishes people for their sins;* most of them openly rejected this concept. Rather than seeing God as punisher, they saw him as both judgment and grace. For them God's judgment always carries grace, and his grace always carries judgment. This balance between judgment and grace provides the person with an assurance of God's responsibility to him.

When a person has found a balance between his need for

authority on the one hand and his need for freedom on the other, he is able to accept responsibility. Wayne Oates states, "The compulsive demand for either authority or freedom to the exclusion of the other is, in both instances, a symptom of ir-responsibility."[27] Within a religion of faith, these two needs are complementary rather than conflicting. In fact, they presuppose each other. The person with a religion of faith sees himself both as freed to unify and organize his immediate world and as one who surrenders himself to those authorities of life of which he wants to be a part. This balance of freedom and authority evokes a consciousness of responsibility to God through creative action and mastery, as well as through self-surrender and openness.

Suffering, in a religion of faith, is seen as that aspect of life which must be accepted and turned to constructive use in the service of mankind and the kingdom of God. In this religious category, therefore, one finds a responsible theology of suffering. Suffering is not to be avoided or denied; it is the pathway to a richer, more mature relationship to life and God. Polly, a seven-teen-year-old girl with a quadraplegic condition, states in her own way her willingness to face suffering bravely and to learn from it:

Chaplain: Would you prefer living without suffering?

Patient: Well, I am sure everyone doesn't want to suffer, but it does help you a great deal.

Chaplain: In what way does suffering help you, Polly?

Patient: It helps you learn more about yourself, and it helps you learn more about other people. It helps you to overcome fear.

Chaplain: What kind of world do you think we would have if we had no suffering?

Patient: I am sure it would be a very boring life. There would be no progress, because man would have everything perfect and laid out for him.

Chaplain: How can suffering take on meaning in your life now?

Patient: Well, by learning from it. When you suffer there are many people around who can help you. You think about the deeper matters of life when you suffer which is meaningful, and you learn new things about your body that are meaningful. You learn to live with your suffering, so suffering is not all bad.

Death for the person with a religion of faith reminds him of his responsibility to God, a responsibility which he carries out

[27] Wayne E. Oates, *The Religious Dimensions of Personality* (New York: Association Press, 1957), p. 259.

through his faith and commitment. Meaning in life is not dependent upon the length of life. Death is not seen as a threat to the possibilities of changing one's way of life. Any length of time is seen as the manifestation of God's grace and mercy and the opportunity for one to affirm his uniqueness before God. Mrs. Lewis clearly illustrates this attitude toward death in the following words:

> Well, Jesus only lived thirty-three years. Many people live to be ninety and have not accomplished as much as somebody else that dies at thirty. I have been able to live sixty-seven years, and I have been grateful for those years. We do not know when we will die, and I don't know how to live any different. I ask forgiveness always for the sins I have committed and omitted. I know nobody lives without sin—that is just human. I ask for forgiveness for that, and I try to live according to the Ten Commandments. I always have, and that is a standard by which we should live. I don't know anything else to do.

Guilt is openly confessed, faced, and channeled into responsible, constructive motivation by the individual with a religion of faith. He is able to confront his guilt, confess his sins, and feel divine forgiveness. There is no morbid preoccupation with irresponsible acts in the past, as well as no denial of those shortcomings and failures which have influenced the pilgrimage of his life. The consciousness of guilt, however, is different from that found in the other categories of religion. In a religion of works guilt is focused on creative values, and the religion of pleasure centers on irresponsibility in relationships to other persons and groups. But in the religion of faith, guilt is conscious and defined as the failure to fulfill responsibility both in terms of autonomous, creative values, and heteronomous, experiential values. Consequently, the person with a religion of faith is freed to develop attitudinal values toward his guilt and affirm his responsibility to God or to life.

The individual with a religion of faith tends to be more accepting of his disability than persons holding to either of the other two religious categories. He moves fairly smoothly throughout the phases of adjustment to disability, and he sees the possibility of a meaningful life as a permanently disabled person. He is able to wait and to accept the long process of rehabilitation. He does not idolize physical normalcy, nor does he resent being seen with other physically disabled persons. He is well motivated to undertake physical therapy, but he is willing to accept his limitations and work with the rehabilitation team regarding his prognosis. A sense of humor is evident in his relationships with other patients and the medical staff. He is able to encourage others and be encouraged by them. Effort is made by him to do as much for himself as he possibly can, but he is willing to seek help when it is needed.

The preceding discussion of the process of adjustment to physical disability and of the three categories of religion, derived from an analysis of the clinical material in the study, has led the writer to three interrelated hypotheses:

1. When a person is excessively concerned with creative values (what he gives to life), he tends to strive for power. When a person is concerned with experiential values to the exclusion of creative values, he tends to strive for pleasure. Therefore, the presence of existential frustration, existential vacuum, even noogenic neurosis, is due to an imbalance of creative and experiential values. Consequently, this preoccupation with either creative or experiential values restricts the person to a one-dimensional consciousness whereby attitudinal values do not become conscious, and the meaning of life is frustrated. This means that the consciousness and expression of attitudinal values are indicative of a proper balance between creative and experiential values.

2. Within the process of adjustment to disability the person will tend to progress from a religion of works to a religion of pleasure until he affirms a religion of faith, that is, if he learns to accept his physical disability. In essence, his religious values may fluctuate, reorganize, and change. During shock and defensive retreat a religion of works appears with an emphasis on creative values, such as what can be done to maintain autonomy and to return to physical normalcy. The phase of acknowledgment reveals an organization of values similar to a religion of pleasure, whereby the person tends to avoid creative responsibilities as a disabled person. Instead, he feels his situation is hopeless and any improvement will involve too many unpleasant experiences, too much suffering. Finally, in the adaptation phase, a religion of faith reveals a balance between authority and freedom, a hopeful attitude toward the future, and the discovery of positive values in suffering.

3. The person who has lived according to a religion of works prior to his disability tends to remain in the phase of defensive retreat. The person with a religion of pleasure prior to disability tends to fixate in the acknowledgment phase. The person with a religion of faith will move much more easily and rapidly through the various stages of adjustment to physical disability.

With these understandings of the concepts of logotherapy, the process of adjustment to physical disability, and the role of religion in rehabilitation, the forms of pastoral care which can be offered to the disabled person will be discussed.

PASTORAL CARE OF THE DISABLED

Any form of pastoral care rendered to the physically disabled person must consider seriously both his religious and emotional needs. The nature of the person's pilgrimage toward an acceptance of physical disability and the character of his religious resources and values are of utmost importance for the pastor-chaplain in the attempt to provide him with a responsible, sensitive ministry. To neglect the developmental aspect of adjustment to disability would result in an irresponsible depersonalization. In other words, every person would be treated the same, regardless of his situation. Also, to disregard the person's specifically religious needs leads to a humanistic approach void of any understanding of man's spiritual nature. Responsible pastoral care, therefore, is the expression of a balance between the freedom of the physically disabled person and the authority of the message and content of the Christian faith.

The correlation of insights gained from logotherapy, the adjustment process to disability, and the religious experiences of twelve permanently disabled persons suggests three forms of pastoral care which can be applied by the pastor-chaplain in his ministry to the physically disabled. These forms of pastoral care are: (1) comfort, (2) catalysis, and (3) challenge. They are distinct, but interrelated, approaches to the care of the physically disabled person. These forms are not definitive, but they are presented as considerations to be proved or disproved in clinical practice.

The forms of pastoral care — comfort, catalysis, and challenge — provide the pastor-chaplain with both a specific and a developmental approach to the needs of physically disabled persons. The following discussion, therefore, treats each of these forms, as well as the various aspects of their interrelatedness.

Comfort

While under the hardship of permanent physical disability, the person experiences desperate need of spiritual strength, emotional support, and a warm, affectionate relationship. Comfort is that form of pastoral care which traditionally is most clearly identified with the Christian minister. The classical meaning of comfort is "to give strength, to impart hope, or to offer help to face reality." Comfort is not necessarily a soothsaying approach; rather, it is grounded in and oriented toward reality. Through a ministry of comfort the pastor-chaplain communicates to the person a genuine acceptance of him for who he is. No heavy demands are made upon the person. Every effort is made by the pastor-chaplain to make clear to the person his right to grieve, to feel bitter, to want to give up, to make unrealistic goals for himself, and to be angry. In essence, through comfort the person hopefully begins to experience a sense of authentic acceptance and a relationship of loving trust whereby he is enabled to affirm his uniqueness and his destiny under God. One of the primary goals of comfort, therefore, is the person's consciousness of freedom and the possibility of a meaningful life.

Comfort is extended to the physically disabled person by the Christian pastor-chaplain through the trinity of *suggestion, catharsis,* and *reassurance.*[28]

By means of *suggestion* the pastor-chaplain's presence reminds the person of God's acceptance of him and unconditional values and meaning which still remain to assure him of the possibility of a new way of life. Through suggestion the person is reminded of God's presence and involvement with him as he struggles for meaning and purpose as a physically disabled person. As the pastor-chaplain visits the physically disabled, he may bring to remembrance for the person a sense of responsibility to God and a sense of God's continuing responsibility toward him in his suffering and despair. As one patient actively involved in physical therapy informed the writer: "I like to see you down here, because you help me to remember that there is a purpose in what I am doing." Thus, by his presence, the pastor-chaplain reminds

[28] Oates, *The Christian Pastor,* p. 166.

the person of his spiritual freedom, his calling to responsibility, his relationship to God in the midst of suffering. The pastor-chaplain suggests the possibility of a new, enriching, and challenging way of life.

Through *catharsis* the pastor-chaplain establishes a durable and meaningful relationship of love and trust whereby the person feels that he is accepted as a unique human being, rather than as an object to be manipulated. By means of catharsis, therefore, the pastor-chaplain communicates to the person the unconditional love and forgiveness of God-in-Christ, that is, the Incarnation. In the early stages of disability the person needs to know that he is loved and valued by someone who is able to enter his system of values with understanding. Such a relationship frees the person to value himself in a positive manner, to become aware of what he has lost, and to visualize those values which can bring meaning and fulfillment to his life. The pastor-chaplain does this in the name of Christ. As he journeys into the disabled person's inner conflict and estrangement and participates in his suffering, the pastor-chaplain mediates to him the incarnate love and forgiveness offered by God-in-Christ, whereby he can be redeemed from the past and freed to determine his own destiny.

Catharsis, therefore, involves the pastor-chaplain's willingness to empathize with the person's fears, confusion, suffering, despair, anger, love, and courage. Such a relationship enables the person "to flush out his system" so that he can pursue creative values, experience community and God for what they really are, and develop a responsible attitude toward God, community, and self. Catharsis is similar to Keith-Lucas's concept of empathy as "understanding how one feels about a problem but not feeling like one oneself." He goes on to say that empathy "is the one thing that helps people tell their hidden doubts and fears and do something about them."[29] Catharsis or empathy, therefore, can set the stage for the disabled person to gain insight into his effective and ineffective ways of handling his problems, his guilt, and his suffering. Theologically speaking, catharsis offers the person an opportunity of confession and repentance whereby he becomes aware of three factors: (1) that his relationship with God is broken due to his idolatrous worship of the past physical

[29] Alan Keith-Lucas, *This Difficult Business of Helping* (Richmond: John Knox Press, 1966), p. 26.

normalcy, and other relative values; (2) that through the unconditional love and forgiveness of God-in-Christ his past and present existence can be changed from meaninglessness into meaning, from estrangement into fellowship, and from conflict into a peaceful existence; and (3) that the proper response to God and life is "to act upon this forgiveness by decisively accepting Christ's love as the organizing center of our identity, as the heart of our existence as a self."[30] Catharsis, therefore, provides the person with the possibility of help necessary for the creation of hope.

Reassurance is an important part of the pastor-chaplain's ministry to the physically disabled. The disabled person needs support; he needs to know that someone is not giving up on him and is continuing to respect him whatever he decides to do and however difficult the future may be. Nevertheless, reassurance must be in keeping with the reality of the disabled person's situation. Pastoral responsibility must be upheld; otherwise, great harm can be done. To reassure physical normalcy for a person with a quadraplegic condition while in the stages of shock or defensive retreat, for example, could only add to his sense of worthlessness and his feelings of guilt and estrangement from God. False reassurance does not communicate understanding, forgiveness, or acceptance of the person as he is; therefore, no real comfort occurs. Reassurance through responsible use of Scripture, prayer, and worship can aid the pastor-chaplain considerably in his reassurance of God's love and concern.

Through suggestion, catharsis, and reassurance the pastor-chaplain represents the trinitarian way in which God has helped us. God the Father reminds man of the reality of his world, his laws, and his judgment. God the Son humbled himself in the form of a man and empathized with man's existence. God the Holy Spirit reassures man of his continuing presence and help.[31]

Catalysis

The second form of pastoral care which can be offered the person with a physical disability is catalysis. "Catalysis" is a derivative of the Greek word *katalusai*, which means "to destroy

[30] Wayne E. Oates, *Christ and Selfhood* (New York: Association Press, 1961), p. 41.
[31] Keith-Lucas, *op. cit.*, p. 26.

or loose." Basically, the term symbolizes the acceleration of action produced by an outside agent which may be recovered practically unaltered at the end of such action. Catalysis, therefore, is a specific type of pastoral relationship in which the pastor-chaplain functions as a catalyst who, by means of empathetic questioning, aims at accelerating the person's acceptance of disability and his discovery of a vocational calling in the kingdom of God. This is done both by aiding the person to discard the false idols which hinder his spiritual becoming and by turning his emotional and spiritual energies to the opportunities and responsibilities of true selfhood as it is found in Jesus Christ.

Pastoral care for the physically disabled person is not only directed toward the person as he is, but also toward what he is capable of becoming under God. In other words, pastoral care must be concerned with man as a sinner and with man as a child of God made in his image. To take him only as he is, therefore, can only make him worse. He must also be related to the person which (by the grace of God) he can become. Whereas comfort centers on God's unconditional acceptance of him as he is, catalysis focuses on God's unconditional affirmation of him as he is created to become. By means of catalysis, therefore, the pastor-chaplain serves the person in his search for his readjusted vocational calling, a calling which can challenge him to a responsible commitment and thereby open him to the grace of God and the experience of expectancy of a full and meaningful life. The primary goal of catalysis is the consciousness of responsibility.

Catalysis is implemented through three methods: *spiritual interrogation,* the *reflective "as if" perspective,* and *"de-reflection."* The pastor-chaplain by means of *spiritual interrogation* relates to the disabled person in a Socratic fashion by asking him relevant, provocative, existential questions. After he has established a meaningful, durable relationship, the pastor-chaplain can provide active help by confronting the disabled person with questions which provoke him to discover meaning in life, particularly as it is related to his relationship to God through the Lordship of Jesus Christ. Thus, the pastor-chaplain must aid the person in his search for the durably meaningful things of life as they are isolated from those things more transient. He should attempt to relate to the individual in such a way as to enable him to set aside his defenses, his denial of need and fear of suffering so that he can begin to face the crucial spiritual questions of his existence. Questions concerning spiritual destiny should be raised. The meaning of life, God, suffering, death, love, and work are all important matters that need to be confronted by the physically disabled person himself.

The *reflective "as if" perspective* is derived from Viktor Frankl's concept of de-reflection. It also is a method which involves the asking of relevant, provocative questions, but the questions are asked in an "as if" fashion in order to motivate the disabled person to reflect upon the possibility of future positive goals and values. Depending upon the stage of the person's acceptance of disability, this method may or may not be concerned with de-reflecting the person from his preoccupation with the problems at hand to the positive values which await his fulfillment. In the stage of defensive retreat, for example, the person seeks to reflect on what it would be like to live the rest of one's life with a permanent disability. However, this needs to be done in an "as if" fashion whereby the person can have emotional distance from the reality of his situation, yet at the same time begin to face it. Such a question as "What is life going to be like *if* you should have to walk with braces the rest of your life?" illustrate what is meant by this reflective "as if" perspective of pastoral care for disabled persons. The raising of questions in this fashion can do much in preparing the person to face constructively the limits of his possibilities, and it can aid him considerably by providing him with several alternatives of action when he finally acknowledges his permanent condition. Therefore, through this reflective "as if" perspective, the pastor-chaplain aids the physically disabled person in his search of hope and his true calling or vocation in the kingdom of God.

By means of *de-reflection* the pastor-chaplain attempts to turn the disabled person's attention away from his demonic worship of the past and his idolatrous concern with physical normalcy toward the discovery of a personal calling in life in service to God's kingdom. Through his discovery of positive values the disabled person begins to move from a comparative to an asset value system, where the emphasis is upon what remains for him to be or do, rather than a preoccupation with what he has lost, such as is found in the stage of acknowledgment. De-reflection, when successful, leads the person to a responsible assessment of his abilities and to a constructive approach to suffering, guilt, and death. De-reflection, therefore, involves the finding of positive values which can attract full devotion and service as a nucleus for the reorientation of the disabled person's whole life. The ultimate goal of the Christian pastor-chaplain is that the disabled person's positive values will focus upon his relationship with Jesus Christ, who out of his grace can give him a distinctly personal identity in the body of Christ, the Christian community, and the kingdom of God. The question "How can you turn the suffering that you have experienced with your disability into a positive experience?" illustrates how de-reflection is implemented.

Challenge

Once comfort has been given and the important catalytic questions have been asked, the pastor-chaplain must turn to a specific challenging of the person. The disabled person may be fully comforted, fully aware of the positive values which await fulfillment, but he may lack the motivation to commit himself to them. This aspect of human nature is the most frustrating for the pastor-chaplain. At this point he must admit his own limitations and recognize the authority of the individual to decide the outcome of his own destiny. However, the pastor-chaplain can challenge the person toward a commitment through a responsible use of the following methods: (1) by furnishing temporary motivation on the basis of an intimate, meaningful relationship with the person; (2) by an active "as if" perspective; and (3) by supporting the person's successes.[32]

A *warm, understanding, and meaningful relationship* provides the fertile ground for the pastor-chaplain's ministry of challenge. Without such a relationship, challenge would not be possible. Therefore, the pastor-chaplain who has established a responsible pastoral relationship with the disabled person can lead the person toward commitment by communicating to him in a realistic, authentic way that not only does he have the responsibility to find his vocation in life, but that if he will do so, someone will care. The disabled person needs to know that what he does with his life makes a difference to another person and ultimately that

[32] See James C. Crumbaugh, "The Application of Logotherapy," *Journal of Existentialism,* Vol. V (Summer, 1965), pp. 403ff.

it makes a difference to God. Thus, the pastor-chaplain may be able to prime the process toward commitment by referring the person to transient values such as family, occupation, or community; but ultimately he seeks to motivate the person toward a "Christian vocation" within the kingdom of God. Wayne Oates writes:

> Apart from the supreme loyalty that God's forgiveness and gift of the Kingdom creates, men's lives are thrown out of balance by their distorted and misguided idolatry of family, church, philosophical system, and domineering teacher. The impinging power of the Kingdom of God separates the children of darkness from the children of light, weans them from their idols, and frees them from the possessive power of the demonic. The demonic is the finite parading itself as the ultimate.[33]

A second method of challenge is *the active "as if" perspective*. This method differs from the reflective "as if" perspective mentioned previously. Whereas the reflective "as if" perspective concentrated on getting the person to reflect on his existential situation in order to discover the questions being asked him by life and by God; the active "as if" perspective focuses upon provoking the person to "act," to answer the questions being asked. After meaningful pastoral relationships of comfort and catalysis, the pastor-chaplain can ask the person to act "as if" he did have meaning and purpose in life, or "as if" God had not forsaken him, or "as if" he is capable of suffering in a creative, responsible fashion. Even though at first the person may feel somewhat false in doing so, he will find that the more he becomes involved in acting "as if" his life had direction and purpose, the more these positive values gradually become a part of who he really is as well as who he is capable of becoming.

The last method of challenge is that of *reenforcement of the disabled person's successes* physically, emotionally, and spiritually. When he receives praise for his accomplishments or new insights, he is motivated to continue. In essence, this method is the same as that of reassurance, which was discussed previously.

In theological terms, the three forms of pastoral care are the implementation of love, hope, and faith mentioned by Paul (1 Corinthians 13). Through comfort the pastor-chaplain reveals both his love and God's love for the disabled person and a forgiveness or acceptance of him as he is. Catalysis aids the person in his structuring of hope by providing him with an outside

[33] Oates, *The Religious Dimensions* . . ., p. 272.

fulcrum of help whereby he can become conscious of the questions that both God and community are asking him. In catalysis the pastor-chaplain helps the person to open up avenues to be "grasped" by the Spirit of God-in-Christ. Challenge focuses upon the development of commitment or faith. Ultimately it seeks to lead the person to the door of Christian faith, but he must decide for himself. However, none of these forms of pastoral care are possible without love. The beginning and end of pastoral care is a meaningful relationship based upon the love and forgiveness of God-in-Christ. As Paul states: "Faith, hope, love abide, these three; but the greatest of these is love" (1 Corinthians 13:13). Thomas C. Oden describes this empathetic love in pastoral care as follows:

> This is what love does: It bears all things, believes all things, hopes all things, endures all things. It projects itself phenomenologically into the sphere of reference of the neighbor's inner life and receives him, believes his word about himself . . . yearns with him in his authentic intentions, shares with him all things, and endures with him through his quiet afflictions.[34]

As the pastor-chaplain participates with the disabled person in his pilgrimage-like search for the ultimate meaning of life, his ministry has a threefold purpose: (1) that through freedom the person will sense a calling and an enabling to share with others who are afflicted the comfort with which he has been comforted by God; (2) that through a sense of responsibility he will be able to live in the reality of God's love and reflect the hope that "does not disappoint us" (Romans 5:5); and (3) that through faith he shall understand fully, even as he has been fully understood by God.

SUGGESTIONS FOR FURTHER READING

1. LOGOTHERAPEUTIC LITERATURE

Frankl, Viktor E., *The Doctor and the Soul.* New York: Alfred A. Knopf, Inc., 1955.
––––––––––, *Man's Search for Meaning: An Introduction to Logotherapy.* Boston: Beacon Press, 1965.
––––––––––, *Psychotherapy and Existentialism: Selected Papers on Logotherapy.* New York: Washington Square Press, 1967.

[34] Thomas C. Oden, *Kerygma and Counseling* (Philadelphia: The Westminster Press, © 1966 by W. L. Jenkins), p. 157. Used by permission.

Leslie, Robert C., *Jesus and Logotherapy: The Ministry of Jesus as Inter-preted Through the Psychotherapy of Viktor Frankl.* Nashville: Abingdon Press, 1965.
Tweedie, Donald F., *Logotherapy and the Christian Faith.* Grand Rapids: Baker Book House, 1961.

2. LITERATURE ON PHYSICAL DISABILITY

Cohn, Nancy K., "Understanding the Process of Adjustment to Disability," *Journal of Rehabilitation,* Vol. XXVII (November-December, 1961), pp. 16-18.
Fink, Stephen L., "Crisis and Motivation: A Theoretical Model," *Archives of Physical Medicine and Rehabilitation,* Vol. XLVIII (November, 1967), pp. 592-597.
Garrett, James F., and Levine, Edna S., *Psychological Practices with the Physically Disabled.* New York: Columbia University Press, 1962.
Hamilton, Kenneth, *Counseling the Handicapped in the Rehabilitation Process.* New York: The Ronald Press Company, 1950.
Krusen, Frank H., *et al.,* eds., *Handbook of Physical Medicine and Rehabilitation.* Philadelphia: W. B. Saunders Co., 1965.
Palmer, Charles E., "The Role of Religion in Rehabilitation: Part I," *Rehabilitation Literature,* Vol. XXIII (December, 1962), pp. 362-370.
Palmer, Charles E., "The Role of Religion in Rehabilitation: Part II," *Rehabilitation Literature,* Vol. XXIV (January, 1963), pp. 2-9.
Rusk, Howard A., *Rehabilitation Medicine.* St. Louis: The C. V. Mosby Company, 1958.
Wright, Beatrice A., *Physical Disability — A Psychological Approach.* New York: Harper & Row, Publishers, Inc., 1960.

3. PASTORAL CARE AND OTHER LITERATURE

Allport, Gordon W., *Becoming.* New Haven: Yale University Press, 1955.
Clinebell, Howard J., *Basic Types of Pastoral Counseling.* Nashville: Abingdon Press, 1966.
Draper, Edgar, *et al.,* "On the Diagnostic Value of Religious Ideation," *Archives of General Psychiatry,* Vol. XIII (September, 1965), pp. 202-207.
Duncan, Franklin D., "Logotherapy and the Pastoral Care of Physically Disabled Persons." Unpublished Master's thesis, The Southern Baptist Theological Seminary, Louisville, Kentucky, 1968.
Keith-Lucas, Alan, *This Difficult Business of Helping.* Richmond. John Knox Press, 1966.
Kreyer, Virginia, "Feelings of Handicapped Individuals," *Pastoral Psychology,* Vol. XVI (June, 1965), pp. 41-44.
_____, "The Physically Handicapped Person — An Area of the Church's and Minister's Responsibility," *Pastoral Psychology,* Vol. XVI (June, 1965), pp. 5-7.
Lynch, William F., *Images of Hope.* Baltimore: Helicon Press, Inc., 1965.
Oates, Wayne E., *The Christian Pastor.* Rev. ed. Philadelphia: The Westminster Press, 1964.
_____, *Protestant Pastoral Counseling.* Philadelphia: The Westminster Press, 1962.
_____, *The Religious Dimensions of Personality.* New York: Association Press, 1957.
Proeless, E. F., "Ministering to the Physically Disabled Person," *Pastoral Psychology,* Vol. XVI (June, 1965), pp. 8-22.

G. Keith Parker, a graduate of Berea College and Southern Baptist Theological Seminary, is pastor of the Worthville Baptist Church in Worthville, Kentucky. He is pursuing studies for the Th.D. at Southern Seminary where he was Garrett Teaching Fellow for 1967-1969.

8

PASTORAL CARE OF CHRONICALLY ILL PATIENTS

G. Keith Parker

INTRODUCTION BY DANIEL LEB, M.D.

Chief of Renal Services and Director of the Renal Dialysis Center, University of Louisville School of Medicine

Advancements in medicine are not necessarily cures; rather, in some instances, medical progress replaces a painful, debilitating, or fatal illness with a condition more compatible with normal existence. Treatment of patients with irreversible kidney failure is an example of this type of progress. Long-term treatment with the artificial kidney or kidney transplantation can prolong useful life, but both present new problems with major or minor degrees of disability.

When the Artificial Kidney Center in Louisville opened, it was quickly apparent that most patients would have problems in life adjustment. The opportunity to help patients through pastoral counseling, including regular group sessions, has assisted both patients and families in adjusting to the problems involved with a treatment which enables them to live longer, more productive lives. In addition to counseling, Mr. Parker invested considerable energy in the study of this group. The results of his work, which are incorporated in the following chapter, provide new insight into chronic dialysis patients and are a unique study in this area of chronic disease.

Modern medical science is making remarkable advances in the treatment of disease and the extension of life by preventive medicine as well as new techniques of treatment. But these new blessings are not without disadvantages. They present an array of new problems that the average minister will probably confront at some time in his ministry. Uppermost among those problems is the increasing number of chronically ill persons. In being given a "new lease on life" by medical means, the chronically ill face a multiplicity of new problems arising out of their treatment. This chapter will consider some of the difficulties faced in the ministry to chronically ill persons. The material is based upon a research project conducted at Louisville General Hospital in conjunction with the Southern Baptist Theological Seminary's Department of Pastoral Care and the University of Louisville Medical School.

PASTORAL CARE OF CHRONICALLY ILL PATIENTS

G. Keith Parker

THE CONTEXT OF THE PROJECT

Funded mostly by federal grants and staffed by University of Louisville Medical School personnel, the Renal Dialysis Unit of Louisville General Hospital functions as a combined research and treatment center for chronic kidney disease. Approximately twenty patients enter the unit twice weekly to have their blood cleansed of natural wastes. The process, which is called hemo-dialysis, involves the patient's being hooked up to an artificial kidney for a period of eight to twelve hours. Some patients continue with this treatment for an indefinite period; others are awaiting kidney transplants. Without this biweekly washing of their blood, the patients would die.

This writer was a member of the professional team ministering to the peculiar needs of the patients, their families and the staff, as well as to occasional kidney donor families in times of cadaver and live transplants. Most of his work was conducted in relation to the immediate problems of patients on the hemo-dialysis machines. The method of ministry was twofold: (1) a basic one-to-one contact with individual patients and family members, and (2) a biweekly group therapy session with spouses of patients. Working closely with the doctors and social worker, this writer led the patients and families in examining their feelings and faith in order to call upon their best resources in both areas.

The purpose of the following discussion is to consider some of the unique problems faced by the chronically ill, to determine how their religious ideation fits the situation, and to suggest some ideas for constructive pastoral care. Key issues are the "hope" and the "values" of these patients. These two concerns will be examined as major dynamics in solution of the problems of chronically ill persons. Some additional comments will be made in reference to closely related issues that face the modern minister. It should be noted that the material used comes from both clinical observations and specific clinical research data.

For the purpose of the study two basic tests were employed. The Allport, Vernon, Lindzey *Study of Values* was implemented to examine the basic value structures of chronic renal patients and their family members.[1] This test not only was easy to administer, but it also served as a unique tool with which to challenge the patient concerning his own value system. The test is designed to measure the relative prominence of six basic motives (or interests) in personality: the *theoretical, economic, aesthetic, social, political,* and *religious.*

Draper's religious psychiatric interview (with a fourteenth question added: What is your most persistent temptation?) was employed to gather additional information about the patient's religious understanding.[2] This test also served to gather data for the chaplain and psychiatrist for further reference and ministry.

An attempt was made to administer both tests to all patients and to at least one member of the patient's family, preferably the spouse. Twenty-eight Allport tests were given; twenty-three were returned. Twenty-eight religious interviews were given;

[1] Gordon W. Allport, Philip E. Vernon, and Gardner Lindzey, *Study of Values: Personality Measurement* (rev. ed.; Boston: Houghton Mifflin Company, 1952).

[2] Edgar Draper, George G. Meyer, Zane Parzen, and Gene Samuelson, "On the Diagnostic Value of Religious Ideation," *Archives of General Psychiatry,* Vol. XIII (September, 1965), pp. 202-207.

twenty were returned. The data was gained from the twenty-three Allport tests which were separated as follows: ten were male patients; three were female patients; seven were female family members; three were male family members.

LIFE SITUATION OF THE RENAL PATIENT

The kidney patient is a unique person with unique problems in his chronic, if not terminal, illness. The development of the artificial kidney has given him the possibility of a longer life to care for his family, to work at his job, and to try to fit his niche in society. He was selected for treatment from among many others whose kidneys failed for one reason or another. He was chosen because he was a better "risk"; consequently, he lives while others will die. His life will no longer be the same, for he is a chronically ill man who must submit to an extremely rigorous and difficult diet, will suffer occasional excruciating pain, and must twice a week allow his blood to be pumped through a machine which is able to accomplish the chore his kidneys cannot do.

Medical and Financial Problems

To his friends the kidney patient may look the same except for protective dressing over the tubes in his arm. He goes to work and to church. But to those who *really* know him, he is not the same, for the many psychological, social, medical, and financial problems which he faces are almost overwhelming.

Although given a medical "hope" for longer life, he is faced by uncertain odds. If he remains on the artificial kidney machine indefinitely, he may live for a few months or a few years. If he is a candidate for a kidney transplant, he has from a 20 to an 80 percent chance for a few years' survival, depending upon the source of the new kidney. The ominous shadow of death which hangs over him is accentuated by the occasional medical crises that arise. He may react to a medicine, or he may drink too much water and thus come into a precarious physical state. Because he must adjust to the rigors of treatment, he must be very cooperative with the medical team and maintain his emotional stability. The care he must give the tubes that connect him to the machine to prevent infection or bleeding is no less exacting than his extremely thorough diet.

Whether or not the kidney patient can adapt his way of living to reassume a near-useful life is most important in his rehabilitation. Under the many stresses some tend to feel "in-valid" and thus become invalids. Giving up or losing interest adds further stress to the situation.

Medical emergencies and uncertain life expectancies are not the only burdens. Financial strain is a major concern. Although the federal government has funded the major centers in the country, patients are being encouraged to pay their own way or to buy a machine for home treatment. Depending on many variables, this means a possible initial cost of $10,000 plus $2,000 to $4,000 per year afterward. Even if he stays at a center he must pay for drugs and other elements of his care. If he loses the usual two days' work while he is being dialyzed, the loss of pay increases the financial burden.

In the series of psychological tests given to the patients and their families, the economic factor proved to be a very strong matter, especially with the wives of male kidney patients — so much that it appeared to change their basic value-structure. These wives had very low esthetic values in comparison to the average American woman. These women were not as concerned with form, beauty, and harmony, nor were they as individualistic as they might have been expected to be. They had to be very practical in money matters, because the breadwinner was threatened. These families felt a total sense of dependency and loss of self-sufficiency. Life became very practical because of the expensive treatment. There is little freedom when a wife knows that her husband must be connected to a machine twice a week and subject to sickness at other times. Threats to her security are very real.

Psychological Problems

The many psychological stresses upon the patient and family units seem to increase with time on dialysis. Former conflicts are often opened up as defense mechanisms are broken down. An early enthusiasm often degenerates into despair and hopelessness in the face of pain and waiting. The problems brought to the fore by the stress of illness quickly show themselves in treatment and ministry.

A deeply hostile patient, for example, manipulated everyone, including the doctors. Her hostilities, which the chaplain finally drew out, were toward her parents for having her so late in life and toward the reality of approaching death. Because she had been abandoned by her first husband, she wanted to strike back at all men. Her flirtations with death by intentional (and near fatal) diet-breaks frustrated the staff as she sought to get back at all who were caring for her. Her religious interview gave clues to the dynamics of her problem. Her favorite Bible story was David and Goliath, and she felt the greatest sin one could commit was to molest children. So obsessed was she with her own childhood, feeling that she had been molested and had not been taught or properly cared for, that she bore great hostility against authority figures. Her first wish was for her children to be cared for, and she felt God functioned through her to teach her children.

Some families who had shaky interpersonal relationships and personality problems began to have even more difficulty under this extra stress. For example, feelings of sexual inadequacy were amplified in some individuals because this chronic illness often brings impotency. Those who had early feelings of inadequacy began to worry when they realized that their sex life would be altered. The wife of one patient expressed great fear that she was unattractive and failed her husband, since he was no longer interested in her. She was very relieved to learn that his biological inadequacy, not her personhood, was the reason. One male patient constantly struggled with his masculinity and sexuality. Having been a sort of "big man on campus," athletically inclined and self-centered, he flirted with the nurses and always left his pajama shirt open showing his hairy chest. In answering the question on the Draper interview "What is your greatest temptation?" he mentioned "sex." He constantly struggled with his sexuality.

An actual or threatened loss of body function was very closely related to the struggle over sexuality. Two patients confessed their fear of the doctor's knife "making a mistake" or "going too far" in the removal of their kidneys. It was not uncommon for patients, both male and female, to attempt to "prove" their sexuality in graphic demonstrations. One formerly dignified executive created a constant problem by dressing and undressing in the open (mixed) ward even after extensive reprimands to either pull a curtain or go to the men's room. Two female patients made obvious efforts to expose their breasts as if to say, "See, I am still a woman!"

One young female patient worried about her decreased function as a mother. Her favorite Bible story was the birth of Christ since "it is so gentle and beautiful." Her struggle over her sexuality was graphically illustrated in her answers to questions 9 and 10 on the Draper interview. In an apparent mistaken exchange of answers she answered the question "What is the most religious act one can perform?" with "This is a very hard question. Adultery or taking someone's life." The next question "What do you consider the greatest sin one could commit?" received the following answer: "I guess keeping one's body pure and thinking of others." Her struggle was apparently with feelings of sexual inadequacy and guilt over those feelings.

The Draper interviews revealed that many of the patients struggled with similar problems of repressed sexuality, though not all as graphic as the above examples. For most of the patients, their favorite Bible character was David because, in their words, he "did wrong" or "tarried from the way" and was forgiven.

Closely related to the problem of repressed sexuality is that of hostility. Perhaps no greater area of inner conflict is opened up by these stresses than this. The Draper interview revealed that most of the patients struggled with repressed hostility. A number were hostile toward God and asked, "Why did God do this to me?" Some rebellion toward their minister and their church indicated a rebellion toward a God who would allow this fate. The counseling process revealed that much of this general hostility was directed at authority figures or at the kidney machine itself. The impersonal references by hostile patients to "that thing" stood in contrast to the attitudes of some more adjusted patients who were more affectionate and appreciative of their "lifeline." More subtle forms of hostility were directed at the staff and at authoritative family members. Small violations of the diet created headaches for all, as well as problems in treatment. These violations were a convenient way of venting negative feeling, much like a small child who hurts himself to get back at his mother and to establish his independence.

One well-educated patient was a "problem child" to all, especially to his large, overbearing wife. His lethargy was the cause of much concern. Some even felt that he might have received brain damage which had rendered him incapable of feeling. Deep-seated hostility showed graphically in the administration of the Draper interview. As his wife dismissed herself before the test began, she said sarcastically, "I'll leave you boys to your games." When the patient was asked "Who is your favorite Bible character and why?" he quickly responded with feeling, "The *boy* David who slew the *giant*." Further questions revealed a deep hostility toward his wife for her overbearing ways. His favorite Bible portion was the Twenty-third Psalm, "For the feeling it imparts and the sense of *comfort* it gives." In answer to the question, "What do you consider the greatest sin one could commit?" he gave two: "murder, an overt or covert act; and adultery (pause), being a family man." He had withdrawn into a world of apparent lethargy as a defense mechanism both to control his anger and to endure the nagging of his spouse.

The important area of a man's social and family life is also affected. The loss of membership in groups (clubs, hobbies, church work) often occurs because the patient may have to withdraw from his most significant community activities. A complete change in one's way of life is experienced as he adjusts to the dialysis schedule and to unpredictable health. Future plans and ventures must be modified for the entire family due to the physical and financial stress. Vacations may no longer be possible, since the biweekly dialysis is necessary to life itself. Frequently, actual loss of status (home and financial) accelerates the faltering ego of the renal patient. This faltering ego may also be the family ego.

For example, one closely knit family was shattered by the chronic illness of the teen-age son. They felt they must "do something" and were impatient with the staff for not curing their son and thus ending the problem. The family had previously been able to handle any crisis. The father solicited blood and attempted to manipulate others to maintain his family ego. But he went too far in his compulsion to be helpful, and nearly crushed the ego of his son. In becoming so overprotective and overbearing he actually threatened the self-identity that the son had struggled to achieve. The chaplain finally confronted the family with the need to give the patient more freedom and room to prove himself. They were asked to stop forcing him into being an invalid. With some coaching they cooperated, struggling to realize why a nineteen-year-old boy *needed* to drive the car by himself, to date, and to be as normal as possible. When they saw that strengthening his own ego and self-sufficiency was a part of therapy, the job was easier for everyone.

For some persons the idea of being attached to a machine is a shock. The initial hopeful acceptance of the dialysis machine sometimes degenerated after long periods of treatment. This seemed to be especially true of those who had dependency needs. One immigrant wife who waited many months for a kidney transplant had high dependency needs. She constantly sought approval. She had left her homeland very early and barely remembered her parents. Her whole life centered upon her children, with whom she was overpossessive. But she could never accept the machine — "it" was "so cold and impersonal." "I hate it," she once said, "and dread being hooked up."

Another patient, a young male newlywed, had been rejected by his family. His mother would occasionally visit him to pacify her own guilt, but then she told him he would die on the operating table or that (she hoped) the doctors would find cancer, too. He craved love from a mother, and his wife became a mother substitute. In spite of his great dependency needs he had a mental block in accepting the cold, impersonal, polished metal machine that could give him no warmth or love. He eventually became a transplant candidate because of his inability to tolerate the machine.

Another psychological problem often encountered is the fear of death. This is a mixed sort of feeling and usually is not just a fear of death but also a desire for it. The "odds" or chances of continued life vary from month to month. Each patient in his own way conveyed to the chaplain his realization that "his time would come" (like others of their community of suffering). For some the months of suffering brought on depression. For those patients whose treatment had not been greatly effective for one reason or another, death became a very real possibility. Their paradoxical feelings about death were graphically acted out. Several of those who were in this depressed category would overtly abuse their strict diet and in a critical condition rush to the hospital for help. Such suicidal gestures were most common among the ones who were giving up hope as they struggled between their desire to die and their fear of death. It was interesting to note that these were not bloody bizarre attempts by poison, guns, or even by simply releasing a clip on the tube in their arm. But these ways were "more acceptable" to society — drinking enough water or eating enough candy to put their blood in a poisoned state.

A young female patient revealed a desire for peace of mind. Her husband said she "put on a good front," but he knew that she was worried about something. In answer to the question about the greatest sin, she wrote, "death, not just physical but mental." She was very faithful to her small sect-type religion and saw death (or mental losses) as a type of sin. This apparently motivated her into extensive defensive mechanisms to prove to the staff her mind was alert. She frequently smiled and joked with the staff, even when in pain.

Guilt is the most important psychological and religious stress related to chronic illness. Guilt is affected by the patient's ability to cope with it both in psychological and religious terms. The expressions of the guilt-laden patients come out in a great many ways. Many suspect that their kidney disease may be a punishment for a past sin or failure. In addition, many guilt feelings arise from the stresses of treatment.

One patient was so guilt-laden that it affected his treatment and attitudes toward almost everybody. Some years earlier his negligent driving had caused the death of his first wife on their honeymoon. He felt the kidney disease was God's punishment for his negligence. He sought to placate God for it. He was converted from Protestantism to an active Catholicism. He said that each time he hooked up to the machine he thought of "running that stop sign." In answer to the questions, "What does prayer mean to you? If you pray, what do you pray about?" he said, "To forgive my soul for things done wrong." In later answers he kept bringing in comments on forgiveness. His response to what God can do was, "I believe he can just [sic] forgive your soul." His response to the question on the greatest sin was, "Murder, harder to be forgiven for that than anything else." He believed he had murdered his wife and couldn't be forgiven.

He eventually settled down but couldn't get free from his albatross of guilt. His problem was especially noticeable in his behavior when a minister or priest was on the ward.

THE RELIGIOUS DYNAMICS OF RENAL PATIENTS

This group of chronically ill patients represented a cross section of religious persuasions including Roman Catholics, mainline and smaller sect Protestants, Jewish, and "nonbelievers." However, most of these patients had greater religious values than normal Americans, even though their family members did not score unusually high in this area. This almost universal interest and concern for religious matters was obvious even without the test results. Their openness to the chaplain was notable, even though several were openly opposed to him and "antireligious."

Religious Concern

Faced constantly with the possibility of death, as well as continued ill health and the multiplicity of associated problems, these patients were more concerned with religious values than the average healthy person. Since the norms used were those set by the tests and not by the patients pretested prior to illness, it would be difficult to say dogmatically whether this difference from normal indicated a basic change of values due to chronic illness or whether the illness uncovered values that were there all along. Two other clinical factors would indicate, however, that the former is the case. One is the fact that many of the patients pictured themselves as irreligious prior to illness. A few felt a sense of pride in their "unfaith." However, all but one displayed strong feelings about matters of religion, especially in attempting to cope with the situation at hand.

Another facet of this study is the work done by Chaplain Franklin Duncan with rehabilitation patients. He has shown that those patients pass through definite stages of adjustment, then of value change. An initial defensive retreat or denial of illness is followed by an acknowledgment (and subsequent mourning, despair). Permanent values are restricted. The third stage is one of adaptation in which an enlargement of values must occur. Then the patient must subordinate the values of body function or physique. An arousal of dormant values must occur as one moves from the comparative to more unique (or individual) values.[3]

These chronically ill patients also seem to react in like manner. They tend initially to deny the illness and talk as if the kidney will begin to function; they act as if the treatment is only to get them "over the hump." When they face the reality of their situation, they often suffer grief and seek sympathy. Because most of their values are built upon good health, poor health is a severe blow. If they can accept the reality of the situation, they adapt their values to something beyond standard body functions.

It is safe to say that the patients develop an interest in religion as a result of their condition. Whether or not this interest and use of religious faith is healthy depends upon the patient and his particular religious ideation.

The religious interviews reveal how these high religious interests or values are interpreted by the individual patients. For some, religion is a grasp for a pragmatic or useful God to help them out of a tight spot. Prayer is the seeking of answers to personal problems in a childlike way. In answer to the question, "How does God function in your personal life?" one replied, "For a jam I pray to him." For others God is "out there" and is to blame for the illness. For a few persons their simple faith tells them that God cares and they appreciate the care given to them by others. Those who had great feelings of guilt and hostility toward God were the patients who created the greatest problems in treatment.

Forms of religion varied from a fundamentalist legalism to much more nebulous sympathies. But about 80 percent were hoping to face their current problems with some religious means.

All of the psychological and social stresses previously discussed had religious connotations as well. A particularly difficult problem for many patients was their inability to handle guilt and hopelessness. A few Protestants were able adequately to utilize their faith to resolve such inner conflict as were at least two Catholics who had the advantage of a more structured confessional ministry.

[3] Fuller details are included in this book in Chapter 7, "Pastoral Care of Disabled Persons," by Franklin Duncan.

This almost universal problem of guilt proved to be a barrier to communication with other members of the professional team, and it was with this dynamic that the chaplain had a unique responsibility.

The implications of the study were as important in prospect as in retrospect. The data gathered about individuals not only helped in understanding why a person reacted to treatment and to other persons as he did, but it also offered several clues for both a ministry to and a treatment of the individual patient. (These two aspects are far from being mutually exclusive.) The actual administration of the tests opened several avenues of self-understanding for some patients as well as clarifying the previous observations made about others. No matter how the patients verbalized their feelings, all of them were much interested in religious matters for a variety of reasons, good and bad. The task of the minister who needs to relate to the chronically ill must be to help filter their feelings and religious resources, so that the patients may utilize what is healthy and discard what is unhealthy.

Hope and Values

The hope and value structure of most patients was built upon complete health and normal activity. Since these two items are clues to an understanding of the chronically ill and to an effective ministry to them, a brief definition of terms is in order. In the case of each term a brief discussion of current usage will be more helpful than a dictionary definition.

Within philosophical and religious ideation, the idea of hope has a multiplicity of meanings. Even within Christianity some variety of interpretation exists. Some would limit a concept of hope to a purely eschatological expectation with little relevance to current life. Others would limit it to a self-realization with little meaning beyond the individual. For purposes of definition this work will allow a broad interpretation of hope which would allow the individual patient to find some hope in a peace and tranquility, a "righting of things" beyond the way they now stand. This could include an expectation of personal fulfillment and a better life beyond this one.

The role of goals and values, objects for which men strive, has taken in recent years an increasingly important place in the study of human behavior.[4] Man's behavior is being interpreted more in terms of purposive action than as a reaction in a mechanistic chain of cause and effect. This shift in emphasis does not deny the basic drives but seeks to correct an overemphasis upon them as the prime motivation of behavior. Thus, a consideration of the psychodynamics of a healthy personality must include a study of a man's motivation, his values, and his hopes.

This approach assumes a constant striving for unity on the part of the individual. Prescott Lecky speaks to this in defining "the personality as an organization of values which are felt to be consistent with one another. Behavior expresses the effort to maintain the integrity and unity of the organization."[5] All of these values are organized into a single system, the preservation of which is essential.

> The nucleus of the system, around which the rest of the system revolves, is the individual's valuation of himself. The individual sees the world from his own viewpoint, with himself as the center. Any value entering the system which is inconsistent with the individual's valuation of himself cannot be assimilated; it meets with resistance, and is likely, unless a general reorganization occurs, to be rejected.[6]

The resistance, Lecky declares, is an essential part of the maintenance of individuality. Thus, the individual organizes his life around his own scheme of values. As one grows he assimilates his own value structure, and as he gets older it becomes more firmly established as adaptability decreases. When his behavior or life violates his conception of himself, remorse or guilt occurs. "Grief is experienced when the personality must be reorganized due to the loss of one of its supports."[7]

In a similar way Stephen Pepper sees personality as a *"system of dispositions for purposive behavior."*[8] There seems to be a sort of "selective system" in each individual who adjusts and corrects his values to help integrate his personality.

Allport's concept of a mature personality sees this system of values coordinated by some unifying philosophy of life. These

---

[4] Gordon W. Allport, "The Trend in Motivational Theory," *The Self*, Clark E. Moustakas, ed. (New York: Harper & Row, Publishers, Inc., 1956), p. 89.

[5] Prescott Lecky, "The Personality," Moustakas, *ibid.*, pp. 25-43.

[6] *Ibid.*, pp. 89-90.

[7] *Ibid.*, pp. 92-96.

[8] Stephen C. Pepper, *The Sources of Value* (Berkeley: University of California Press, 1958), p. 463.

goals or values involve not only the integration of one's personality and his conscience but also his religion. The mature religious sentiment is defined as:

> a disposition, built up through experience, to respond favorably, and in certain habitual ways, to conceptual objects and principles that the individual regards as of ultimate importance in his own life, and as having to do with what he regards as permanent or central in the nature of things.[9]

Viktor Frankl, famed psychiatrist of Vienna, posits a dynamic view of humanity based on man's search for meaning. He feels the basic characteristic of being human is that search for a goal of meaning. His method of logotherapy is to help face meaninglessness. He contends that social values are universal meanings, "general" meanings that are known throughout society, but each person's own meaning or value system must be discovered himself.[10]

Religious feeling, in whatever form (positive or negative), seems to be related to one's value structure. This has to do with meaning in life as an integral part of individuality. Since life's norms are, for the most part, set by a person's values, Tillich says one's values or intentions focus on one's individuality. It is not always personal doubt that changes values, but usually the fact that values do not speak to our existential situation. Thus, when one faces existential fear or anxiety, he may modify his basic structure in order to cope with the situation. This state of anxiety is related directly to the fear of the unknown, of uncertainties and ambiguities in life situations.[11]

At the point of religious faith, one's values and hope come into focus. The two terms or phenomena are not mutually exclusive, but rather closely related. In the context of difficult life situations, such as that of chronic illness, a basic value system is threatened and usually modified. If the value system is too rigid to be sufficiently adaptable to face the crisis of such illness, despair often results. Degrees of despair (or hopelessness) affect the lives and treatment of most patients in a hospital set-

⁹ Gordon W. Allport, The Individual and His Religion (New York: The Macmillan Company, 1952), p. 56.

¹⁰ Viktor Frankl, Man's Search for Meaning (Boston: Beacon Press, 1965), pp. 97-111.

¹¹ Paul Tillich, The Courage to Be (New Haven: Yale University Press, 1953), pp. 36-37, 48-50.

ting. The questions now faced in a clinical setting are related to the three items: values, religion, and hope.

A brief word study points out several interesting aspects of the usage of the word "hope." Hoping is not a wild wishing or dreaming, but an earnest expectation or desire with some confidence that something can be obtained. The archaic usage of "hope" to designate arable land surrounded by swamp is graphic, for it almost pictures a person cut off from others by the swamp, hoping to reach that island of fruitfulness. The Hebrew concept shows a bond of security that is involved as well as a measure of one's life.

One's values and hopes are interrelated in an important way. If one hopes for and binds his life by certain expectations, hope and value come to sharp focus when they are threatened. If in that value system those hopes are unreal or inadequate, they must be adjusted. For a great many whose hopes are centered on good health, jobs, and families, the crisis of illness threatens their whole value system. Some continued their hope for health, but made the kidney machine or a transplant the object of their hope. But "hope that is seen is not hope" and short term goals prove inadequate to sustain the long waiting that becomes a way of life. In "hoping for health" by way of dialysis or transplant, an unrealistic outlook on life is often utilized in spite of the doctors' admonitions that the patient is "in-valid" and will always be limited in comparison to other people. A gradual despair often overtakes those who set good health as their main goal in life. They fail to adapt their values and begin to feel the futility of reaching their standard.

In both the meaning of the word and the clinical situation, hope may be involved with a fear or apprehension of the undesirable. Among the renal patients the fear of death is very real. Much guilt is felt by some because of their conscious and subconscious desires to die mixed with a hope for death. In attempting to deal with these tensions in some patients, it was discovered that they felt these tensions most strongly during the periods of depressions, especially after long periods of waiting for a transplant.

Two of three patients, who during counseling openly expressed a wish to die, had been grossly mishandling their diets and had serious complications. One eventually died as a result.

The other could only explain her nearly suicidal weekend diet breaks as due to some mysterious uncontrollable urge when she felt so depressed, alone, and hopeless. After venting her many guilty and hostile feelings toward herself, her family, and husband, and admitting her possible suicidal gestures, she began to adapt her value system. Her first change was in realizing that the staff cared for her because she was a *person* and that acceptance was not contingent upon her complete health. She began to accept herself and those around her, feeling that God must also care for her. Before and after her transplant she confessed her strengthened religious feelings, that she was happy whether or not the kidney worked — *still desiring the short-term goal but feeling her greater hope was far beyond failing health.* Thus, she could face the uncertainty of life and health by looking beyond herself into a faith, a greater hope.

The question of religious faith in this context is a very real one. Although the value of "foxhole religion" may be questionable (if such religion indeed exists), the fact is that the chronically ill are thinking in religious realms. Whether or not it is healthy thinking depends upon the person and his ideation. But his questions, his hostile feelings, and his guilt feelings will be directed toward or picked up by the minister who should be able to handle them appropriately. These feelings are closely related to treatment and to patient behavior. The families, also, are involved intimately in these situations.

Many of the medical aspects are given religious interpretations far beyond the more common, "Why did God do this to me?" Sexual inadequacies, changes of personality, health problems, and hereditary questions that have medical basis (from kidney failure) are frequently referred to the minister with guilt feelings. Although intellectually the patients accept the doctors' answers, at the feeling level they still are perplexed. This calls for even closer teamwork between the doctors and ministers. Thus, the minister may reassure and reaffirm the patient, but at the same time reach for the dynamics behind the questions.

THEOLOGICAL ISSUES IN CHRONIC ILLNESS

In the course of the work with the renal unit several unique opportunities have occurred that would raise further reflective theological issues as well as practical problems. Especially in dealing with situations involving the transplantation of a kidney has this been true.

Resurrection

One issue is that of the resurrection of the body. One would think that some who believed strongly in a literal, physical resurrection might object to the removal of an organ on the grounds of their belief. In ten situations, however, such was not the case. This objection was never raised, although in six situations the persons were asked specifically if this were an issue. Although affirming their belief (for most) in some sort of resurrection, none of them felt the loss of an organ would affect it. "It would not affect it," as several put it, "anymore than the loss of a finger or a leg or my hair." Most expressed a type of mystical feeling about the resurrection and cited such acceptable activities as eye banks and skin grafts as secular proof for their feelings.

Only one woman even hinted toward resistance on this basis, but her feelings of hostility toward doctors and authority figures quickly came out in the issue. She hinted by saying, "He *must* be left like he came into this world." On indirect querying if this related to the resurrection she admitted, "Heavens no. I just don't want those medical students experimenting on him."

A "perfect-body" idea of the resurrection does not appear to be an issue with those who are faced with the question. In the religious interviews the comments in answer to the question, "What are your views of an after life?" reveal that most (fourteen of twenty) believe in some form of after life. Four had mixed feelings, and only two raised specific doubt about it. Only one, the husband of a patient, mentioned a "perfect body." The term resurrection was not used by any of the interviewees.

In a sense the doctrine of the resurrection symbolizes the wholeness of personality. As these patients seek to readjust their value systems to maintain their individuality and unique personality, a healthy hope may well allude to a concept of the resurrection. Perhaps this is where a "hope that is not seen" is expressed as a simple trust. Realizing he is not a complete person but is hoping for a final correction of things, a person is able to face his limitations. In a very practical way some individuals seem to hope for some kind of resurrection, yet are not worried about the technicalities or mechanics of it. These cases seem to indicate that such nondefinitive understandings are able to give valid hope to people who really need it.

Election

A closely related issue is that of "election." This is a most sensitive matter for doctors who must accept or turn down patients for dialysis or transplant (and thus decide who lives and who dies.) At every juncture this is a most difficult decision. In each case the doctors must deal with their own guilt feelings. This subject is far too broad for extensive comment, but it is a real issue because the doctors admit that they "play God." At the same time the physicians ask serious questions about the nature of life and death and about the patient's right to die. Where life can be mechanically sustained for indefinite periods, by various means, with extreme prolongation of pain or no "sign of life" at all, is it ethical to continue? Does a person have a "divine" right to die? What of the patient who is in pure hell on the kidney program? *Can* he be given the right to face death honorably without extended physical, mental, and financial pain? What of the patient who begged, "Let me die, oh please, let me die!" At what point is the value of a person subordinate to the value of "life" *per se?*

Ethical Responsibility

These questions about life and death are the focus of ethical and theological attention. In numerous discussions and panels great interest has been expressed in these issues, especially in light of current heart transplants. In that context two basic issues are unresolved and pose the greatest medical and theological problems: What is life? And what is a person? Both of these are related to hope, especially in the realm of resurrection. Is a person limited to the totality of his somatic functions? Is he something more? Does the removal of part of his body remove part of his personhood? These are the issues. Can an adequate hope be found — not necessarily one that gives glib answers — but one that speaks to suffering men where they are?

To examine the maze of ethical questions surrounding transplants is a perplexing and complex endeavor, whether they be questions about economics, experimentation, or donor-recipient choices. In answering the questions two basic considerations would be whether or not the experimentation is linked responsibly to therapy and the degree of the risk as compared to the possibility of help. Historically, the great advances in medical science have been made through practical research (although perhaps not as dramatic or with as much publicity as the current transplants). Through modern efforts, men may soon have organ transplants from animals or portable mechanical organs which will be as common as the current replacement of heart valves or eye corneas. But in the meantime great *care* is necessary on the part of the physician and society. Personal fame and medical research, *per se*, must not obliterate the long-range goals or the individual needs of a particular patient. The freedom to choose donors and recipients and to transplant organs involves a certain kind of medical power over life and death. That freedom and power can only be handled properly when corresponding responsibility goes with it. As long as the medical profession handles that responsibility in an ethical way, the community should share a covenant of support. The oft-quoted phrase, "The greatest good for the greatest number in the long run," must be qualified by the principle, *primum non nocere* ("First, to do no harm.")

PASTORAL CARE OF THE CHRONICALLY ILL

Positive pastoral care to the chronically ill is an area of great need. The average chronically ill person may or may not actively seek out his pastor, even though he is greatly concerned over religious matters. In the group of patients studied, only two felt their ministers understood or demonstrated enough concern to go to them. Some persons felt they had been abandoned by their pastor and church because of the hopelessness of their situation (i.e., the pastor or church couldn't "do" anything, since the problems were medical). One found his pastor more of a hindrance than a help in problems of guilt because the pastor naively urged the patient to reveal a past sin to hang the blame on. Several areas of concern are very important for one who seeks to minister to the chronically ill.

Reality Testing

In the first place, the pastor should recognize the value of reality testing both for himself and the patient. This does not mean a denial of the past and future for the sake of seeing only the present but rather a frank admission of the situation as it really is so that together the pastor and patient can face the problems responsibly. This is especially true in accepting the finiteness of the situation and the concepts of God posited by those involved. The minister who apologizes for God's distant but "ultimate love" only adds insult to injury. If the pastor is unwilling to face death as a real possibility, he is no help.

Patience

"Be patient and wait on the Lord" points up another area of concern. Rarely seen in our culture, patience and waiting are a difficult experience for the average "high-speed" man. A minister on the run who schedules a five-minute visit with a chronically ill person does not communicate the value of patience. Long and lonely hours of thinking open old and new avenues of thoughts as well as guilt patterns. The alert (and patient) pastor will serve a ministry of confession and help filter out feelings and worries.

Grief

The pastor will also find a prolonged grief situation, both anticipatory and real. The person suffers a very real grief in his ill status, much the same as one who has lost an arm or leg. But he also faces the grief of his own death that hangs over his head. Some families refuse to discuss the possibility and suffer silently. Some adjust well, continually working through the grief; and they are able to talk openly of the death and even make plans for the family "after Daddy is gone." (One female patient even jokingly described to her husband the kind of "replacement" he should get.) In any case, the pastor is the one to lead a family through the entire grief situation.

Death

Another area of major concern is the interpretation of death, perhaps helping the patient to develop a theology of death. Whereas most people find no time to consider seriously their own death, chronically ill folk live with it constantly. Most feel that their faith has given only token answers that do not meet their needs. Although most had been taught that death was to be accepted, at the feeling level they were scared. A pastor must be able to face death himself in a Christian context and even admit, with the patients, that it may be anticipated if one possesses a greater hope that gives a positive affirmation that God cares.

Hope

The prevailing existential problem for pastoral care is not death, but continuing life. At this point hope and values are paramount. The Christian pastor must possess and administer a theology of *Christian* hope to aid the chronically ill.

What a man lives for determines who he is and how he lives. Hope was the original impulse of theology, but it has been transmuted into utopian ideals, secular movements, and speculation over sin, evil, and death.[12] People now tend to shy away from hoping in anything beyond short-term tangible goals because of philosophical stereotypes of hope. In the face of suffering and pain, and in meeting new problems created by technology, a reevaluation must be made of man's need for a valid hope.

Much of the Christian faith has to do with hoping. Faith itself is defined in terms of hope. "Now faith is the assurance of things hoped for, the conviction of things not seen" (Hebrews 11:1). This hope is one that "does not disappoint us" (Romans 5:5) as many others do. Only in times of despair can one really begin to experience a real hope. Christian hope helps men to realize in the midst of suffering that they are humans and need God. When a person begins to realize that he, as a human, is limited, he can learn to trust God and expect — or hope — that in the final analysis God will care for him. This hope involves patience, which is sorely needed in chronic illness (Romans 8:25). The psalmist said: "I waited patiently for the Lord" (Psalm 40:1). Such trust enables one to experience not only hope but also a deeper faith and character (Romans 5:1-5). Hope involves the mutual love of others. This type of hope in others gives strength and help in a caring way (1 Thessalonians 2:19). The care given

---

[12] Ernst Benz, *Evolution and Christian Hope* (Garden City: Doubleday & Company, Inc., 1966), p. viii.

by others in time of despair, as in the case of those who treat sickness, helps one experience a Greater Hope.

Perhaps it could best be said in the words of the psalmist:

> Out of the depths I cry to thee, O Lord!
> Lord, hear my voice!
> Let thy ears be attentive
> to the voice of my supplications!
>
> If thou, O Lord, shouldst mark iniquities,
> Lord, who could stand?
> But there is forgiveness with thee,
> that thou mayest be feared.
>
> I wait for the Lord, my soul waits,
> and in his word I hope;
> my soul waits for the Lord
> more than watchmen for the morning,
> more than watchmen for the morning.
>
> O Israel, hope in the Lord!
> For with the Lord there is steadfast love,
> and with him is plenteous redemption.
> And he will redeem Israel
> from all his iniquities (Psalm 130).

SUGGESTIONS FOR FURTHER READING

1. ON THE CHRONICALLY ILL

Allport, Gordon W., *The Individual and His Religion*. New York: The Macmillan Company, 1967.
_____. "The Trend in the Motivational Theory," *The Self*, Clark E. Moustakas, ed. New York: Harper & Row, Publishers, Inc., pp. 25-43.
_____, Philip E. Vernon, and Gardner Lindzey. *Study of Values*. Boston: Houghton Mifflin Company, 1960.
Draper, Edgar, *et al.*, "On the Diagnostic Value of Religious Ideation," *Archives of General Psychiatry*, Vol. 13 (September, 1965), pp. 202-207.
Fromm, Eric, "Values, Psychology and Human Existence," *New Knowledge in Human Values*, A. H. Maslow, ed. New York: Harper & Row, Publishers, Inc., 1959, pp. 151-164.
Lecky, Prescott, "The Personality," *The Self*, Clark E. Moustakas, ed. New York: Harper & Row, Publishers, Inc., 1956, pp. 86-97.
Schreiner, George W., and Maher, John F., "Hemodialysis for Chronic Renal Failure: Medical, Moral and Ethical and Socio-Economic Problems," *Annals of Internal Medicine*, Vol. 62, No. 3 (March, 1965), pp. 551-557.
Shea, Eileen J., Bogdan, Donald F., Freeman, Richard B., and Schreiner, George E., "Hemodialysis for Chronic Renal Failure: Psychological Considerations," *Annals of Internal Medicine*, Vol. 62, No. 3 (March, 1965), pp. 558-563.

Wright, Robert G., Sand, Patricia, and Livingston, Goodhue, "Psychological Stress During Hemodialysis for Chronic Renal Failure," *Annals of Internal Medicine,* Vol. 64, No. 3 (March, 1966), pp. 611-620.

2. ON MEDICAL ETHICS

Fletcher, Joseph, *Morals and Medicine.* Boston: Beacon Press, 1960.

Readers' Guide to Periodical Literature lists many articles, both in popular and technical periodicals, that deal with medical ethics. See especially: "Transplantation," "Medical Research," "Ethics," "Experimentation on Man," and "Euthanasia."

Some of the better articles are:

"Doctors as God," *Current,* October, 1967, pp. 35-38.

"Heart Surgery," *Time,* March 15, 1968, p. 66.

"Heart Transplants: How Many, How Soon?" *Medical World News,* February 16, 1968, pp. 51-58.

"Repairs, Implants, Transplants . . .," *U.S. News and World Report,* January 22, 1968, pp. 58-59.

"When Are You Really Dead?" *Newsweek,* December 18, 1967, p. 87.

3. ON PASTORAL CARE

Draper, Edgar, *Psychiatry and Pastoral Care.* Philadelphia: Fortress Press, 1968.

Erikson, Erik H., *Insight and Responsibility.* New York: W. W. Norton & Company, Inc., 1964.

Frankl, Viktor, *Man's Search for Meaning.* Boston: Beacon Press, 1963.

Lynch, William F., *Images of Hope.* Baltimore: Helicon Press, Inc., 1965.

Oates, Wayne E., *Christ and Selfhood.* New York: Association Press, 1961, pp. 103-135.

——————, *Protestant Pastoral Counseling.* Philadelphia: The Westminster Press, 1962, pp. 75-100.

Pruyser, Paul W., "Phenomenology and Dynamics of Hoping," *Journal for the Scientific Study of Religion,* Vol. III (Fall, 1963), pp. 86-96.

Scherzer, Carl J., *Ministering to the Physically Sick.* Philadelphia: Fortress Press, 1963.

Sharpe, William D., *Medicine and the Ministry.* New York: Appleton Century, 1966.

Takaji Mitsushima is the General Chaplain of the Seinan Jo Gakuin Baptist Girls' Institution in Japan. He has studied in Japan and the United States and has served as pastor in Japan in addition to his work in the field of education.

9
PASTORAL CARE
AND SOCIAL DISASTERS
Takaji Mitsushima and Wayne E. Oates

The present generation of theological students and some pastors are too young to have known a time when the threat of nuclear attack was not hanging over their heads. Yet they have not experienced what life can be like for a pastor at a time of disaster. Nevertheless, they live as pastors likely to be called upon to care for people in such a crisis. If he does not find himself in a war, a minister may be caught in the maelstrom of other lesser, but nonetheless crucial, pastoral situations. He might have been a pastor in the Watts area of Los Angeles, or in Detroit or Chicago during the summers of 1967 and 1968. He might have been a pastor in the little hamlet of Aberfan, Wales, when the slag pile covered the school building full of little children, or a missionary in Saigon during the Tet Offensive of 1968.

In such situations pastoral care becomes something more than knowing how to counsel on a one-to-one basis, as important and imperative as this approach may be. Pastoral care in times of social disaster becomes the involvement of a pastor in the shock, panic, numbness, and catastrophic suffering of masses of people.

Shortly after World War II, Michihiko Hachiya, a Japanese physician, wrote a personal journal during the days August 6 to September 30, 1945. He ministered to an entire population that had "been reduced to a common level of physical and mental

193

weakness. . . . They were so broken and confused that they moved and behaved like automatons."[1]

More recently, George W. Baker and Dwight W. Chapman have edited a book entitled *Man and Society in Disaster*. Both these books are worthy of careful reading by a pastor. However, the following paper by Takaji Mitsushima, now a chaplain at the Seinan Jo Gakuin Girls' School at Kitakyushi, places his own personal experience as a Japanese soldier in the context of the resources and hopes of the Christian faith. The autobiography speaks for itself. As a postscript to it, some of the specific ways and means of pastoral care in the crucial situation of great social catastrophes will be identified.

SUICIDE AND HOPE IN THE FACE OF WAR
(An Autobiographical Account)

In the spring of 1945, the Japanese soldiers in China, at least those of us who were stationed near the coast, somehow had a feeling that there would be no chance to see the loved ones back home again. Much time had passed since we had received a supply of resources from Japan, both men and equipment. We no longer had a hope of hearing from our families and friends from the homeland.

In the middle of August we received an order to move up to the north in order to fight against the Russians who had just begun to come down into Manchuria from Siberia. Only the officers knew that our next destination was Manchuria, but every one of the soldiers sensed it when they were handed gas masks. All of us had already spent two to five years or more in the battlefields, and there was nothing that would surprise us. We quickly fastened our bundles and got on board the train — a freight train, of course.

There was not any excitement or any particular anxiety or horror. We had already experienced and come through all possible anxieties and hardships. We had become accustomed to moving around without much knowledge of the new places where we were going. Perhaps the only thing that ran through our minds was what the Russians would look like and what kind

[1] Michihiko Hachiya, *Hiroshima Diary*, Warner Wells, trans. and ed. (Chapel Hill: University of North Carolina Press, 1955), p. 55.

of tactics they would use. Unlike the Japanese soldiers and sailors in the South Pacific, we had never experienced any defeat except occasional tactical retreats in our battles against Chinese.

I do not recall how many hours or days we had been in this train when it suddenly stopped and remained for a long time at a "no-place" — no village, no station, and no person was to be seen. (Later we found how lucky we were to have stopped there; otherwise, most of us would have died a terrible death in Siberia, a kind of death which is not less miserable than that of Auschwitz.) We only knew that we were still in central China. But the Brigadier General had just received a special order from General Headquarters in China. He was told to stop where he was and wait for the following orders. Very soon everyone was told that the war was over. We remained about one month in this freight train, always ready to fight against any enemy. Nobody felt that we were to surrender. My company was kept busy in the receiving and dispatching of orders for the Brigade Commander.

In September our train moved forward for several hours and stopped again, this time at a small town. We left the train and entered the town to be settled down in a certain block. We moved there smoothly and immediately built barbed-wire entanglements as we had been accustomed to do. These later became our confinements.

Prisoners of War

When the Chinese officials came into the town in order to disarm us, they gave us a blow which not only crushed our pride but left us in a state of anxiety we had never experienced before. They were also afraid of us and only pointed out when and where we should hand over our arms, horses, police dogs, and carrier pigeons. They let the officers carry their swords for another two months, the swords being symbols of the spirit of the Japanese warriors.

Thus we became prisoners of war. We were confined in a temporary concentration camp which we ourselves had prepared. Everyone began to wonder what was going to happen to him. Some were well educated and very sensitive soldiers, but outwardly they appeared no different from the rest. No one attempted suicide. In my company two soldiers had killed themselves before surrender: one did so when he had a cipher-dictionary stolen in town; the other, who had majored in literature in college, could not endure the inhuman society of the Japanese army. Thus, those who might have wanted to kill themselves would have done so before our confinement. Later we heard of some officers who did commit suicide when they were told to surrender.

Now, to live, instead of daring suicide, meant first of all to realize the fact that we were prisoners with no liberty. It was painful to know ourselves to be different from ourselves of yesterday. We experienced anxiety because we did not have any knowledge of the dark future. We were in a foreign land, and even thousands of the Japanese who also were in the same Chinese nation did not know where we were and how we were getting along. "Front-haziness," as we called it half-jokingly, was now mixed with apathy. The fact that we still had our organization ranks and orders kept us from a deeper apathy, as well as from more confusion.

We were told to live on what we had. We were not told how long we were to stay in this concentration camp. There were rumors — some said that we would have to wait only until New Year's Day, others said several years, and still others said for good. We had to suffer from the scarcity of food. Everyone gradually became like a child. How many times we talked about food! How many times we talked about the delicious meals which we would enjoy when we came home — such Japanese delicacies as raw fish, *sukiyaki* or *ochazuke*! "We must survive even for the Japanese delicacy!" we said to one another. We also missed the hot, really hot, deep bath. In the beginning we could enjoy baths in drums, but the fuel became scarce, as well as the food and lamp oil.

There were not any Christians among us. Every one of us was from Buddhist background and could become a Buddhist when faced with death, even though Buddhism was not a religion which was lived daily except by a very few real Buddhists. Also, we all shared a Shinto background, which was expressed in the daily Emperor worship. We were not conscious of different attitudes toward the circumstances into which we were thrown so abruptly, although there were "swines" and "saints." We found great difficulty in existing without a fixed point in the future. But there were some other elements which made us survive. We survived because we still had our organizations and orders and because every one of us still believed in the Emperor and his representatives, that is, our officers. We had been taught to wait for orders from higher castes or ranks through a long period of feudalism. The Japanese people want either to dominate or to submit, and do not recognize gradations in between. This dangerous trait helped us to exist and survive even though the higher ranks in whom we had faith were defeated ones. When the news came that the Emperor had declared that he was not divine, it literally shattered our faith. And yet, the shattered faith still had strength to hold us, strange as it may sound.

Now the anxiety concerning the future, including the fear of death by either hunger or bullet, irritated us day and night. We thought of our loved ones all the more. Rather, we imagined the happiness of meeting them again. This also intensified the problem of scarcity of food, too.

News of Hiroshima

Sometime in December we were informed of the atomic bomb in Hiroshima. Most of us were from Hiroshima and its vicinity. In August, the news which we received only said that a new kind of bomb had been dropped in Hiroshima and the damage seemed to be severe. That was all we knew, and since by that time almost all the cities and towns in Japan had been destroyed, we did not pay special attention to it, but just hoped that our families were safe. Someone brought two pictures from a torn English magazine — Hiroshima before and after the atomic bomb. We all, including patients suffering from undernourishment, eagerly gazed at the pictures. They did not look like another American propaganda piece! My home was very near the center of the blast, according to the picture. There were many who recognized the same thing. But what we said then was, "Even if all the citizens of Hiroshima had been killed, my parents, my wife, my children must have evacuated to somewhere, and must be alive!" I heard only one exception, and it was a joke told a month later. An officer, an ex-dentist who had been drafted for the second time, was saying to the general, "I would like to ask you, sir, to find a beautiful young lady for me in case my wife was killed by the A-bomb after we go back to Hiroshima." The general, in turn, promised the young officer on the condition that he should also try to find a beautiful lady for the general if his wife had been killed. I am not sure if it was a joke. (Both of their young wives were found alive, and their hopes were in vain!) Indeed, the hope to see our loved ones again was the strongest focus by which we could interpret the life-in-threat constructively.

After New Year's Day, 1946, we were becoming more and more ill-nourished, anxious, and irritated. The rumors made it worse. However, some time in February, we finally were told to pick up our things and get on board the freight train going to Shanghai, from where we were supposed to sail for Japan. The train was unusually slow, but we arrived at a concentration camp in Shanghai toward the end of February. There were many other troops who had been waiting for their boats, and we joined them. We went through several examinations, another very humiliating experience. There had been reported some incidents of soldiers who were killed because they were hiding parts of pistols, and of their officers in command receiving life sentences. We had to be careful in every way. If any one of us became suspect of epidemic, our turn of getting aboard would be postponed indefinitely.

The day finally came for us to get aboard. The voyage back to Japan took three days. We threw away our rank badges at the bay of Fukuoka, Kyushu Island, Japan, where we landed on March 29, 1946. This trip from the first concentration camp to Japan was a long and hard one, but I had spent many hours in meditating on how I would greet my parents, on how I would explain the years I had spent away from them, and on how I would express my love and gratitude to them. And every time I meditated on these things I was filled with anticipated joy of seeing them again. Yes, this was a freedom by which I could take my own attitude toward the circumstances on our way home. And the fact that I had a hope of seeing my parents again made me *exist* even in the cold, stinky, dark freight train or in the crowded and rolling cabin. We had heard of the total destruction of Japan, especially of Hiroshima, but we had not seen it. We were more concerned about the fact that we were on our way home, which we had not seen for years.

Besides, there was a girl whom I had seen a few times as a high school girl and then as a college girl. We were not in love. I doubt if we were friends to each other. But after I was sent over to China as a soldier, our parents engaged us. She was the only child of the family, and her parents wanted to adopt me as their son and at the same time as their daughter's husband, that is, their son-in-law. They wanted the family name and their silk business to be perpetuated. So we had become engaged even though each of us did not feel anything like love at all. And yet, on my way home, I was thrilled to think of a girl who was supposed to be faithfully waiting for my homecoming.

Arrival in Hiroshima

I arrived at Hiroshima on the last day of March, 1946. I still do not know of any language by which I could describe the hellish feeling I had upon seeing the site of the former city even though more than half a year had passed since the bomb. I found nobody and nothing waiting for my homecoming except the ashes and rubble there. (I would meet my two brothers and one younger sister later, but not at the time when I came home.) A stranger told me that my parents had been killed and how miserable my mother had been during the thirty days she survived after the bomb.

There was only one person whom I could meet again, and that was the fiancée who had grown up beautifully. She was now a reporter for the largest newspaper in Japan. It took her a little time to recognize me when I went to see her in Kokura. The only word she said to me was that she did not want to marry me any more. Her parents were still alive, and they tried to persuade her to marry me, but in vain. Perhaps it was natural for her to refuse to marry someone who did not have any home or job and who looked very dirty and hazy and terribly undernourished.

I was left alone in the midst of the rubble of a former Hiroshima. I did not know what to do. I did not have anyone with whom I could talk. If there had been anyone, he would have been in similar circumstances, and I did not know what to say after all.

There was no place for me to stay. While spending nights in the waiting room and under the eaves of the damaged railway station, I began to think seriously about life. I could not experience a bit of joy of homecoming at all, which made me even more skeptical. When I grew up and was drafted into the army, I had the Emperor who was divine. "In the name of the Emperor Divine" was the almighty key word by which we could endure all difficulties at the front. I was literally ready to give my life for his cause, like many other soldiers. Now, my mother was gone, and the Emperor was not divine! There was nothing left which could be a stay within me. What meaning did all of my service with its pain and hardship have? Could it have any meaning at all? What is the meaning of life?

In the midst of my perplexity I found myself a tottering drunkard (drunken with the cheapest Japanese whiskey obtained from the black market) in the middle of a long suspension bridge which rose from one darkness and reached another. I had been running on this bridge with much sweat on my brow, not knowing where I came from, why I was running, or where I was going. What an idiot! A living corpse!

The Alternative of Suicide

Thinking about those officers who killed themselves, I decided to kill myself. I thought that I could not keep standing on that bridge any more. The desperate circumstance encouraged me, perhaps, to jump off the bridge. And it would also help me to take revenge on that girl. Everyone and everything were in abnormal conditions then and there, and probably I was not an exception. I thought about killing myself for about two nights. Such logical thinking concerning the meaninglessness of life drove me to suicide, which was not a logical thing at all. (It is not really a matter of either logic or illogic to kill oneself.) Anyway, I did not have or could not think of the courage, if it was a courage — I could have only suffered from self-hatred or hatred of self-hatred. After all, I was a soldier, a very honest and simple soldier, too simple to stand known absurdity.

I took out a long razor and slashed my throat!

The Lord did not allow me to touch the jugular vein. When I came to myself, I realized that I could not even commit suicide successfully. I had to face myself as the failure of failures. During my recuperation I began to try many things to escape from myself, or at least to forget myself. Drinking, gambling, and some other foolish amusements were the last resorts that I tried. But none of them worked for me. There was no place where I could hide from myself; there was no way by which I could forget myself.

The Christian Encounter

Strangely enough, it was at this time that I began to receive invitations from the Baptist college, Seinan Gakuin, in Fukuoka, Kyushu, to enroll as a student. (Much later I found that it had been that girl, having become a Christian at the campus church of the Baptist Girls' School, Seinan Jo Gakuin, Kokura, Kyushu, who secretly worked so that I would enter the Baptist college to hear the gospel. She refused to marry me, but she wanted me to know Jesus Christ and thought that it would be best for me to enter the college.) The final decision was made one Sunday morning (I did not know it was Sunday myself) when I saw a group of people, some fifteen or sixteen in number, in the rubble of Hiroshima. I was just wandering in a former street. These people were coming along the street, quietly and peacefully. I watched them and I was shocked. They were also in simple clothes of the postwar period and not different from others, but when I watched their faces I was really shocked. They looked so peaceful. Their eyes were different. The way they walked seemed to be different. I instantly thought these people must have had something I did not know. "Who are they?" And then I looked at the place where they seemed to have been standing together. It was the place where a Methodist church used to be. I noticed the two stone posts of the gate still standing there. I used to take a walk along this street very often when I was a middle-school boy. I recalled the church building which was conspicuous in that neighborhood. Yes, they were having Sunday morning service at the place where their church building used to be. They were the ones who had narrowly survived the atomic bomb about half a year ago. My thoughts raced: "Yes, they are what are called Christians! Can Christianity give anything that I do not know? Can Christianity teach me the meaning and purpose of my life? Why are these people so quiet and peaceful against this hellish scene? They may have something that I do not know and yet I need badly. Perhaps I should go and enter that Christian college to study the Bible — "

I decided, and finally entered the Seinan Gakuin College, majoring in English Literature. For the following two years I was a faithful seeker. Even when I could not attend classes because of my work, I went just to listen to the chapel speaker at school. It was a difficult time for me, both financially and spiritually. I started as a shoeshine boy to earn a livelihood and then changed to other manual labor jobs. On the one hand I was struggling to reach an understanding of a personal ethical life, and on the other hand to find a spiritual God. Gradually I came to know the truth that a man should not live by bread alone. But still there were questions: "Why Jesus, a Jew?" "Why a free salvation?" I was a man who had been brought up in the Japanese culture of *shame* and *obligation*. As for the culture of shame, I had been taught from my boyhood to pay most attention to whether-or-not-people-laugh-at-you. Rather I wish I had been taught to live in terms of whether-or-not-sinful-against-God. But the Japanese culture does not even have the word for sin! As to obligation, which along with shame drove many classic warriors to *harakiri*, I could not follow a free salvation. I thought I should pay something for my salvation. But I did not have anything that I could give to anybody — no money, no position, no knowledge except that of warfare, no willpower, no discipline, and no good manners.

At the end of the second year in the college I was filled with despair for myself for the second time. But this time I asked God to give me something with which I could pay him for my salvation, because I found that there was an opening upward even though there was no exit all around. He gave me a Person for that purpose, who was and is himself in Jesus Christ. The Holy Spirit touched and moved my heart to receive Jesus as my personal Christ. And I was given the power to become one of God's children.

When I was born again, God taught me that now I was not a traveler on the long and high suspension bridge which spanned two entire darknesses. He taught me that he had created me according to his plan (I did not just happen to be born); that he had given me the ability to respond to his call when he molded me after his image (this is where my responsibility came from); that he wanted me to live in close fellowship with him so that he might use me as one of his tools for his plan of salvation (this gave me the purpose of life); and that now I had everlasting life. These things God taught me by his Spirit through his Word.

This realization is the reason why I came to experience a peace which I had never known before. This is the reason why I came to be able to testify that "in everything God works for good with those who love him. . . ." Yes, in everything, even in the A-bomb which so miserably killed my parents, relatives, and friends. When I think of God who used my experiences of the concentration camps and Hiroshima in order to draw me to himself, I am tempted to make a selfish and self-contradictory confession that I am even thankful for those events, through which I could meet Christ Jesus.

After my conversion, my former fiancée started to write to me. She wrote many letters to me. "But if you think that I would answer a girl who had spurned my approaches, you do not know Japanese men," I once said to my American friend. However, one afternoon I happened to see her outside the classroom window at school. There she was standing! She had come to see me! My pride crumbled. And my heart tumbled. We became engaged for the second time — this time by our own choice.

Her parents, who were still devout Buddhists, however, were not willing for their daughter to marry a future Christian minister. They threatened her by saying that they would disown and disinherit her. At last, they gave me two conditions: firstly, to forsake my family name, Hidaka, and take their family name, Mitsushima, to perpetuate it, and secondly, to take over the silk business to perpetuate that. So I compromised and took their family name. They also had to compromise in giving up their desire for me to run the business. We married. When our first son was born at his grandparents' home (because I was still a student), I wrote down on a scroll with a brush, "my son's business, his faith and his marriage, no one can force!" and hung it on the wall. Of course everyone knew that the newborn baby could not read it! Then, I entered the Seinan Baptist Theological Seminary, Fukuoka, Kyushu, to prepare myself for the mission given to me by God — a rejoicing and willing participation in the loving pain of God. Certainly, God had given to me a wholly different outlook upon life from that which I had when I first returned to the ruins of Hiroshima.

SPECIFIC SUGGESTIONS FOR
PASTORAL CARE AMID DISASTER

The story of Mr. Mitsushima is still going on though it has not been written. We chose this autobiography because it is a first-hand account of Christian experience in face of disaster, because it stirs up the kinds of emotions necessary for relatively affluent pastors to sense the peril of disaster, and because of the ambiguity of war in a time when pastors are tempted to assume that the solutions of war disasters can be simply achieved by resolutions of solemn assemblies. In spite of the most sincere and feverish protests, the veteran pastor should know that disasters like assassinations, war, flood, fire, famine, and all manner of catastrophes are going to happen. As professionals, pastors must be trained in the processes of reaction and, like doctors, pray for health and prepare for disease! The following suggestions are put forth with pathos and prayer that pastors may be a part of bringing order out of chaos and that they may never overlook the fact that even though things are being shaken, things that cannot be shaken will remain. In all things God is at work with both his goodness and his severity to bring reconciliation among men.

With this attitude in mind, the following basic responsibilities of Christian pastors are outlined for use amid times of disaster:

Understand the process through which a population goes. A disaster situation moves through typical periods of time within the course of the disaster:

1. the phase of warning
2. the phase of threat
3. the phase of impact
4. the phase of inventory
5. the phase of rescue
6. the phase of remedy
7. the phase of recovery

In the phase of warning, the pastor and his fellow pastors should be in such close contact with each other that they can keep the spreading of rumors to a minimum. A thorough study of Gordon Allport's *The Psychology of Rumor* will help here. Mr. Mitsushima's autobiography pinpoints how rumor was separated from fact.

In the phase of threat, the pastor can use his influence to persuade people to remain calm, avoid panic, and take all precautionary steps, such as evacuation of an area.

In the phase of impact, pastors can provide the physical facilities of the church to those in need, be a sustaining presence as a fellow sufferer, and freely assist existing reliable community leaders and civil defense personnel in the community. Because of his knowledge of the families and his acquaintance with their habits, the pastor may be able to help persons discover the whereabouts and well-being of others in their families. This need to know about the well-being of the family stands out vividly in Mitsushima's account.

The phase of inventory continues with the rendezvous of families. The inventory is the actual collection of personal belongings which may take on an intensified symbolic value because they represent loved persons who may have been killed. As one person in a disaster said, "He found my diamond ring; he found his own ring and a few little things that you know that I wanted to save — never could replace, memories that I cherish."

The phase of rescue brings the temptation of exhibition into full expression. The pastor is no exception to this temptation. Response to this temptation usually takes the form of unnecessary risk-taking, exaggeration of what really did happen, and hyperactivity. The latter is apparently the most common. For this reason alone it would be helpful for the pastors of a community to be trained by the Red Cross in first aid and disaster relief. This training would be a very profitable use of several Monday morning pastors' conferences. Through such training talk could be converted into muscular action in time of disaster.

The phase of remedy calls forth the organizational skill of the pastor. He participates with people in the repairing of the damages, the burial of the dead, the comfort of the sick, and the relocation of refugees into more permanent places to live. He incarnates the concern of the church and the compassion of Christ.

The recovery phase of a community from a disaster may involve pastors in committees and programs to prevent similar disasters. However, the building of adequate community ceremonies of a distinctly religious nature is the great ministry of the pastor. For example, when the Passover is celebrated by the

Jewish community, the ceremony represents their deliverance from a disaster of mass deaths among the children of their city. The great rituals of the church and synagogue have often been built around deliverance and/or recovery from a disaster. Before World War II the celebration of November 11 as Armistice Day was a major community ritual. In contrast, after the experience of World War II, the Korean War, and the Vietnam War, even religious people have become inured, even hardened, to the disaster of war. Where are the rituals that celebrate peace? The little children of Aberfan will never be forgotten, but the pastors of a community such as that could help to make the memory of the victims meaningful by providing a time of prayers and comfort for their loved ones. Communities make legends of events such as these, and the endowment of the legend with high religious meaning seems to me to be imperative. The Watts community has itself developed anniversaries of the disastrous riot. Have the churches of the Los Angeles community chosen to give these anniversaries "religious reminder value," or is this ceremony, too, a part of the "secular city" rather than the City of God?

SUGGESTIONS FOR FURTHER READING

Allport, Gordon, *The Psychology of Rumor*. New York: Holt, Rinehart, 1947.
Ardrey, Robert, *The Territorial Imperative*. New York: Dell Publishing Co., Inc., 1968.
Baker, George W., and Chapman, Dwight W., *Man and Society in Disaster*. New York: Basic Books, 1962.
Galbraith, J. K., *The Great Crash, 1929*. Boston: Houghton Mifflin Company, 1955.
Grinker, R. R., and Spiegel, J. P., *Men Under Stress*. New York: Blakiston, 1945.
Oates, Wayne E., *Pastoral Counseling and Social Problems*. Philadelphia· The Westminster Press, 1966.